Praise for *High Performance Drupal*

"Tag1 has been my go-to partner for performance and scalability for the last decade. This book, based on their experience scaling the largest (Drupal) sites on the Internet, is a must-read for any Drupal developer or system administrator."

— *Michael Meyers*
Vice President, Large Scale Drupal at Acquia

"An exhaustive, baremetal-to-browser treatment of both the factors governing Drupal performance, and the tools for working in each layer."

— *Sam Boyer*
Manager, Enterprise Architecture at NBCUniversal

"It's been wonderful to work with the brilliant minds at Tag1 Consulting (Jeff, Narayan, Nat and others) on a number of enterprise-class Drupal projects. I'm always blown away by the depth of their knowledge and how they're able to apply what they know to troubleshoot performance bottlenecks.

This book is a wonderful window into this team's collective experience and skills. Anyone who's serious about Drupal will have this book on their "must have" list of Drupal references."

— *Kevin Millecam*
Partner, WebWise Solutions

"Jeff and Narayan have always amazed me with their knowledge and experience with high performance hosting, especially with regards to Drupal. From their experience at the OSU Open Source Lab working on Drupal.org to working at Tag1 they are very much my go to resource for high performance knowledge."

— *Lance Albertson*
Director, Oregon State University, Open Source Lab

High Performance Drupal

Jeff Sheltren, Narayan Newton,
and Nathaniel Catchpole

Beijing · Cambridge · Farnham · Köln · Sebastopol · Tokyo

High Performance Drupal

by Jeff Sheltren, Narayan Newton, and Nathaniel Catchpole

Published by O'Reilly Media, Inc., 1005 Gravenstein Highway North, Sebastopol, CA 95472.

O'Reilly books may be purchased for educational, business, or sales promotional use. Online editions are also available for most titles (*http://my.safaribooksonline.com*). For more information, contact our corporate/institutional sales department: 800-998-9938 or *corporate@oreilly.com*.

Editor: Meghan Blanchette	**Indexer:** WordCo Indexing Services, Inc.
Production Editor: Christopher Hearse	**Cover Designer:** Karen Montgomery
Copyeditor: Rachel Head	**Interior Designer:** David Futato
Proofreader: Amanda Kersey	**Illustrator:** Rebecca Demarest

October 2013:   First Edition

Revision History for the First Edition:

2013-10-11:   First release

See *http://oreilly.com/catalog/errata.csp?isbn=9781449392611* for release details.

ISBN: 978-1-449-39261-1

[LSI]

Table of Contents

Preface

Drupal has come a long way since becoming an open source project in 2001. What was once a fairly limited content management system has become a very powerful framework that runs millions of websites. Everything from personal blogs and small neighborhood businesses to Internet startups, universities, governments, and global companies are running Drupal. There are hundreds of Drupal-focused companies offering development, hosting, and performance tuning services, and new Drupal sites, small and large, are coming online everyday.

Does Drupal Scale?

The three of us authors all work at Tag1 Consulting, where we focus specifically on the performance and scalability of Drupal websites. If there is one question we see asked more than any other, it's, "Does Drupal scale?" The question may be asked in many different forms: "I want to do X (insert super dynamic, cool feature here), and it needs to support millions of users"; "We're thinking of using Drupal for this project, but we hear that using Views is terribly slow"; or focusing on the infrastructure components, "We're confident in Drupal, but pretty sure that MySQL can't keep up with our traffic." In the end, it all boils down to, "Can Drupal scale?" because when we say "Drupal" in this context, we actually mean the entire stack of infrastructure and software that supports a Drupal site. The short answer is, of course, "Yes," but if it were that simple, this book could start and end with this introduction. As you might expect, the actual answer of how to achieve performance while scaling up a large Drupal site is much more complicated.

We deal with clients of all types and with many varying needs. We repeatedly see many of the same issues arise: pages aren't caching properly, servers are overloaded, database queries are running too slowly. All of these issues contribute to the overall question of whether and how Drupal can scale. While it would be impossible to cover all the possible reasons for any potential problems in a single book, the best practices and guidance provided here will cover the most common problems encountered while scaling Drupal websites. We provide a strong base of knowledge that can be used to plan for and over-come more difficult or unique performance issues.

Goals of This Book

The primary goal of this book is to help you solve Drupal performance and scalability issues. Drupal makes creating websites incredibly easy; however, if you aren't careful, it can quickly turn into a performance nightmare. This book is full of information on best practices for running a high performance Drupal site. This is not just limited to "enable these performance settings in the Drupal configuration"; rather, we take a holistic approach to website performance, covering Drupal internals, coding, and infrastructure techniques that all come together to build a high-performing and scalable website.

This is a technical book providing in-depth explanations and examples of common methods used to improve Drupal site performance. It is expected that readers of this book have a basic understanding of Drupal and the LAMP stack and are familiar with common hardware and infrastructure concepts. We've designed this book to be useful to both developers and system administrators. A site cannot perform at a high level unless attention is given to both code and infrastructure.

Supported Drupal Versions

The main focus of the book will be on Drupal versions 7 and 8, with Drupal 8 planned for release shortly after this book goes to press. There are still many websites running Drupal 6, and while our infrastructure advice and examples are still very relevant for older versions of Drupal, be aware that the code examples and discussion of Drupal internals have generally changed for the newer versions of Drupal.

How This Book Is Organized

We cover a wide range of topics within this book and have grouped them into the following topical sections.

Performance Analysis

Chapter 1, *Beginning a Performance Project*, discusses the various aspects of a website that all contribute to the big picture of website performance. Here, we also introduce a process for analyzing websites and approaching performance improvement projects.

Application Performance

This section covers a wide variety of Drupal application performance issues, starting with Chapter 2, *Frontend Performance*, where we describe best practices for frontend optimization, looking at network utilization, code optimization, and issues specific to mobile performance.

Chapter 3, *Drupal Performance Out of the Box*, discusses Drupal configuration settings that can improve performance. This includes an overview of the Drupal caching system, CSS and JavaScript aggregation, and other configuration options related to Drupal core.

We go into more depth on code-level optimizations in Chapter 4, *Drupal Coding for Optimal Performance*. This chapter covers important issues that should be addressed when writing or extending custom code in Drupal, giving best practices for items such as entities, the cache API, and the use of queues and workers. On the flip side, Chapter 5, *Drupal Coding for Abysmal Performance*, talks about common pitfalls that should be avoided, and explains why certain code can greatly reduce website performance.

Chapter 6, *Verifying Changes*, outlines the importance of tracking performance metrics for a site and using that information to understand how changes to the site affect performance for better or worse.

Infrastructure

We begin the section on infrastructure issues with Chapter 7, *Infrastructure Design and Planning*, which describes best practices for designing and infrastructure to host a Drupal website and related services. Early planning of infrastructure design will help a website to easily scale as it grows.

Chapter 8, *Service Monitoring*, covers how to monitor services and infrastructure in order to be alerted of potential issues before they affect a website and how to track performance and usage baselines in order to better understand how services react under load.

Chapter 9, *"DevOps": Breaking Down Barriers Between Development and Operations*, introduces many common infrastructure ideas and best practices to break down barriers between development and operations. This chapter discusses revision control systems, system configuration management, deployment workflow, and development virtual machines.

Chapter 10, *File Storage for Multiple Web Servers*, analyzes the difficulties faced with sharing a single Drupal *files/* directory between multiple web servers and gives examples of common file sharing options including NFS, rsync, and GlusterFS.

Chapter 11, *Drupal and Cloud Deployments*, introduces the idea of virtualized hosting and cloud-based infrastructures. Here we discuss the performance and scalability benefits of using a virtualized infrastructure, as well as some of the trade-offs between using virtual servers as opposed to physical servers.

Chapter 12, *Failover Configuration*, explains how to provide highly available services, using technologies such as Heartbeat to handle failover when a service goes offline.

Databases

Chapters 13, 14, and 15 all cover MySQL database information related to Drupal. Chapter 13, *MySQL*, provides an in-depth look at MySQL performance considerations and general configuration settings. It also contains an introduction to MySQL storage engines, with specific focus on InnoDB for performance and scalability. Chapter 14, *Tools for Managing and Monitoring MySQL*, introduces a number of tools commonly used for tuning, managing, and monitoring MySQL servers. Chapter 15, *MySQL Query Optimization*, wraps up the MySQL discussion by focusing on methods for locating and optimizing slow queries.

Chapter 16, *Alternative Storage and Cache Backends*, describes how alternative database and data storage engines can be used with Drupal to improve performance. This chapter includes examples on how to implement Memcache, Redis, and MongoDB backends with Drupal.

Chapter 17, *Solr Search*, discusses using Solr as an alternative search option for Drupal. We look at some of the benefits and added functionality that can be achieved by shifting the search backend out of MySQL.

Web Servers and Reverse Proxies

For an optimally performing site, it's important to have a properly tuned web server. Chapter 18, *PHP and httpd Configuration*, discusses how to best configure the web server and PHP for a Drupal website. *httpd.conf* is nothing to be scared of—we cover thread settings, keepalive, logging, and other useful configuration options for Apache *httpd*. This chapter also discusses PHP configurations and the importance of using an opcode cache.

Chapter 19, *Reverse Proxies and Content Delivery Networks*, introduces the concept of using a reverse proxy to cache website content. We give detailed examples of how to use Varnish with Drupal, including specific Varnish Configuration Language (VCL) configurations that can dramatically increase website performance. This chapter also covers content delivery networks (CDNs) and explains options for integrating Drupal with a CDN.

Ongoing Testing

One important lesson in this book is that website performance is not a one-time task; it's something that needs to be done continually in order to have a website perform at its best and be able to scale to meet increasing traffic needs. Chapter 20, *Load Testing*, discusses load testing tools and the importance of ongoing testing in order to catch performance issues before they become major problems.

Where to Next?

Wrapping up the book, Chapter 21, *Where to Next?*, provides some external resources to extend upon ideas presented in the book.

Conventions Used in This Book

The following typographical conventions are used in this book:

Italic

Indicates new terms, URLs, email addresses, file and path names, and file extensions.

`Constant width`

Used for program listings, as well as within paragraphs to refer to program elements such as variable or function names, databases, data types, environment variables, statements, and keywords. Also used for commands and command-line options.

`Constant width bold`

Shows commands or other text that should be typed literally by the user.

`Constant width italic`

Shows text that should be replaced with user-supplied values or by values determined by context.

 This icon signifies a tip, suggestion, or general note.

 This icon indicates a warning or caution.

Using Code Examples

Supplemental material (code examples, exercises, etc.) is available for download at *https://github.com/tag1consulting/high-performance-drupal*.

This book is here to help you get your job done. In general, if example code is offered with this book, you may use it in your programs and documentation. You do not need to contact us for permission unless you're reproducing a significant portion of the code. For example, writing a program that uses several chunks of code from this book does not require permission. Selling or distributing a CD-ROM of examples from O'Reilly books does require permission. Answering a question by citing this book and quoting example code does not require permission. Incorporating a significant amount of example code from this book into your product's documentation does require permission.

We appreciate, but do not require, attribution. An attribution usually includes the title, author, publisher, and ISBN. For example: "*High Performance Drupal* by Jeff Sheltren, Narayan Newton, and Nathaniel Catchpole (O'Reilly). Copyright 2014 Tag1 Consulting, 978-1-449-39261-1."

If you feel your use of code examples falls outside fair use or the permission given above, feel free to contact us at *permissions@oreilly.com*.

Safari® Books Online

 Safari Books Online is an on-demand digital library that delivers expert content in both book and video form from the world's leading authors in technology and business.

Technology professionals, software developers, web designers, and business and creative professionals use Safari Books Online as their primary resource for research, problem solving, learning, and certification training.

Safari Books Online offers a range of product mixes and pricing programs for organizations, government agencies, and individuals. Subscribers have access to thousands of books, training videos, and prepublication manuscripts in one fully searchable database from publishers like O'Reilly Media, Prentice Hall Professional, Addison-Wesley Professional, Microsoft Press, Sams, Que, Peachpit Press, Focal Press, Cisco Press, John Wiley & Sons, Syngress, Morgan Kaufmann, IBM Redbooks, Packt, Adobe Press, FT Press, Apress, Manning, New Riders, McGraw-Hill, Jones & Bartlett, Course Technology, and dozens more. For more information about Safari Books Online, please visit us online.

How to Contact Us

Please address comments and questions concerning this book to the publisher:

O'Reilly Media, Inc.
1005 Gravenstein Highway North
Sebastopol, CA 95472
800-998-9938 (in the United States or Canada)
707-829-0515 (international or local)
707-829-0104 (fax)

We have a web page for this book, where we list errata, examples, and any additional information. You can access this page at *http://oreil.ly/HP-Drupal*.

To comment or ask technical questions about this book, send email to *bookques tions@oreilly.com*.

For more information about our books, courses, conferences, and news, see our website at *http://www.oreilly.com*.

Find us on Facebook: *http://facebook.com/oreilly*

Follow us on Twitter: *http://twitter.com/oreillymedia*

Watch us on YouTube: *http://www.youtube.com/oreillymedia*

Acknowledgments

This book has been quite an undertaking for all of us, and we couldn't have done it without the help and support of many people. First of all, thanks to all of the Drupal contributors who have made Drupal into the amazing platform it is today. Specifically, we would like to thank our wonderful technical editors for their thoughtful reviews and ideas: Fabian Franz, Rudy Grigar, and Mark Sonnabaum.

We'd also like to give a special thanks to Jeremy Andrews for his endless hours spent reviewing the book, for providing ideas for concepts to cover, and for constantly pushing us to provide better explanations for things we may take for granted. His encouragement and ongoing assistance with all aspects of the book were absolutely priceless. The book would not be anywhere as good as it is without him.

We also need to thank Tag1 Consulting, our employer, for providing us the flexibility to work on the book over such a long period of time. And thanks as well to Meghan Blanchette, our O'Reilly editor, for pushing for us to write this book, and for putting up with our seemingly endless delays.

From Jeff

First and foremost I need to thank my wife, Sara, for being so supportive and encouraging throughout this process, and also for her understanding throughout all of the late nights and weekends I spent cooped up in the office writing. Thanks also to all my family and friends for your support and excitement about the book, in spite of the fact that it does not involve a zombie apocalypse.

This book was a true collaborative effort, and I really appreciate the hard work done by Narayan and Nat, who both brought their amazing expertise and insight. I can't even imagine how Nat was able to write so much content for the book even as he was in the midst of the Drupal 8 release as the branch maintainer.

From Narayan

Firstly I need to thank Jeff, who was the major motivation for getting this book done and the driving force to keep it moving forward. Secondly, I must thank my very tolerant wife, Candice, who somehow didn't get too upset at the concept of us doing just one more thing. Lastly, we all very much thank Jeremy, Peta, and all of our coworkers at Tag1 Consulting for creating the time for us to work on this.

From Nat

Massive thanks go to my wife Shoko and daughter Amile for putting up with yet another Drupal project, Jeff for keeping the book on track, Tag1 Consulting for interesting consulting projects that allow me to spend more time on these issues than is probably healthy, and all of the Drupal core and contributed module contributors for working on the software that both runs into these issues and also attempts to solve them.

## CHAPTER 1

Beginning a Performance Project

So you're ready to jump in and start improving your website's performance. This can be a daunting task. There are so many services, underlying technologies, and possible problems that it can be difficult to pick a starting point. It is easy to run around in circles, checking and fixing many small issues but never addressing your major problems (or even discovering what they are). Knowing where to start and which issues are of high priority can be one of the most difficult parts of optimizing a site.

Due to these common issues of discovery and prioritization, good performance engineers and system administrators tend to do a lot more gathering of metrics and statistics than most people think. A complete understanding of the problem points of a website (problem pages, blocks, or views) and server metrics during average- and high-load situations is a requirement for making good decisions. Whenever we approach a new infrastructure or website project, the investigation and metrics collection period is often the most important time and will determine how effective the entire optimization project is.

Getting Started with Performance Improvements

We will discuss tools and methodologies for collecting performance information in later chapters. For now, let us assume we have a spreadsheet of problem pages or requests and some server information (CPU, load, I/O usage, etc.) during some peak load periods. The next important step in optimizing a site is defining goals and usage patterns. This is important for similar reasons to having accurate metrics: it prevents you from endlessly fixing issues that may be legitimate, but are not the problems preventing the site from meeting its goals. For example, if you have a site that needs to serve 10,000 pages a day to only anonymous users, you can review all of the Views for this site and ensure they are all performing well, but it would be a waste of time when you could get better performance faster by ensuring the page cache is working effectively.

Everything we have discussed so far is considered quite pedantic and seems to be little more than bookkeeping. As technical people, we like to walk into a bad situation, immediately pinpoint the problem, and fix it in a few minutes. It's nice when this works, but often it fails or succeeds only partially, or worse, temporarily. The methodology we are proposing of performing a robust discovery phase and having a lot of quality information (metrics, expected site usage, and goals) for the site is much better for both the long-term sustainability of the site and your own longer-term sanity. You cannot always immediately pinpoint the problem, but a method based on information and metrics is always going to be effective.

There are a number of approaches that can be used to collect this information and develop a performance plan. However, we typically follow a straightforward approach that attempts to focus on low-hanging fruit and the real site problems. We also tend to focus on iteration, as often when you solve one large problem, it uncovers other issues that used to be hidden.

Let's outline the steps involved in this process—we will go into more detail on each step later in this chapter:

1. Measure and record the current site performance. This is your "performance baseline," which will be used to analyze potential performance improvements. Document any known issues with the site, such as individual or groups of pages that are consistently slow, servers that are always under high load, or anything else that might have an effect on performance or scaling. We will go into the tools and methods for doing this in later chapters, as its a very broad topic and can be a somewhat nebulous task.

2. Define goals and requirements for the site. For example, "The front page must load in under two seconds for anonymous traffic," and "A site search must not take more than three seconds on average to return results." The "must" and "should" wording in these statements is important, as it separates requirements ("must") and goals ("should")—more on this in the next section.

3. Actually perform your review. This often involves running a load test, reviewing configuration files, profiling pages, and reviewing slow query logs. Many engineers consider this the only step, but the problem with such an approach is that it lacks baseline information and a structured list of goals, as defined in the previous two steps. There will be many chapters in this book on the various topics that this step encompasses.

4. Define a list of potential improvements based on the site goals and requirements, using the information gathered in the performance baseline and your review. The list should be prioritized based on a few factors:

   - Does the item contribute to achieving a requirement or goal for the website?
   - What is the expected benefit of the change?

- What is the cost of the improvement, both in terms of staff time and any hardware or software purchases that may be necessary for the change?
- Once an improvement has been made, what impact does it have?

If you are working for a client, step 4 is particularly important. However, even if you are working for yourself or for your company, it's incredibly important to develop a list of potential improvements and ensure they are both prioritized and tracked for effectiveness. Returning to a site two or three weeks later without a good record of what was done previously and the impact of those changes will make your job much more difficult.

As to the prioritization of fixes, there is no hard and fast rule, but a good approach is to work on items that will give you the most bang for your buck—that is, those fixes that either don't take much effort compared to their impact or provide a vast improvement.

Establishing a Performance Baseline

Measuring current website performance will give you a baseline that you can compare to the performance after making a change. Knowing how the site was performing initially makes it easy to tell whether changes have had the expected effect, or when they resulted in only a minor improvement—or worse, decreased performance! Depending on your needs, determining the performance baseline could be as simple as tracking full page load times for a selection of pages on your site, or as intricate as tracking memory and CPU usage for key functions used to display one or more pages on your site. What's important here is that you decide what measurements are important to you. If this is a first pass at improving the performance of a site, generally it will be sufficient to choose one or two pages of each type that you have on your site (e.g. "article category display," "article," "author bio," "forum overview page," "forum topic page"). For each of those types, you'll want to measure some predefined set of data—what data is tracked will vary based on your needs, but if you're looking simply to improve page load time, there are a few data points that can be focused on to start:

Time to first byte
> This is how long it takes your server to start to deliver data back to the client after the client's browser has requested the page from your site. It is at this point that the user's browser can begin displaying data on the screen and, more importantly, begin fetching CSS and JavaScript files.

Time for a full page load
> This is how long it takes for an entire page to be loaded in a user's browser window.

Frontend display times
> This includes the JavaScript completion time, DOM load time, etc. We won't cover this in much depth in this book, as an entire books have been written on this subject.

While frontend display times are very important for user interaction, a slow frontend usually won't bring down a backend server.

Before fully understanding the performance implications, many people assume that the full page load time will be the most important factor in the site feeling fast to a user. In fact, the time to first byte can be much more important (there are exceptions, of course), because it's at that point that the user's browser starts working on displaying the data sent from your site. That's not to say you should focus entirely on the time to first byte, though it's quite important to at the very least look at both of these measurements.

Setting Goals for Website Performance

Once you have a good understanding of the website's baseline performance and have started to track down some of the current bottlenecks, it will be possible to start setting some well-defined and attainable performance goals for the site. Setting realistic goals is important for a number of reasons:

- Performance improvements on a website are a continual process. Setting concrete goals allows for work to be split up incrementally.

- Defining a set of goals with site developers can help prevent the addition of features that may be "nice to have" but have a serious adverse affect on performance. If goals have been well defined and have buy-in from all involved parties, they can be referred to later as a reason why or why not to implement certain features and technologies on the site.

- If goals are arbitrarily set without knowing the current performance of the site or the actual near-term requirements, you may set yourself up to fail with goals that are impossible to achieve with the resources you have at your disposal. Always focus on reality, not what you would like reality to be.

Potential improvements could include (but are not limited to) the following:

Reducing average page load time
This could be set as an overall goal for the site, and also more specifically for certain page types or common entry points into the site (the front page, marketing landing pages, etc.). Example goals: "Decrease the average page load time for all pages across the site from five seconds to three seconds. Average page load time for the front page should be under two seconds."

Decreasing maximum page load time
Again, this goal could be set overall for the site as well as for specific pages or page types. Example goals: "The maximum page load time across the entire site should always remain below eight seconds. Article pages should have a maximum page load time of five seconds. The front page of the site should have a maximum page load time of three seconds."

Improving page load times for first-time visitors

How long are your pages taking to load for visitors who do not have any of your assets (think images, JavaScript, etc.) cached locally in their browsers? This can be drastically different than page load times for visitors who have been to your site recently and may have most of those items in a local browser cache. If first-time visitors are important to you (and they likely are!), then it's important to consider page load performance specific to that group of users. Example goal: "The average page load time for the front page of the site should be under three seconds for first-time visitors and under two seconds for repeat visitors."

Once you've created a list of performance goals for the site, you can start to look at specific tasks that will help you to achieve those goals and problems with the current site preventing you from reaching those goals. Much of the rest of this book is dedicated to giving specific examples of common slow points on Drupal websites and ways to improve performance for those specific issues. As you start to dive in to make adjustments to the site, always keep an eye on the goals and requirements that you have developed. As you work, some of the goals may need to be adjusted because they were either too optimistic or perhaps didn't take into account certain aspects of your site or infrastructure that you are unable to change.

The Many Aspects of Drupal Performance

Websites—especially Drupal websites—are built up of multiple components, each of which could be suffering from a performance problem. Some of the major aspects that should be examined are:

- Frontend performance: page rendering time in a site visitor's browser
- PHP execution time on the web server
- Time spent for the web server to serve a request
- Time spent fetching and storing items in the cache
- Database query execution time
- Network traffic for each link along the path of a request: user→web server→cache server→database server, etcetera
- External requests, either server-side or client-side—for example, code that calls an external API (think Twitter, Facebook, etc.) or pulls in external files or images

All of these items contribute to the big picture of how a website performs. By breaking down requests and analyzing the performance of each of these various pieces, we can isolate the worst-performing parts of the site and focus our improvement efforts on those in order to get the most benefit from our work. In addition, understanding where the performance bottlenecks are can save you from blindly working on general performance improvements that may not have much effect on the overall performance of the site.

For example, consider a page that takes five seconds to deliver the first byte of data to a client browser. Let's say that one second of that is spent on the web server serving the request and executing PHP, 3.75 seconds are spent on database queries for the page, and 0.25 seconds are spent pulling items from cache storage. Now, it's pretty clear that there is not much benefit to be had by working on the caching layer. The best place to start performance work in this case would be to look at the queries that are being run on the database to figure out which of them are slow—we may be able to improve the query speed by changing the logic, or figure out a way to better cache the query results to avoid running queries repeatedly. Had we not broken down the different components, we could have wasted a lot of time trying to improve PHP execution time or trying to increase the speed of cached requests when those are not likely to give us much overall improvement in the performance of the page.

We'll get into more specifics on how to measure and analyze performance for various aspects of a site later. It is a complicated topic, and one that much of this book is devoted to. For now, it's just important to understand that there are multiple pieces contributing to overall page load performance. Understanding where the bottlenecks are makes it possible to focus performance improvements on areas that will have the greatest effect on the overall page load time.

Creating a Prioritized List of Improvements

During a performance review or site analysis, it is important to either have very detailed notes or to build your "prioritized list of improvements" during the review. As we have already explained, a single page load is a complicated matter. We are all "standing on the shoulders of giants" in the computer industry; those giants created the subsystems, drivers, architectures, services, caching daemons, *httpd* daemons, and opcode caches we rely on, and even Drupal itself. Although many were not particularly tall (Dries— the founder of Drupal pictured in Figure 1-1—is a notable exception), they are not called giants for nothing—each layer is immensely complex, some more so than others.

Due to this complexity, if you don't consistently keep priority in mind and look for the "low-hanging fruit", it is very easy to lose your way or forget something you've found. Perhaps while instrumenting the Apache process of your site, you noted that too many directory lookups are happening. However, if you have SQL queries on your home page that are taking five to six seconds to execute, are Apache's foibles your highest priority? For every performance engineer solving client-facing problems, there is at least one other optimizing something entirely pointless.

Figure 1-1. Dries Buytaert

Not only does keeping a priority list or priority-driven notes force you to focus on real problems, but it also allows you to cross reference and remember what you've seen. The issues you observe in different subsystems may be related, but it can be hard to draw the correct correlations without the issues noted down. Not everyone can connect the dots entirely in his head.

Once you have your list of issues, you can review them and prioritize them based on what you believe are the most important issues, or the ones that will be very easy to solve relative to their impact. Because you started building them during the review, most of the list items should be fairly detailed and actionable.

## CHAPTER 2

Frontend Performance

The principles of frontend performance apply regardless of the underlying application used to create a website. The browser receives an HTML document and, based on its contents, downloads CSS, JavaScript, fonts, and images; it then renders the page using all of these. The 14 rules defined by Steve Souders's *High Performance Websites* (O'Reilly) remain a good reference point for examining the pages served by a site and identifying areas for improvement (see this page (*http://stevesouders.com/hpws/rules.php*) for a refresher). Google's PageSpeed (*https://developers.google.com/speed/pagespeed/*) and Yahoo!'s YSlow (*http://developer.yahoo.com/yslow/*) will quickly grade a single page of your site and identify the highest-priority areas for improvement. For this chapter we're going to assume you have a working grasp of the rules (cacheable headers, compression, minimizing HTTP requests, etc.) and, rather than discussing them, we'll look at the challenges specific to developing Drupal websites when implementing those rules.

Limiting HTTP Requests

Drupal provides CSS and JavaScript aggregation via a configuration option. This allows potentially dozens of individual requests for CSS and JavaScript files to be reduced to just a few. While enabling this option in production should be one of the first steps you take to optimize frontend performance, there are several other steps you can take to minimize HTTP requests that require some more work on your part. Especially on mobile devices, or slow Internet connections in general, the number of HTTP requests can have the most serious negative impact, taking into account both back- and frontend performance. HTTP request latency applies for every file required to build a page, and can be hundreds of milliseconds multiplied by the number of files on the page. Assuming your code and infrastructure can scale to handle the traffic that comes to the site, this should be the very next thing you look at with regard to the overall user experience and performance of the site.

Audits

Many Drupal sites operate without any custom JavaScript and, if using a stock contributed theme or base theme, may only have a small amount of custom CSS. This, however, doesn't mean that the site itself is running with a small amount of JavaScript or CSS, as both core and contributed modules provide their own files. As with many other Drupal performance issues, the most common cause of problems is particular combinations of configuration and site structure and how these interact with modules that are unable to know exactly how they're used on every individual site.

When identifying bottlenecks, select two or three pages of different types to start with. Ideally these will be the most popular types of page on the site—for example, article pages or user profiles, as well as a landing page such as the front page.

What you audit depends on your priorities for optimization. When auditing, start by disabling JavaScript and CSS aggregation, then view the pages as either an anonymous user or an authenticated user. This allows you to see all the individual CSS and JavaScript files being added to the page. Do not look for performance issues while logged in as an administrator unless you're specifically trying to find issues affecting administrators, since toolbars, contextual links, and the like add a lot of page weight that will often show up as frontend (and sometimes backend) performance issues, obscuring issues that affect users without access to those features.

Once you're ready, look at the CSS and JavaScript requests in a tool such as Firebug (*http://getfirebug.com/*) or Chrome Developer Tools (*https://developers.google.com/chrome-developer-tools/*).

If there are no JavaScript-heavy features such as carousels or slideshows on these pages, the first thing to check is whether any JavaScript is loaded at all. If it's not necessary, loading no JavaScript at all saves the most possible HTTP requests (no requests are better than any nonzero number of requests), as well as other overhead such as initialization of jQuery.

Drupal 6 and Drupal 8 will not add any core JavaScript to the page if no modules or themes add their own (this isn't the case for Drupal 7 at the time of writing, but see *https://drupal.org/node/1279226* for a core bug report). However, it's often the case that contributed or custom themes will add small (or even large) JavaScript files to every page for every user via the `scripts[]` property in *.info* files, or via `hook_init()`.

In addition to serving pages without any JavaScript at all, Drupal 8 also makes it more likely that pages can be served without jQuery. For basic event handling, DOM selection, etc., native JavaScript functions are often perfectly adequate with modern browsers, and core JavaScript is being refactored to take advantage of these where possible. Scripts that require jQuery should explicitly declare it as a dependency, and if you have only a handful of *.js* files on a page but jQuery is one of them, look at whether both the files themselves and the jQuery dependencies within them are really necessary.

If you're not expecting to see any JavaScript on the page you're looking at, take a note of each filename, then `grep` the code base for where it's added. Start with the files loaded last, since the early files like jQuery and *drupal.js* may only be loaded due to dependencies. While all pages on Drupal sites will include CSS, a very similar approach can be taken when trying to reduce the amount of CSS loaded overall.

There are several common reasons why files might be added to a page despite not being actually needed:

- The file has been added via the `scripts[]` or `styles[]` *.info* property, despite not being needed on every request. Try to find which markup the file actually affects, then file a bug report for the module on Drupal.org to add it conditionally via `#attached` instead. For example, if a JavaScript file is only used when nodes are displayed in full view mode, it can be moved from *.info* to `hook_node_view()` as follows.

  Before:

  ```
  example.info
  name = Example
  description = Example module
  core = 7.x
  scripts[] = js/example.js
  ```

After:

```php
<?php
/**
 * Implements hook_node_view().
 */
function example_node_view($node, $view_mode, $langcode) {
  if ($view_mode == 'full') {
    $path = drupal_get_path('module', 'example') . '/js/example.js';
    $node->content['foo']['#attached']['js'][$path] =
      array('every_page' => TRUE);
  }
}
?>
```

- The file is associated with a feature that is only available to users with a certain permission but has been added to the page outside the permission check. File a bug report for the module on Drupal.org to make including the file conditional on the access check.

- Often CSS and JavaScript files apply to more than one feature. Following core guidelines for CSS organization ensures that admin-only CSS is only served to admins, and that files are easier to override for themes. Similarly, with JavaScript, it's worth evaluating if a file should be split up—aggregation puts it back together when needed anyway.

- Sometimes files are related to a specific feature but are still added site wide. This is usually an error, but in some cases, there might be CSS that applies to a search box, header menu, or similar feature that appears on every page, or a very high percentage of pages. Having this CSS in the site-wide aggregate saves it being duplicated in each per-page aggregate, reducing their size and increasing the effectiveness of the browser cache. In general this makes more sense for CSS than JavaScript—all pages need CSS, but some might render without any JavaScript at all.

After reviewing the site with aggregation disabled, reenable it and view the pages again. This time it won't be possible to see which individual files are being included, but instead you can look at the resulting aggregates of the pages and their comparative sizes.

A common problem with both the Drupal 7.x/8.x and Drupal 6.x aggregation strategies is that they're fragile when files are added incorrectly—for example, if they're added in different orders by different modules, or if the every_page option is set for conditionally added files. This can have the result that even if very similar JavaScript or CSS files appear in two or more pages, different aggregate filenames get created, resulting in lower cache hit rates, more bytes to download, and a greater workload server side generating the aggregates.

To track down issues like this, first compare the list of aggregate filenames, locate any filenames that are unique to any of the pages being compared, and then look at the size and/or contents of those files to see if they're actually different. On a live site that's been running for some time, checking the number and date of aggregates in the *css* and *js* directories can also be an indicator of how many unique aggregates are being created. One or two small aggregates differing between pages is expected if the JavaScript added is genuinely different, but very minor changes between files or several files changing may indicate an underlying issue.

A further option to reduce HTTP requests with JavaScript, assuming only minimal JavaScript usage on a site (i.e., no jQuery dependency), is to add it inline rather than using an external file. Drupal's JavaScript API supports this via the inline option.

Image Requests

Images embedded in content via the <img> tag are relatively hard to optimize in terms of the number of requests. You can optimize images for bandwidth using image derivatives, which ensure the images are scaled or cropped to the size they will be served at. Drupal 8 goes further by supporting responsive images via the Picture (*https://drupal.org/project/picture*) module (also available in Drupal 7 as a contributed module), so that the correct image derivative—and only that image derivative—is loaded based on breakpoints. For very image-heavy pages, you may want to explore more advanced techniques like deferred image loading via JavaScript.

For images loaded via CSS, there are more options. Go back to Firebug or Chrome DevTools to look for image requests; the paths will tell you whether they come from core, contributed, or custom modules, or themes.

Most Drupal 8 modules do not provide much default styling, with the exception of content forms, administrative features and user-facing menus which do have some icons.

There are several approaches for reducing image requests:

- *Image sprites* combine several images into a single file, then use CSS to display only the specific image needed. Creating and maintaining sprites can be quite time-consuming, but tools like SASS allow for automation of this process.

- Images can be base64 encoded within CSS files using `data-uri`. This means they are served as part of the CSS file itself rather than downloaded separately, saving an HTTP request for each image that's inlined. Remember that the larger your CSS file is, the longer it takes before the browser can download and parse it and move on to other things (like downloading images served via `img` tags), so this is a trade-off that needs to be made carefully if at all. This is supported by a contributed module for Drupal called CSS Embedded Images (*https://drupal.org/project/css_emimage*) that automatically inlines images when the CSS is preprocessed.

- *Icon fonts* allow for arbitrary images to be combined in a single font file. This has the same advantages as a sprite in terms of reducing HTTP requests, but since fonts use vector graphics, it also allows the icons to be scaled or presented in different colors without any modification to the original image. Fonts can be embedded into CSS using `data-uri` as well, saving a further HTTP request.

- Another approach is to use browser support for scalable vector graphics (SVG) directly. As with fonts, this allows for scaling, recoloring, etc., without modification of the original image. Since SVG files are XML, it's also possible to style the SVG itself with CSS. SVGs can be used via a URI, embedded into CSS via `data-uri`, or embedded into HTML using either `data-uri` or the SVG format itself, which provides a great deal of flexibility in terms of how they're served.

Both icon fonts and SVG have significant advantages over the older techniques of sprites and base64 encoding of binary images; however, some older browsers don't support them, so you may need to include a polyfill library if your site requires them.

Minification

Drupal provides very rudimentary on-the-fly CSS whitespace and comment stripping as part of the core aggregation support. There is no core support for JavaScript minification—files are concatenated together when aggregation is enabled, but the contents are left unchanged.

This leaves three options for minifying/uglifying JavaScript files, as discussed in the following sections.

Minification On the Fly

Drupal 8 has added the Assetic (*https://drupal.org/project/assetic*) library, which amongst other things provides support for minification of JavaScript and CSS via preprocessors. At the time of writing, the work to replace core's own file aggregate generation with Assetic has not been completed; however, if this lands for Drupal 8, it will allow files served from Drupal to be preprocessed via any of the pluggable backends that Assetic supports. It should be simple to implement as a contributed project if support isn't available in core. The main advantage of Assetic over previous on-the-fly preprocessors from contributed modules is that it supports native JavaScript backends such as *uglify.js*. While *uglify.js* (which requires *Node.js*) introduces an additional hosting requirement, the resulting minified code is much more efficient than that produced by PHP preprocessors, which are not well supported, use more server resources, and result in larger files.

Preminification for Modules/Themes

Drupal core ships with minified versions of jQuery and other external JavaScript libraries. Minification does not yet happen for JavaScript provided by Drupal core itself, nor for many contributed modules and themes that provide dedicated JavaScript files. Ensuring that external libraries are shipped as their minified versions (or both minified and unminified) allows sites to serve these by default without taking any additional steps, but it does introduce overhead for core or contrib developers whenever a file changes, and thus far there is not a system in place to support this. The Speedy (*http:// drupal.org/project/speedy*) module provides minified versions (via *uglify.js*) of core JavaScript files, which is a good one-stop solution for core, even if it will leave contributed projects unminified until they're individually supported. Preminification also solves the problem of retaining license information in minified files, which is a requirement for open source JavaScript libraries.

Minifying During the Build Process

If you have automated code deployment, minification could be added as a step in building releases (this is also something that could be considered for Drupal.org project packages). This is really a site-specific version of using/contributing to the Speedy module and is only mentioned here for completeness.

Compression

Serving files with gzip compression and respecting `Accept` headers allows file size to be reduced drastically. Drupal handles this via PHP for cached pages via a setting, and via *.htaccess* rules for JavaScript/CSS aggregates (both gzipped and uncompressed files are saved during the aggregation process, then the *.htaccess* rule rewrites them). Compression for uncached HTML pages is not supported by core so needs to be handled at the server level via `mod_deflate` or equivalent, in which case the PHP gzip support for cached pages should be disabled via configuration as well. You may want to disable PHP gzipping of CSS and JavaScript files as well and handle this at the server level. This can be done via *settings.php* or `variable_set()` in Drupal 7, or via the configuration API in Drupal 8. You will also need to edit your *.htaccess* to comment out the rules for rewriting filenames, since the Apache module will be handling serving the correct file instead. Note that there's no UI provided for this in the administration screens. To see the configuration options in Drupal 8, either review the aggregation code itself, or look at *system.performance.yml*:

```
cache:
  page:
    use_internal: '0'
    max_age: '0'
css:
  preprocess: '0'
  gzip: '1'
fast_404:
  enabled: '1'
  paths: '/\.(?:txt|png|gif|jpe?g|css|js|ico|swf|flv|cgi|bat|pl|dll|exe|asp)$/i'
  exclude_paths: '/\/(?:styles|imagecache)\//'
  html: '<!DOCTYPE html><html><head><title>404 Not Found</title></head>
          <body><h1>Not Found</h1><p>The requested URL "@path" was not found
              on this server.</p></body></html>'
js:
  preprocess: '0'
  gzip: '1'
response:
  gzip: '0'
stale_file_threshold: '2592000'
```

Cacheable Headers

Drupal sets cacheable headers for all CSS, JavaScript, and images, as well as for cached HTML pages. The HTML `max_age` value of the `Cache-Control` header can be set via *admin/config/development/performance* or the configuration API; assets are set to have an `Expires` header of two weeks via *.htaccess* if `mod_expires` is enabled in Apache. For sites that aren't undergoing frequent releases, you may want to tweak this upward. If you're not using Apache, you'll need to ensure that you handle cacheable headers for static assets in the web server you're using.

CDNs

Content delivery networks have two primary goals. First, they allow files (and potentially whole pages via custom configuration) to be served from a location as close as their infrastructure allows to the visitor requesting a site. Therefore, a site hosted in the US but visited by a user in France may have all JavaScript, CSS, and images served from servers in France, dramatically reducing the latency of those requests. As a secondary benefit, they reduce the number of requests to your own infrastructure, freeing up bandwidth and server resources to serve only uncached requests that can't be handled by the CDN.

See Chapter 19 for more information on CDNs.

Keep Third-Party Libraries Up to Date

Drupal 6 and 7 have frozen versions of jQuery. This means that the latest stable Drupal 6 release ships with jQuery 1.2.6 (released in 2008) and the latest stable version of Drupal 7 ships with jQuery 1.4.4 (released in 2010). jQuery's release schedule is considerably faster than Drupal core's for major releases, which means its developers often drop support for the version of jQuery shipped with the latest stable version Drupal core while the new Drupal release is still under development. To compensate for this, the contributed jQuery Update (*https://drupal.org/project/jquery_update*) project exists: it includes more recent versions of jQuery, as well as replacing particular core JavaScript files dynamically if they're incompatible with the newer versions. While sites usually install jQuery Update due to a frontend feature that specifies it as a dependency, the jQuery team is constantly adding optimizations to jQuery with each release. Simply installing *jquery_update* may result in both a smaller file size and access to performance optimizations within jQuery itself, such as faster selectors.

Drupal 8.x at the time of writing includes jQuery 2.0.0, and unlike Drupal 6 and 7, it's intended to update third-party JavaScript libraries as they become available with point releases of Drupal 8, with an option for a site to pin/downgrade its jQuery version to the older one if necessary. This will be a first for Drupal core but may mean that jQuery Update is not necessary for Drupal 8 sites.

jQuery Update

jQuery Update also provides an option to serve the minified jQuery file via Google's CDN rather than from the module folder. If you're not already using a CDN, this allows quite a large file to be served via a CDN "for free." There's also the potential that site visitors will have visited other sites that serve the same jQuery version prior to visiting yours and already have it cached, although how likely this is depends on the traffic patterns of your site's visitors and overall adoption of the Google CDN. If you have a family of sites all running Drupal with lots of traffic between them, the chances of this happening might be increased.

However, this does mean an extra DNS request, a dependency on Google's infrastructure, and an extra HTTP request, since jQuery will no longer be included in aggregates, so be aware that there are trade-offs in both directions.

External Scripts

Regardless of the quality and performance of Drupal core, contributed modules, and your own custom module or themes, all of that optimization and thought can go to waste—or at least be cancelled out—as soon as you add analytics, social widgets, advertising, and similar external services to a site.

Services like these often drive either revenue or traffic (or both) to websites, and when building commercial or community websites, there's often a lot of pressure (from either end users or business owners) to add as many as possible. This can result in many different JavaScript snippets from different services being included, which in turn may load other JavaScript files, CSS, and images.

All external services are different, but there are several rules of thumb that apply to most. We'll look at some of them in the next section.

Single Points of Failure (SPOFs)

When JavaScript is loaded synchronously, browsers block all rendering until the file has finished downloading. If an external service is down or having performance trouble, this may cause a script included on your page to take longer than usual to load, or fail to load altogether.

Synchronous loading just means putting a normal JavaScript file in a normal `script` tag:

```
<script>http://example.com/some/file.js</script>
```

If *example.com* is unable to serve the request in a timely manner, browsers will wait until either it eventually serves the request, or the request times out before rendering the full page. This can result in large blank sections below where the script is included or even entirely blank pages, depending on the browser and the location of the `script` tag, not to mention potential delays of 30 seconds or more. Most of the optimizations in this chapter have focused on changes that are likely to save milliseconds, hundreds of milliseconds, or perhaps a couple of seconds at most; yet a single external script can render a site unusable—potentially as unusable as an outage on your own infrastructure, in terms of the end user experience.

 The SPOF-O-Matic (*https://chrome.google.com/webstore/detail/spof-o-matic/plikhggfbplemddobondkeogomgoodeg*) browser plug-in by Patrick Meenan both flags likely single points of failure and can simulate complete failure for any external script it finds on your pages. This allows SPOFs to be found easily and provides an easy way to demo just how bad they are to anyone who might question the importance of handling external scripts carefully!

Many of the more popular services now provide asynchronous snippets that will not block page rendering; this is usually achieved by providing inline JavaScript, which then dynamically creates a `script` tag so that the JavaScript is loaded asynchronously.

Even scripts loaded asynchronously can block the browser `onload` event, on which real user monitoring, analytics, and in some cases site functionality might rely. A further optimization is executing the JavaScript within a dynamically created iframe so that it's isolated from the parent window's `onload` event. Note that techniques in this area change frequently; some services still support (and advertise in their documentation) snippets they provided several years ago and that might be found on sites in the wild, and some services have ignored these techniques and exclusively provide snippets that will cause a SPOF.

To avoid this, ensure you audit sites for SPOFs; SPOF-O-Matic is great for this. When adding scripts, avoid any temptation to embed markup or `script` tags directly into a *page.tpl.php*, *head.tpl.php*, or any other template or custom block, and use Drupal APIs such as `#attached` and `drupal_add_html_head()` instead. Better still, if a contributed module supports the service, consider enabling the widget or analytics via that module instead of custom code, as the contributed project has a better chance of keeping up with newer versions of the snippet than you do.

As well as SPOFs, it's also worth checking for cacheable headers on any assets that scripts load themselves. Frontend audits of sites have often found CSS or secondary JavaScript files from external services loaded without minification or compression, and without cacheable HTTP headers—whoops!

For social widgets in particular, also consider their usage on the site itself. Most sites present lists of content on a single page, and it's quite possible to have several social widgets enabled for each node teaser on such pages. For example, let's take a page showing 20 node teasers. If widgets make requests back to services to load information such as Like/comment/+1 counts, that's 20 times as many of those requests, as well as the JavaScript itself being executed 20 times for each request. A poorly optimized widget that appears once is bad enough, but when there are 20 of the same thing on a page, it could go from a sluggish response to crashing a browser.

## CHAPTER 3

Drupal Performance Out of the Box

Drupal provides several features and configuration options both in the core install and in contributed modules that can affect a site's performance and scalability. Making use of these can provide dramatic improvements in site performance compared to Drupal's default settings. While many of these settings are essential when running a large Drupal website in production, they are not enabled by default on new installs and can easily be forgotten when moving a site from development to production. It's therefore quite common to see newly launched sites with one or more configuration options disabled, leading to performance and scalability issues that could have been avoided with, in many cases, just a few minutes work.

In addition to modules and configuration options that provide quick wins for improving performance, we'll also discuss some common pitfalls.

Page Caching

The majority of requests served by a Drupal site will either be requests for full HTML pages served to browsers or read-only requests for content in other formats, such as RSS or JSON-LD. Serving a request from Drupal involves the following:

- Parsing the request
- Loading various necessary services and modules
- Locating the correct route controller and executing it
- Rendering in the desired format

The single biggest improvement to application performance that can be made is simply to skip as many of these steps as possible via page caching. When a request comes in, the URL itself (and other request context in Drupal 8) is used as a cache identifier. If there's a cache hit, the output is sent from the cache rather than built from scratch in PHP.

While cached pages are served in a fraction of the time of a "normal" Drupal request, how much benefit a particular site might get from page caching varies greatly based on site usage. Understanding the strengths and limitations of page caching is important when considering more advanced optimization techniques.

When Should You Use Page Caching?

As a general rule of thumb, page caching is effective as long as the time saved by cache hits exceeds the overhead of having page caching enabled for cache misses.

Let's take an example of a site with a very low cache hit rate—say, a 1:30 hit/miss ratio. Note that all the numbers here are entirely for illustration purposes and don't necessarily reflect any real websites:

```
Time to serve a page without caching: 300ms
Overhead of page caching on cache misses: 2ms
Time to serve a page from cache: 5ms
```

The 30 cache misses add an additional 60 ms across all requests (time spent checking and then writing back to the cache).

However, the single cache hit saves 295 ms compared to building the page from scratch, meaning that there is a net gain of 235 ms across all requests even with such a low hit rate.

The numbers will vary dramatically depending on the site, although 300 ms can be quite conservative to generate a full page on a complex site.

There are various types of sites and traffic patterns that can lower hit rates or make page caching unviable:

Authenticated traffic
> Page caching does not work if a visitor has an authenticated PHP session. By default, Drupal customizes pages for authenticated users, for example, displaying their username or administrative links based on their roles. A site that has 100% authenticated traffic—for example, a private intranet or ticket tracker—will not get any benefit from full page caching.

Breadth of content
> If a site has a large number of articles or similar content and regularly gets traffic to this content via search engine referrals, external links, crawlers, etc., page caching can be of limited value. To show this contrast, consider that one page visited 1,000 times within the length of the cache TTL will give 999 cache hits, whereas 1,000 pages visited once each during the same period will give 0 cache hits. Many sites will have traffic patterns that encompass both of these extremes. Due to the relatively

low cost of writing a page to cache versus building it each time, it's usually worth enabling page caching.

Frequent updates

By default the page cache is invalidated every time content is posted, deleted, or updated on the site. This means you can enable page caching without being concerned that site visitors will see out-of-date content. However, it also means that a site that is updated every minute will invalidate the entire page cache every minute, vastly reducing the chance of a cache hit. On the other hand, if you have infrequently posted content, flurries of activity with long pauses in between, or updates at particular times of the day, page caching will be effective for the bulk of the time. This situation may be improved for both cases in Drupal 8, which has introduced cache tags for smarter cache invalidation. Cache tags allow cache entries to be associated with the specific content entities that are rendered so that they can be invalidated when those entities are updated or deleted; however, at the time of writing, this has not been integrated with the page cache.

PHP sessions for anonymous users

The page cache is bypassed for any anonymous users with a PHP session. Since Drupal 7, PHP sessions are initialized on demand when something is written to $_SESSION, so whether a user has a session depends on enabled code and user activity. Actions such as adding an item to a shopping cart often trigger a PHP session, and this is something to be generally aware of when writing code for custom or contributed modules.

Customized content based on request parameters

Some sites customize the user experience for anonymous users at the same path. This may involve using browser settings for preferred language to determine which translation of a text to show, showing region-specific content based on IP address, changing rendered output based on a cookie, switching to a mobile-specific theme based on user agent, or showing content in different formats based on Accept headers. Since the path is used as the cache key, Drupal is only able to cache and serve one copy of the content, meaning that users see incorrect content when such a feature coexists with core page caching. Drupal 8 natively handles Content-Type Accept headers as part of the page cache key, so that different versions of a page will be saved for different content types, but it does not handle the other cases yet.

Internal Page Caching

Drupal core provides its own internal page cache. The configuration option is accessed via *admin/config/development/performance* and allows the full rendered HTML output to be stored using Drupal's own cache API. When the option is enabled, Drupal loads and executes the minimum possible PHP code to check the cache item and serve the page request. This can require as little as one database lookup, meaning pages can be served from PHP in a matter of a few milliseconds.

The configuration settings `$conf['page_cache_invoke_hooks'] = TRUE` and `$conf['page _cache_without_database'] = TRUE` allow Drupal 7 to skip even more of its usual bootstrap when serving cached pages, so that pages may be served without any database or cache lookups except for the page cache item itself.

This can make the difference between a site being able to serve tens of requests per second or hundreds, including in shared hosting environments.

Drupal also provides an option to compress cached pages. This makes use of gzip compression when the client supports it, which can dramatically reduce the payload of HTML sent to the browser. If you have control over your server configuration, however, you may want to enable compression within your web server or reverse proxy instead of from within Drupal. Drupal's own page compression only works for pages served from the internal page cache, whereas `mod_deflate` and similar work for all requests to the site, whether cached or not.

Reverse Proxy Caching

The "Expiration of cached pages" option is located at *admin/config/development/performance*. Setting this option affects the `max_age` value of the `Cache-Control` header sent by Drupal, which allows reverse proxies to cache pages. The most common reverse proxy used for Drupal sites is Varnish, so we'll use that as the example here; however, many of these assumptions also apply to other caching options such as serving pages via a CDN, or Nginx proxy caching.

Using a reverse proxy such as Varnish to serve cached pages has advantages over the internal page cache, since Varnish is able to serve the entire page request without having to call back to Apache and PHP. This significantly reduces server load by completely avoiding the web server, PHP, and the database. Note that Varnish is not typically available in a shared hosting environment and may not be an option for everyone, although many Drupal-specific hosting providers do offer it.

When serving cached pages, there is one limitation that Varnish has compared to Drupal's internal page cache: Drupal, by default, can't expire pages from Varnish when content is updated.

There are two options for handling this:

1. Set up Drupal to purge Varnish entries via the command interface or a PURGE HTTP request based on updates to the site. This requires a custom Varnish configuration, so it may not be available to all site owners. Assuming you have this option, though, contributed projects such as the Varnish (*http://drupal.org/project/varnish*) HTTP Accelerator Integration module or the Purge (*http://drupal.org/project/purge*)

module make it easy to set up your Drupal site to purge items in Varnish, and more granular purging can be enabled via projects such as the Expire (*http://drupal.org/project/expire*) or Cache Actions (*http://drupal.org/project/cache_actions*) or CacheTags (*http://drupal.org/project/cachetags*) modules.

2. Set the `max_age` to a low value, such as five minutes, while keeping the internal page cache enabled. This keeps pages fresh in Varnish at the cost of a lower cache hit rate, while ensuring that Drupal only builds a full page from scratch when necessary. However, it requires some additional storage since pages are cached in two locations.

CSS and JavaScript Aggregation

Frontend performance best practices recommend combining page resources into as few requests as possible, and Drupal core provides an option to do exactly this out of the box. CSS and JavaScript may be added to pages by Drupal core; any enabled core, contrib, and custom modules; and themes. By default, each file is added to the page individually in the HTML markup, meaning potentially dozens of HTTP requests on each page as each file is requested individually by the browser. Aggregation in Drupal has particular challenges that make it more complex to get this right than it might be for a custom web application. The assets added to the page depend on:

- Which modules are enabled
- Whether the enabled modules define global assets to be added to every page and/or conditional assets added only on certain types of request
- Which theme is active for the request, and whether that theme defines global or conditional assets

Therefore, when assets are added to the page, they're added with particular metadata, and with information about whether they're part of the base application, from a module, or from the theme. The aggregation logic in Drupal 7 breaks these into the following groups:

- Assets from System module added on every page
- Assets from System module added conditionally
- Module assets added on every page
- Module assets added conditionally
- Theme assets added on every page
- Theme assets added conditionally

In Drupal 8 these are being consolidated into two groups, a change that may be back-ported to Drupal 7:

- Assets added on every page
- Assets added conditionally

Files will not be aggregated if they define custom attributes or a specific media type.

Separating files that are added to every page from those added conditionally reduces the potential that users will download multiple large aggregates containing lots of duplicate assets as they browse around different pages of the site. This was the case with Drupal 6's aggregation strategy, which relied on a single aggregate per page.

Two other behaviors are enabled when CSS and JavaScript aggregation are switched on. First, Drupal will write gzipped versions of each file and try to serve them to clients that accept gzipped content via default *.htaccess* rules. You may want to consider disabling this behavior in *.htaccess* if already using `mod_gzip`/`mod_deflate` or equivalent.

Additionally, CSS files are stripped of whitespace and comments. No preprocessing is done for JavaScript files, but several core JavaScript files are already minified, and the Speedy (*http://drupal.org/project/speedy*) module helps by replacing those that aren't with minified versions.

Logging

Also provided by core but requiring a certain level of control over your hosting environment is the *syslog* module. Drupal enables the database logging (*dblog*) module by default, which directs all `watchdog()` calls to the database. Modules that log verbosely or that generate PHP notices and warnings can cause a large number of database writes. Verbose logging and PHP errors should be fixed at source, by auditing the logs periodically and fixing custom code or submitting patches to contributed code to avoid the logging or errors. Switching to *syslog* allows any remaining or unexpected messages to be logged by the operating system rather than the database, which can help to reduce overall load on an overworked database server.

The Cache and Other Swappable Storage

Drupal's cache API (used for internal page caching, as well as many other things needed during the course of a request) uses the database storage implementation by default. As with logging, simply setting up the cache to write to somewhere else will take some of the load off the database server. Additionally, some cache backends have further benefits over database caching, such as improved performance or the ability to scale horizontally. Less frequently accessed but equally swappable are the queue and lock storage backends.

Core doesn't provide a useful alternative storage implementation (except for a null implementation useful for development, or if you believe the YouTube video "MongoDB Is Web Scale" (*http://youtu.be/b2F-DItXtZs*)), but contributed projects are available providing support for Memcache, Redis, MongoDB, APC, and Files.

Cron

Drupal core and many contributed modules rely on hook_cron() for tasks such as indexing or garbage collection. Up until Drupal 7, site administrators were required either to set up a cron job to execute hook_cron() on their servers or to install the Poormanscron (*https://drupal.org/project/poormanscron*) module, which triggers the cron job automatically via PHP upon the first request after a certain time limit. If neither of these was set up, garbage collection didn't run, which could lead to watchdog and cache tables growing indefinitely as expired items were never cleared up.

From Drupal 7, the functionality of the Poormanscron module was moved into core and is enabled by default. Drupal will execute these periodic cron jobs inline during a page request every three hours, meaning the user that triggered the cron run may have page serving delayed by seconds or minutes while the various jobs finish.

To avoid both of these scenarios, ensure that Drupal cron is configured to run frequently. This can be done using a cron job or a more advanced job scheduler, such as Jenkins (*http://jenkins-ci.org/*). Cron also has high resource/memory requirements, so it should be run via *drush* to avoid taking up a web server process and artificially inflating PHP memory limit requirements with mod_php.

Views

Views (*https://drupal.org/project/views*) (both the Drupal 8.x core version and the Drupal 7 contributed module) ships with a built-in time-based caching system, while additional modules can also provide alternative caching implementations.

Caching settings are located under the *advanced* section in the Views UI. After enabling caching, there are two settings available:

Query results
> This caches only the results of the main listing query configured in the View, using the query itself as the cache key. Views allows very complex queries to be created, and caching the results is the quickest way to reduce the performance impact of the queries on a site.

Rendered output
> This caches the rendering of the items in the View, once the results have been retrieved. This can also be expensive—it may involve loading entities, running additional queries for field values, as well as invoking the theme system. Since the

cache is time-based, an entity update such as changing a node title won't be reflected in the cache until the items have expired.

Where possible, both of these should be set to the maximum possible time. If you're concerned about cache coherency, setting a longer value for query caching and a shorter value for rendered output is a good compromise.

Configuring caching for Views is often forgotten in the process of site building, and this is one of the first simple changes to look at making (after page caching) when a site runs into performance issues.

 If you want to ensure that you never forget to enable caching for a View, consider installing the Views Cache Bully (*https://drupal.org/ project/views_cache_bully*) module, which enforces time-based caching on any View where it's not configured.

## CHAPTER 4

Drupal Coding for Optimal Performance

One of the great things about Drupal is the ease with which you can extend or override core functionality in order to customize it for your specific needs. However, if you are not careful with how you code, you may introduce a huge performance bottleneck into your contributed or custom module. This chapter will give an overview of Drupal APIs relevant to performance and scalability, common coding best practices, and pitfalls to be aware of when trying to approach common tasks.

Context Matters

Before discussing the APIs and patterns that Drupal provides, it's worth discussing which types of issues are often introduced when writing Drupal code.

Performance and scalability issues in code can affect CPU, memory, filesystem, database, and network usage, either individually or in combination. All code uses at least some CPU and memory, and all sites will access the database and filesystem and potentially make network requests. Whether any of these turns out to be a performance bottleneck is always down to context.

There are no hard and fast rules about what makes code "fast" or "slow"—exactly the same code could be acceptable in one situation but not in another, and performance often needs to be balanced against other programming issues such as testability, readability, and maintainability.

When writing or reviewing code, it's important to think of the context the code will be executed in—both the immediate use case and whether it might also be applied to other contexts. The following are some general questions to ask, before you start trying to optimize at all:

- Does the code get executed on every request?

- Could it run more than once during a request? If so, a few times, or hundreds or thousands?
- If the code runs less frequently, will it affect end user performance? And how critical is end user performance in that case?
- Does the code have side effects that could affect the performance of other requests, such as writing to the database or flushing caches?
- Is the code an isolated unit, or will it be affected by other code or the configuration and state of the Drupal installation it runs on? For example, the amount of content, users, themes, or modules installed can dramatically change the characteristics of how code performs.

Only after considering these questions should you attempt to apply one or more of the approaches outlined here.

False Optimizations

It's entirely possible to make the performance of code worse by "optimizing" it. This happens when additional code is added to avoid expensive processing, but the expensive processing happens anyway. The result is that both the original expensive code and the new code run, adding additional overhead to an already bad situation.

An example of this is the fairly common micro-optimization of replacing `array_key_exists()` with `isset()`. (Please note that this is used only as an example, and we're not explicitly recommending doing so!):

`isset()`
    This is a language construct that tells you whether a variable is set or not, and returns `false` if that variable is explicitly set to NULL.

`array_key_exists()`
    This is a function that tells you if an array key exists regardless of the value.

Function calls in PHP have more overhead than language constructs, so `isset()` takes less time than a function call, and while the semantics are different, they can be used interchangeably if you don't need to explicitly check for array keys set to NULL. Hence, a common micro-optimization is to use `isset()` unless it's absolutely necessary to check for NULL.

Let's assume you had some code that definitely needed to use `array_key_exists()` because of the NULL check, but you wanted to try to run the faster `isset()` first, to skip the function call when it's not needed. You might write code like this:

```php
<?php
$array = array('foo' => NULL);
```

```
isset($array['foo']); // returns FALSE.

array_key_exists('foo', $array); // returns TRUE.

isset($array['foo']) || array_key_exists('foo', $array); // returns TRUE.
?>
```

The last example is semantically identical to just an array_key_exists() call, but in the case that $array['foo'] is set to a non-NULL value, only the isset() check needs to be made, avoiding the more expensive function call.

However, if $array['foo'] doesn't exist or is set to NULL, then the code actually has to do more work—checking isset() then the array_key_exists(), as well as the || operator—all of which is going to be slower than just running array_key_exists() in the first place!

The only way to know the effect of this is to create a realistic scenario or test on a real install, and see which code execution path is actually the most common. This comes back to context—it's not so much the content of the code itself that determines its performance, but how exactly it is executed.

Whether this kind of optimization is a problem depends on the relative performance increase you hope to gain.

For example, when checking access rights, you may need to check an administrative permission via user_access() as well as access permissions based on an entity ID, which requires loading the entity via entity_load() first. Both checks are necessary regardless, but the order is important.

While very few users might have the administrative permission, a call to user_ac cess() takes a fraction of the resources that loading and access-checking an entity does and won't cause a measurable delay. It's worth doing the cheaper check first even if the second, more expensive check will run too.

This is the same with almost any pattern that attempts to circumvent code execution rather than completely rewriting it. For example, adding persistent caching to a function that is a cache miss in 99.9% of cases will mean extra time spent checking and writing to the cache, as well as extra space being taken up in cache storage, on top of the original code being executed. However, if the code being executed is very expensive, then the overhead of cache misses may well be outweighed regardless.

With this in mind, we'll first cover a common task for Drupal custom and contributed modules, and look at ways to ensure that this task is executed as fast as possible. Then we'll move on to the APIs that Drupal provides specifically to aid with performance and scaling.

Listing Entities

Whether it's on the front page of a blog or in a gallery of images or a comment thread, much of the work done on a Drupal site involves getting a list of entities and then rendering them.

There are two APIs introduced in Drupal 7, and only slightly changed in Drupal 8, that help with this: `entityQuery()` and `entity_load_multiple()`.

entityQuery()

Rather than a direct database query to entity and field tables, `EntityQuery()` relies on a storage controller to handle building and executing the query for the appropriate entity storage backend. This has the advantage that any query run through `entityQuery()` is storage agnostic, so if you're writing a contributed module or working on a site where it might be necessary to move to alternative entity storage in the future, all your queries will transparently use the new storage backend without any refactoring. `Entity Query()` can be used whether you're writing queries by hand in custom code or via the `entityQuery()` Views backend.

Multiple Entity Loading

Once you have some entities to list, you'll need to load and then render them.

A common pattern would be to loop over each node and load them individually:

```php
<?php
/**
 * Provide an array of rendered entities given the IDs.
 *
 * @param array $ids
 *    The entity IDs to load
 *
 * @return $rendered_entities
 *   The array of rendered entities.
 */
function render_entities($ids) {
  $rendered_entities = array();
  foreach ($ids as $id) {
    $rendered_entities[$id] = entity_view(entity_load($id));
  }
  return $rendered_entities;
}
?>
```

Drupal 7 introduced multiple entity loading and rendering so that tasks such as fetching field values from the database could be done once for all nodes with an `IN()` query rather than executed individually:

```php
<?php
function render_entities($ids) {
  $entities = entity_load_multiple($ids);
  return = entity_view_multiple($entities);
}
?>
```

By using the multiple load and view functions, assuming 10 nodes need to be loaded and rendered, 10 similar queries to the same table can be reduced to just one. Since an individual node load could require 10 or 20 database queries, this can result in dozens or hundreds of database queries saved when loading and rendering multiple nodes at the same time.

Note that this applies to hook implementations as well; for example, hook_enti ty_load() acts on an array of entities.

One often overlooked hook is hook_entity_prepare_view(). Often, custom themes will need to add fields from user accounts/profiles when rendering nodes or comments —this could be the user's full name, avatar, registration date, etc. A common pattern for this is preprocess. Let's take nodes as an example:

```php
<?php
template_preprocess_node(&$variables) {
  $node = $variables['node'];
  $variables['account'] = user_load($node->uid);
  // Set up custom variables based on account here.
}
?>
```

When rendering several different nodes or comments by different authors, this pattern can result in a lot of round trips to the database as each account is fetched individually. The following example provides the same functionality while resolving the performance issue:

```php
<?php
hook_entity_prepare_view($entity_type, $entities) {
  if ($entity_type != 'node') {
    return;
  }
  $uids = array();
  foreach ($entities as $entity) {
    $uids[] = $entity->uid;
  }
  $accounts = user_load_multiple($uids);
  foreach ($entities as $entity) {
    $entity->account = $accounts[$entity->uid];
  }
}
?>
```

Then $entity->account is available in preprocess:

```php
<?php
template_preprocess_node(&$variables) {
  $account = $variables['node']->account;
}
?>
```

Caching

Caching is often the quickest way to solve a performance issue. By adding caching in a particular code path, you can ensure that it will only be executed on cache misses.

Before adding caching, though, there are a few things to consider:

- Is it possible to optimize the code so that it doesn't need to be cached?
- Is there already caching of the code at a higher level, for example page caching, that might affect the hit rate?
- Will the cached code path be considerably quicker than the current code path?
- Does the cache need to be cleared on particular events? Is it OK for it to be stale sometimes?
- Is the code run multiple times with the same output during a single request?

Static Caching

When code is run multiple times per request, a common optimization is to add a static cache around it. For example, you might rewrite the following code:

```php
<?php
function my_function() {
  return something_expensive();
}
```

as

```php
<?php
function my_function() {
  static $foo;
  if (!isset($foo)) {
    $foo = something_expensive();
  }
  return $foo;
}
?>
```

Because $foo is declared as static, it will be held in memory for the duration of the request regardless of how many times the function gets called. This means once this function has run once, it will run the isset() check and then immediately return.

While it only takes a couple of lines of code to add a static cache, doing so has implications that aren't always immediately obvious.

Let's look at the code inside something_expensive():

```php
<?php
function something_expensive() {
  return friends_count($GLOBALS['user']);
}
?>
```

Whoops. If $GLOBALS['user'] changes during the request, then something_expensive() will return different output. This often happens during automated tests using Drupal's *simpletest* adaption, or in a *drush* process that might be sending emails to multiple different users.

It's not impossible to fix this, of course. For example, we can key the cache based on the global user's ID:

```php
<?php
function my_function() {
  static $foo;
  global $user;
  if (!isset($foo[$user->uid])) {
    $foo[$user->uid] = something_expensive();
  }
  return $foo[$user->uid];
}
?>
```

Now, regardless of how many times the global user object is swapped out during the request, our function will return correctly, whilst still statically caching the results.

But the problems don't end there. What if the number of friends the user has changes during the request as well? This might well happen during a functional test or a long-running *drush* job. Additionally, this is where memory usage starts to be a problem: a *drush* job processing one million users could eventually end up with a million items in this static cache.

Drupal core has a solution for this in the form of the drupal_static() function. This operates similarly to static caching, except that the static cache can be accessed from different functions, both for retrieval and for reset.

Now our function looks like this:

```php
<?php
function my_function() {
  // Only this line changes.
  $foo = &drupal_static(__FUNCTION__);
  global $user;
  if (!isset($foo[$user->uid])) {
```

```
      $foo[$user->uid] = something_expensive();
    }
    return $foo[$user->uid];
  }
  ?>
```

Code in unit tests that updates the user's friends count or needs to reclaim some PHP memory can then call `drupal_static_reset('my_function')` to empty the static cache.

Since `drupal_static()` is a function call, it has a lot more overhead than declaring static and including an `isset()` check. This can lead to a situation where static caching is added to micro-optimize a function, then converted to `drupal_static()` for testing purposes, which leads to the function being slower than when it had no caching at all. If you absolutely need to use `drupal_static()` and your function is going to be called dozens or hundreds of times during a request, there's the `drupal_static_fast` pattern:

```php
<?php
function my_function() {
  static $drupal_static_fast;
  if (!isset($drupal_static_fast)) {
    $drupal_static_fast['foo'] = &drupal_static(__FUNCTION__);
  }
  $foo = $drupal_static_fast['foo'];
  global $user;
  if (!isset($foo[$user->uid])) {
    $foo[$user->uid] = something_expensive();
  }
  return $foo[$user->uid];
}
?>
```

This adds testability and performance at the expense of quite a bit of complexity.

There are two issues with `my_function()` now. One is a development process issue, and the other is architectural.

In terms of process, if we look back at the original function, we can see it's only a wrapper around `something_expensive()`. While a real example probably wouldn't be a one-line wrapper, if the only thing that needs caching is `something_expensive()`, this isn't the right place to add that caching. What we should have done was add the caching directly to `something_expensive()`, which also knows about any global state it depends on and any other factors that might influence the result (and, if you're lucky, is in a contributed module rather than your custom code).

When you add caching to a wrapper rather than to the function itself, the following bad things happen:

- Any other code that calls the function (here, `something_expensive()`) does not get the benefit of the static caching.
- If the function or another function that calls it adds static caching at a later point, the same data will be added to the cache twice, leading to both higher memory usage and potentially hard-to-find cache invalidation bugs.

From an architectural/readability perspective, we can see the gradual change from a very simple function to one that is balancing various variables in global state. A major change in Drupal 8 has been the migration from procedural APIs to object-oriented code based on dependency injection. Most classes are loaded via a factory method or plug-in manager, or accessed from the dependency injection container. When this is the case, simply using class properties is sufficient for managing state between methods, and no static caching is necessary at all.

Persistent Caching

Drupal core ships with a rich caching API, defaulting to database caching but with contributed support for files, Memcache, Redis, MongoDB, APC, and other backends.

While static caching allows code to skip execution when called within a single PHP request, persistent caching is shared between PHP processes and can retain data for anything from a few seconds to several weeks.

The Cache interface is well documented on the Drupal API site (*https://api.drupal.org/ api/drupal/core!lib!Drupal!Core!Cache!CacheBackendInterface.php/interface/Cache BackendInterface/8*), and there are numerous examples of basic usage in core modules. Rather than duplicating that information here, we'll discuss some of the lesser known features and ones new to Drupal 8.

Cache chains

A new feature in Drupal 8 is the *cache chain backend*, a means of stringing together different cache storage backends in a way that is transparent to the calling code. This feature is primarily designed for combining two persistent storage backends together —for example, APC and database caching—in order to get the best of both. With an APC and database chain, the cache will check APC first and return immediately if an item is found. If not, it will check the database and then write back to APC if the item is found there; and on cache misses, it will write to both. It's also possible to use the memory backend shipped with Drupal core and any other persistent backend to emulate the static + persistent caching pattern shown earlier, without the code complexity.

Cache bins

Drupal core defines several different cache bins, including "bootstrap" for information required on every request, the default cache bin, and use-case-specific bins such as "page" which is only used for cached HTML pages. The cache API not only allows for storage to be swapped out but also allows it to be changed for each cache bin, via the $conf[cache_backends] variable in Drupal 7 and the dependency injection container in Drupal 8.

The bootstrap cache bin is designed for items needed for every request; it's used primarily by low-level Drupal APIs such as the theme registry or hook system. The cache items in this bin tend to be invalidated infrequently—often when a module is enabled or disabled—and since they're requested all the time will have an extremely high hit rate.

On the other hand, the "block" cache bin is used to cache the output of Drupal's blocks system. Blocks may have different cache items per role, per user, and/or per page, which can result in hundreds of thousands or more potential entries in the bin. The bin is also cleared often on content updates, so it has a high insert/delete/update rate.

In most cases, sites will want to set up a single cache backend such as Memcache or Redis to handle all cache bins, but the option is there to use different backends with different bins if desired.

When using the cache API, you'll likely use the default cache bin, or create a custom bin. A custom bin should only be used if there's going to be a very large amount of data to cache.

getMultiple()/setMultiple()/deleteMultiple()

As with entity loading, the cache API allows for loading, setting, and deleting multiple cache objects at once. Any situation where you know the cache IDs of multiple objects in advance is a candidate for using these methods, and many different storage backends natively support multiple get, allowing a single round trip to the cache storage and a shorter code execution path.

Cache tags

A new feature of the core cache API in Drupal 8 is cache tags.

There is often confusion between cache tags as a concept and cache IDs, so let's explain cache IDs first.

When creating a cache ID in Drupal, the following conventions are important:

- Use the module name or another unique prefix at the start of the cache ID to avoid naming conflicts with others.
- Where a cache ID depends on context, include enough information about this context in the ID to ensure uniqueness. That is, for a cache item that varies per user, you might use:

    ```php
    <?php $cid = 'my_module:' . $uid; ?>
    ```

    If it varies by language as well, then use:

```php
<?php $cid = 'my_module:' . $uid . ':' $langcode; ?>
```

In this case, the semantics of what makes up the cache ID aren't important; all that matters is that one user doesn't get presented content that was cached for another user or translated in a different language to the one they're viewing the content in..

 One exception to this is *key-based invalidation*—using the updated timestamp of an entity as part of the cache key means that when the entity is updated, so is the cache key, resulting in a cache miss and new cache entry without having to explicitly clear the old key.

Cache tags, rather than guaranteeing the uniqueness of cache items, are intended for cache invalidation.

A good example of this is entity rendering. Entities may be rendered on their own with multiple view modes, as part of a listing of multiple entities via Views, as part of a block, or embedded within the rendering of another entity via entity references.

A rendered node may include information from referenced entities, such as the name of the user that authored the node and that user's avatar. A Views listing might include multiple nodes like this.

To maintain coherency when entities are updated, there are two common approaches:

Set long TTLs and clear all caches of rendered content
> The cache will be completely emptied whenever a single item of content is updated, even though the majority of the cache will be unaffected. On sites with frequent content updates, this approach can lead to low hit rates and the potential for cache stampedes. However, the cache will always be accurate.

Set short TTLs so that content is only stale for a few seconds or minutes
> This results in lower hit rates regardless of the frequency of content updates. However, not explicitly clearing the cache all at once when an item is updated means there's less likelihood of cache stampedes.

Cache tags allow for a "best of both worlds" scenario, where all cache items that include an entity are tagged with that entity's ID, and saving the entity invalidates those cache items but no others. This allows for both cache coherency (assuming consistent tagging in the first place) and longer TTLs.

CacheArray

CacheArray was originally added to Drupal 8 but has been backported to Drupal 7, along with several patches integrating it with core subsystems. As a highly dynamic system, and with so much functionality provided by modules, Drupal has evolved to carry a lot of metadata about what functionality is provided from where. This includes the theme registry (a large array of all theme hooks, templates, and preprocessors), the schema cache (which contains metadata about every database table defined by a module, which often reaches 200 or so), and several other registries. On a default install of Drupal core, these usually reach a few hundred kilobytes at most; however, many Drupal sites end up with as many as a hundred or even several hundred contributed modules enabled, each of which may be defining new database tables, theme templates, and the like.

Prior to Drupal 7.7, each subsystem would store these arrays in one large cache item. This meant that for the theme registry, every theme function or template registered on a particular site would be loaded on every page—including theme functions for specific administrative tables that might not be used, or for functionality that might not be exposed on the site itself due to configuration. For the schema cache, while the schema metadata is only used for tables passed to `drupal_write_record()` or `drupal_sche ma_fields_sql()`—often as few as 10–15 tables on most sites—metadata about every database table on the site would nevertheless be loaded from the cache for every request.

`CacheArray` (*http://api.drupal.org/api/drupal/core!lib!Drupal!Core!Utility!CacheAr ray.php/class/CacheArray/8*) provides a mechanism to drastically reduce the size of these cache entries by emulating a PHP array using `ArrayAccess`. When an array key is requested that hasn't already been cached, it's treated as a cache miss and looked up, and then the array is populated with the returned value. At the end of the request, any newly found array keys and values get written back to the cache entry so that they'll be a cache hit for the next request. This allows the cache item to be built on demand, populated only with data that is actually in use on the site and often excluding infrequently accessed items such as those used for administrative pages that may not be visited during normal site operation. Relatively few contributed modules need to maintain as much metadata as some of these core subsystems, but `CacheArray` provides a solution to this problem when you run into it.

 CacheArray is in the process of being replaced by `CacheCollector` (*https://api.drupal.org/api/drupal/core!lib!Drupal!Core!Cache!Cache Collector.php/class/CacheCollector/8*) in Drupal 8. `CacheCollector` has the same internal logic but uses public methods for `get` and `set` instead of `ArrayAccess`.

Render caching

Drupal's render API takes a structured array of data and converts it to HTML, running it through the theme system and collecting associated assets such as CSS and JavaScript. One of the more powerful but underused features of the render system is its integrated cache handling.

When writing code that generates HTML, there are two main phases that the content goes through:

- Building the array of data (e.g., a list of nodes based on the results of a query)
- Rendering the array to HTML, which mainly involves running it through the theme system

Render caching allows the majority of time spent in these operations to be skipped. We'll take the example of a custom block that shows the five most recently published article titles, taking it from no caching at all to using the render cache as much as possible:

```
/**
 * Implements hook_block_info().
 */
function example_block_info() {
  $blocks['example_render_cache'] = array(
    'info' => t('Render caching example.'),
    'cache' => DRUPAL_CACHE_CUSTOM,
  );
  return $blocks;
}

/**
 * Implements hook_block_view().
 */
function example_block_view($delta = '') {
  switch ($delta) {
    case 'example_render_cache':
      $query = new EntityFieldQuery();
      $query->entityCondition('entity_type', 'node')
        ->entityCondition('bundle', 'article')
        ->propertyCondition('status', 1)
        ->range(0, 5)
        ->propertyOrderBy('created', 'ASC');
      $result = $query->execute();
      $nids = array_keys($result['node']);
      $nodes = node_load_multiple($nids);
      $titles = array();
      foreach ($nodes as $node) {
        $titles[] = l($node->title, 'node/' . $node->nid);
      }
      $block['subject'] = t('Render caching example');
      $block['content'] = array(
        '#theme' => 'item_list',
        '#items' => $titles,
      );
      break;
  }
  return $block;
}
```

When the block is rendered with each request, first the hook_block_view() implementation is called. Then the resulting render array is run through drupal_render() (the second phase).

Just adding #cache to the render array would skip theming, but the entity query and loading would continue to happen with every request without some reorganization. Render caching allows us to skip that work as well, by moving that code to a #pre_ren der callback. This is the most complicated aspect of using render caching, so rather than adding the cache first, we'll start by moving that code around.

hook_block_view() now looks like this:

```
/**
 * Implements hook_block_view().
 */
function example_block_view($delta = '') {
  switch ($delta) {
    case 'example_render_cache':
      $block['subject'] = t('Render caching example');
      $block['content'] = array(
        '#theme' => 'item_list',
        '#pre_render' => array('_example_render_cache_block_pre_render'),
      );
    break;
  }
  return $block;
}

/**
 * Pre-render callback for example_render_cache block.
 */
function _example_render_cache_block_pre_render($element) {
  $query = new EntityFieldQuery();
  $query->entityCondition('entity_type', 'node')
    ->entityCondition('bundle', 'article')
    ->propertyCondition('status', 1)
    ->range(0, 5)
    ->propertyOrderBy('created', 'ASC');
  $result = $query->execute();
  $nids = array_keys($result['node']);
  $nodes = node_load_multiple($nids);
  $items = array();
  foreach ($nodes as $node) {
    $items[] = l($node->title, 'node/' . $node->nid);
  }
  $element['#items'] = $items;

  return $element;
}
```

hook_block_view() now returns only the minimum metadata needed; the bulk of the work is transferred to the render callback, which will be called by drupal_render() itself when the element is rendered.

Once this is done, adding caching requires only a small change to hook_block_view():

```
/**
 * Implements hook_block_view().
 */
function example_block_view($delta = '') {
  switch ($delta) {
    case 'example_render_cache':
      $block['subject'] = t('Render caching example');
      $block['content'] = array(
        '#theme' => 'item_list',
        '#pre_render' => array('_example_render_cache_block_pre_render'),
        '#cache' => array(
          'keys' => array('example_render_cache'),
        ),
      );
    break;
  }
  return $block;
}
```

Adding #cache means that drupal_render() will check for a cache item before doing any other processing of the render array, *including* the #pre_render callback. Profiling a page with this block before and after should show that the EntityFieldQuery and node loading has been removed on cache hits. See Chapter 6 for more information about how to check this.

Queues and Workers

Drupal core ships with a robust queue API, defaulting to MySQL but with contributed projects providing support for Redis, Beanstalkd, and others.

The queue API is most useful when you have expensive operations triggered by actions on the site. For example, saving a node or comment may require updating the search index, sending email notifications to multiple recipients, and clearing various caches. Performing all of these actions directly in hook_node_update() will mean the request that actually saves the node takes considerably longer, and introduces single points of failure in the critical path of updating content. Depending on the implementation, failures in search indexing or sending emails may show up as errors to the end user or interrupt the content saving process altogether.

Instead of doing all this work inline, in your hook_node_update() implementation, you can create a queue item for that node; then, in the worker callback, you can perform whichever tasks on it are necessary.

This has the following advantages:

- Expensive processing is taken out of the critical path of saving nodes into a background process. This allows the Apache process to be freed up quicker and pages to be served more quickly to users.
- The background process may be run by *drush* or a queue daemon. Any operations that require high memory limits won't bloat Apache, and they don't necessarily need to run on the main web server at all. If queues are processed by Jenkins, it's also possible to isolate reporting of failures for particular queues.
- Multiple queue workers may run at the same time, allowing infrastructure usage to be maximized when there are lots of items in various queues. In contrast, Drupal's hook_cron() only allows one cron invocation to run at a time.
- Queue items are processed individually and can be returned to the queue if not successful. For example, if a queue item needs to call an external service but the API call fails with a 503 response, it can be returned to the queue to be retried later.

In sum, pages can be served to end users faster, you have more flexibility when scaling up your infrastructure, and your application will be more robust against failures or performance issues in external providers.

Cache Stampedes and Race Conditions

As sites reach large numbers of simultaneous processes, the potential for stampedes and race conditions increases.

A stampede can happen when a cache item is empty or invalid and multiple processes attempt to populate it at the same time. Here's an example with Drupal 7's variable cache:

- Process A requests the variable cache, but there is no valid entry, so it starts loading the variables from the database and unserializing them.
- Process B then comes in; there is no cache entry yet, so it also queries the variables from the database.
- Process C comes in and does the same thing.
- Process A finishes building the page and caches it.
- Process D requests the page and gets the cached item.
- Processes B and C finish and overwrite the cache item with their own identical versions.

In this case, only one cache item was needed, but it was created three times.

If this is an expensive task, it can put the server under high load as multiple different processes all do duplicate work.

There are two approaches to handling this scenario:

- When it's OK for a few requests to be served an invalid cache item, it's possible to use the $allow_invalid parameter to $cache->get() so that invalidated but still present cache items are returned by the API. The first request to get an invalid cache item can acquire a lock using Drupal core's lock API, then proceed to build the new cache item and return it to the caller. Subsequent requests will fail to acquire the lock and can immediately return the stale cache item; this will happen until the new cache item is available.

- When the cache item must be up to date at all times, or if a cache item is completely empty, it's not possible to serve stale content. The first process to get a cache miss will still acquire a lock and proceed to build the fresh cache item. If the item is very expensive to build, then subsequent requests can be put into a holding pattern using $lock->wait(). This will return as soon as the lock is released, after which the cache should be available.

Using the locking system can have its own problems—when a cache stampede turns into a lock stampede—and it would be remiss not to discuss these:

- By default, acquiring a lock requires a database write, and polling for locks queries the database quite frequently. Locking to save one inexpensive database query can be counterproductive in terms of performance since it may have as much overhead as rebuilding the cache item. The lock API has pluggable storage, so this can be improved by installing one of the alternative backends.

- Items that are cached per page are less likely to be requested simultaneously than items cached once for the whole site. Where there is very little chance of a cache stampede, the extra overhead of acquiring the lock is not worth it for these items.

- Items that are invalidated very frequently—say, every 10 seconds—will result in a constant acquiring and freeing of locks. Since processes that don't acquire locks usually poll to see if the item is created, they may miss the window of the valid cache item and continue to poll.

If you are running into issues with locking, consider whether the lock may be making things worse rather than better. Alternatively, it may be necessary to rethink the functionality altogether; for example, refactoring a per-page element to work across all pages on the site.

## CHAPTER 5

Drupal Coding for Abysmal Performance

Having looked at some Drupal best practices for performance, we'll now take a look at some worst practices and antipatterns. No one intentionally writes abysmally performing code, but as with any system, misuse of Drupal APIs can lead to unexpected and hard-to-predict performance issues that are often hidden in the implementation details of a specific API.

It's not possible to provide an exhaustive list of antipatterns in Drupal that are bad for performance, but one API in particular gets abused very frequently and can cause quite serious and hard-to-track-down performance issues on high-traffic sites with particular configurations.

variable_set() Abuse

The variables system prior to Drupal 8 is one of the simplest, most central, and most commonly used APIs, to the point where it's very rare to find a module that doesn't use it. It's also one of the most frequently abused APIs, including in Drupal core, so it provides a good example of how a simple API can come to be misused over time as use cases change. As you'll see, this API no longer exists in Drupal 8.

We'll start with a brief explanation of the API and its implementation in Drupal core.

Variables are stored in a single table with a name and a serialized value. Early in each page request, every variable is loaded into the $conf global from the cache (or the cache item is rebuilt if it's missing). Individual variables are accessed, set, or deleted via the variable_get(), variable_set(), and variable_del() functions. system_set tings_form() provides a degree of automation between administrative configuration pages and the variables they control.

Over the years, as well as storing configuration, the variables system has been used for storing other things as well:

- Cache items that are updated infrequently and expensive to rebuild
- Site "state," or metadata tracking the status of a specific site, which can't be recreated in the same way a cache entry should be (so can't be deleted when all caches are flushed), but is set dynamically by code rather than triggered by configuration UI changes

Prior to Drupal 8, core did not provide a dedicated key/value store, so the variables system was reused for this as the next closest thing.

Examples of where variables are used to store state in Drupal core include for tracking whether outgoing HTTP requests are failing, the time of the last cron run, and the filenames and file collections for generated CSS and JavaScript aggregates.

When a variable is set, three things can happen:

1. The database row is updated. Updating the database invalidates the MySQL query cache and may cause issues with locking on high-traffic tables, but is usually a fast operation with a well-indexed query affecting just one row.
2. The cache is cleared. Clearing a cache itself is very cheap.
3. The next request to the site discovers that there's no cache entry for the variable table, so it loads every variable (sometimes 2,000–3,000 of them on complex sites) from the variables table, unserializes them, then writes the cache entry. This could take anything from a few milliseconds to a couple of hundred milliseconds depending on the number of variables, site load, etc. No Drupal request can be served without all variables being loaded, so if a previous request has cleared the variable cache, the next request will try to rebuild it. If multiple requests hit the site before the cache item has been set, one of the following occurs:

    - (Drupal 6) All requests that get a cache miss will each rebuild the variables cache entry and write it back to the cache table.
    - (Drupal 7 and Drupal 6 Pressflow) The first request acquires a lock, rebuilds and writes back the cache entry; other requests wait for the lock to be released, then either build it if there's still no cache entry, or read from the cache and continue.

If `variable_set()` ends up being called very frequently, this can result in either a cache stampede, where dozens of requests are constantly updating the cache entry, or a lock stampede, where processes are constantly waiting for a new variable cache entry that may be invalidated again before they're able to retrieve it from the cache.

What makes this problem worse is that it can be relatively hard to track down the cause, for a few reasons:

- When profiling a page, `variable_set()` won't show up as one of the most expensive operations—the set itself is fairly quick, so it could easily be skipped over.

- While generating the variables cache entry is quite expensive, there's no way to tell from these requirements why the variables cache was empty. It's not possible to know which variable was cleared without reviewing code or debugging, so even profiling a page where the variables cache was previously invalidated doesn't give an indication of whether this was due to state tracking or via a configuration form submission.

If you find a module doing this in Drupal 7, consider checking that the value of the variable has changed before saving it, converting the code to use the cache system if that's feasible, saving the value in a dedicated table if it's not requested frequently, or, like `drupal_http_request()`, just logging the change via `watchdog()`.

In Drupal 8, the variables system has been completely removed and replaced with three distinct APIs:

Settings
Low-level configuration required before storage is available to the system as a whole; settings can only be changed in *settings.php*.

Configuration
The majority of module configuration is stored as YAML, providing the ability to stage configuration changes between sites.

State and key/value store
A new key/value store interface and implementation have been added, and a "state" service is made available by default using this API. All the things that previously would have been abusing the variables system to store state can now use the state service. Since state is separated from overall site configuration, updating values in the state system won't invalidate the entire configuration cache.

External Requests

Increasingly, site development includes interacting with external APIs, whether for social sharing, login, content sharing, or similar purposes. When making HTTP requests from PHP code, it's easy to introduce a single point of failure in your architecture, and in the case of requests to an external API, it's one that you will have no control over if the service happens to be sluggish or go down due to network or infrastructure issues.

Examples of where this can go wrong include features such as allowing users to specify an RSS feed in their profile pages and then displaying it in a block, or using the PHP APIs for services such as Facebook and Twitter. If the request to the external service takes several seconds, times out, or returns a bad status code, will your page still be served in a timely manner, or at all?

External HTTP requests can also be a hidden cause of performance issues on a site, since they may be intermittent and will not cause high CPU or disk load in the same way poorly optimized PHP algorithms or slow database queries can.

There are several steps that can be taken to reduce the potential for catastrophic failure. We'll use a user-specific RSS feed displayed in a block on the user's profile page as an example:

1. Add caching. A call to an external API can easily take 200–300 ms. If that call is a simple GET request for a list of posts or the like, it will be very straightforward to cache the results using Drupal's caching API. If the site has empty caches, this won't prevent downtime, so just adding caching won't be sufficient, but it will mean that sites with a warm cache entry won't depend on the service being available.

2. Add a timeout. If an API can't respond within a second or two, can you afford to wait any longer before serving the page? If not, adding a timeout to the HTTP request ensures that your code will continue.

3. Move the HTTP request out of the critical path. It may be possible to move the HTTP request to hook_cron() (for example, precaching the RSS feeds for each user once per hour instead of checking each time the block is viewed) or a queue. Alternatively, the block could be moved to an AJAX callback, with JavaScript on the parent page requesting the block and inserting it into the DOM (known as a client-side include). You can also use both methods: if the HTTP request fails, cron might take a bit longer, or the AJAX request might not return, but the main request itself will still be able to complete and be served.

Sessions

Since Drupal 7, sessions are only created for unauthenticated users once something is actually put into $_SESSION. Once a user has a session, page caching is disabled to avoid serving incorrect content based on the contents of the user's session, such as the contents of a shopping cart, or status messages. This happens when using both the internal page cache and a reverse proxy, if using a standard configuration.

$_SESSION should therefore only be used for situations where storing the information for the anonymous user should also prevent pages being cached for that user. An example would be a user's shopping cart choices, where the shopping cart contents may be displayed on each page, and the site may want to preserve the choices in the session when the user logs in. While adding items to a shopping cart is a valid reason to disable caching, attention should be paid if a user removes an item from the cart. A common mistake is to set `$_SESSION['foo'] =''` or `$_SESSION['foo'] = array()` when emptying out a session variable; using anything other than `unset($_SESSION['foo'])` will leave the session open.

Excessive Cache Granularity

When you're working on a project, requests may come in to make particular content user specific (per user, geolocated), or to vary things on every page—for example, excluding the article in the main content area from a list of featured articles in the sidebar. Often these requests are unavoidable, but the details of how this extra information is added to or removed from pages can have profound effects on a site's performance.

Let's take for example a snippet that shows the latest three articles added to a site. A simplified version of the block on a Drupal 7 site might look like:

```php
<?php
  $nids = db_query_range('
  SELECT nid
  FROM {node}
  WHERE status = 1
  ORDER BY created DESC', 0, 3)->fetchCol();
  $nodes = node_load_multiple($nids);
  return node_view_multiple($nodes, 'block_listing');
?>
```

However, when you're on the *node/n* page for one of the nodes in this block, you might want to exclude it from the list and show the fourth-most-recent node instead:

```php
<?php
  $current_node = menu_get_object();
  $nids = db_query_range('
  SELECT nid
  FROM {node}
  WHERE status = 1
  AND nid <> :nid
  ORDER BY created DESC', 0, 3, array(':nid' => $current_node->nid))->fetchCol();
  $nodes = node_load_multiple($nids);
  return node_view_multiple($nodes, 'block_listing');
?>
```

Only one condition was added, but this fundamentally changes the performance of this block. With the first version, despite potentially being displayed on tens of thousands of node pages across the site, the query was always exactly the same. This allowed it to be cached in a single cache entry, both by the MySQL query cache and in Drupal's cache API if desired. With the second version of the query, however, a different version will be run on every node page. A million node pages might mean a million variations on the query, vastly reducing the effectiveness of both the MySQL query cache and Drupal's own cache layer.

Rather than excluding the current node ID in SQL, we could do it in PHP:

```php
<?php
  $current_node = menu_get_object();
  // This time load four nodes.
  $nids = db_query_range('
  SELECT nid
  FROM {node}
  WHERE status = 1
  ORDER BY created DESC', 0, 4)->fetchCol();

  foreach ($nids as $key => $nid) {
    // If one of the nodes is the current one, remove it.
    if ($nid == $current_node->nid) {
      unset($nids[$key]);
    }
  }
  // Ensure only three nodes are loaded.
  array_splice($nids, 3);
  $nodes = node_load_multiple($nids);
  return node_view_multiple($nodes, 'block_listing');
?>
```

This allows the same query to be cached across the whole site again, but still the markup will need to be cached per page. A further optimization in terms of cacheability would be to render four nodes every time, then implement the same logic for removing either the current node or the fourth-most-recent node in JavaScript, allowing the block to be safely cached in a reverse proxy via edge-side or client-side includes. At this point, it's a trade-off between caching the rendered output and the additional JavaScript requirement.

A similar issue exists with per-user markup. Drupal traditionally adds per-user markup to many site elements: for example, "new" or "updated" markers on nodes and comments based on the last time the user visited a node, or quick administration links such as contextual links. Drupal 8 will continue to add user-specific markup in these places, but it does so via JavaScript replacement so that the markup generated for the blocks themselves is the same regardless of the user. For examples of this implementation, see the Comment and History modules in Drupal 8.

PHP Errors

While Drupal core complies with E_STRICT by default and has fairly comprehensive test coverage, it is common when reviewing a live site to find PHP notices and warnings logged on every request (in some cases, tens per request). When using Drupal's default database logging (*dblog*) module for logging, this means potentially hundreds of additional database writes per second on a high-traffic site. Even if using *syslog* or another alternative log implementation, PHP error handling is expensive and should be avoided.

PHP errors and notices may well be a sign of underlying functional bugs, but even if they're not, there's no excuse for writing and deploying code that's not E_ALL compliant.

Debug Code in the Code Base

Code review as part of the development process should prevent this, but "emergency" fixes can result in debug code being committed to the live code base. This could include things like clearing the entity cache before loading entities, disabling the theme registry or locale caching, excessive logging, and various other operations that are both expensive and unnecessary on a production site.

Development Settings

While not strictly a "coding" matter, a common issue on live websites is leaving one of the many debug features provided by modules and themes enabled, such as rebuilding the theme registry on every request. Settings like this should never, ever be enabled in the user interface, but rather overwritten by settings.local.php in $conf, which can be different for development, staging, and live environments (see Chapter 9). Similarly, development modules should be enabled locally by developers after each database refresh and never enabled on a live environment. While this may be standard practice for some readers, others may recognize the frustration of discovering that a downtime issue was due to a forgotten development setting that was never switched off.

## CHAPTER 6

Verifying Changes

When optimizing a site that's under development or in production, the most important step before any other is to gather data on what the performance and scalability bottlenecks are. Without data, a lot of effort can be expended on optimizing code that's actually performing OK, and conversely, poorly performing code might be overlooked. Without being able to identify and quantify specific performance issues, it's not possible to verify that improvements have been made. A site might seem "faster" after a change was rolled out to production, but you'll never know whether this was because of the change itself, or perhaps because crawler traffic or even a distributed denial-of-service (DDoS) attack subsided at the same time.

Analyzing Frontend Performance

Frontend performance monitoring falls into roughly four categories:

- Getting a summary of a page's performance based on rules for high-performance websites
- Waterfall and timeline charts for individual pages
- Real user monitoring
- Profiling of CSS and JavaScript

YSlow and Google PageSpeed

Often the first step toward analyzing a site's frontend performance is looking at the summary report produced by a tool such as YSlow (*http://developer.yahoo.com/yslow/*) and PageSpeed (*https://developers.google.com/speed/pagespeed/*). Given a URL, or via a browser plug-in, they'll analyze a request to an individual web page and give you scores for specific areas such as number of HTTP requests, cacheable headers, etc.

Drilling down on these items will show specific recommendations. Both of these tools are very easy to use and have great documentation, so doing a walkthrough here would be redundant. However, the reports they generate are only useful if you have an understanding of the underlying principles of frontend performance and the effort it's likely to take to fix the issues that are identified. Chapter 2 goes into detail about Drupal-specific advice on how to deal with many of these issues, based loosely on the categories that are highlighted by these reports.

While generating a summary report from YSlow or PageSpeed is a very quick task, this is commonly treated as a manual step to be taken by an individual developer and so can often be overlooked during the development process, or done much less frequently than changes are made that impact the frontend performance of the site. However good your intentions may be, automating frontend performance testing as part of your continuous integration process helps to ensure that your site is regularly put through its paces and helps you discover changes that may negatively impact performance before they're deployed.

 PhantomJS is a headless WebKit implementation including a Java-Script API for which there is a YSlow plug-in. This allows you to trigger a YSlow report from the command line and write the output in a structured format such as JUnit.

Once you have a summary of a page's performance, it's often necessary to drill down to individual requests to see what's going on.

Waterfall Charts

Waterfall charts show the sequential process of loading a web page. Primarily this shows page resources as they're requested and downloaded by the browser, as well as timings for "start render" and "document complete" events, represented by the green and blue vertical bars on the chart. See Figure 6-1 for an example waterfall chart, created for a load of *http://drupal.org*.

Each horizontal bar on the waterfall chart represents a separate request. Each request is further broken down into the following components:

DNS lookup
> The address lookup for each domain that resources are served from. This occurs once per domain/subdomain rather than once per resource on the page, and may be skipped if the browser implements DNS caching and has a warm cache for the domains on the page.

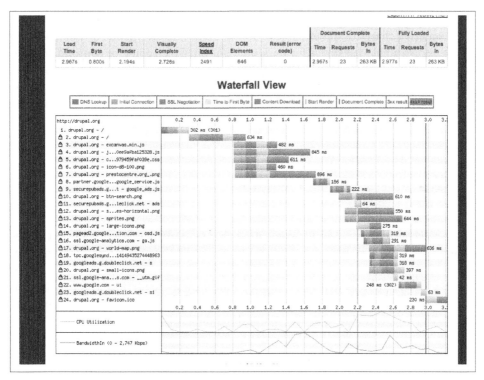

Figure 6-1. Waterfall chart for the Drupal home page

Initial connection

The upstream connection to request the resource from the server. This is constrained by upstream bandwidth, so tends to be worst for mobile connections. It's also affected by the number/size of cookies that the browser needs to send with each request—these are sent upstream for every request the browser makes that it has cookies set for.

SSL negotiation

The process of checking SSL certificates (only for SSL requests, of course).

Time to first byte

The time until the browser downloads the very first part of the resource. This depends on the speed of response of the server (is it under load, and was the file served by Varnish from memory or by Apache from disk, or even generated by PHP dynamically?).

Content download

This depends mainly on file size—whether the file is optimized to the correct size, gzipped, etc.

Drupal.org is quite well optimized at 23 requests on the front page, but looking closely at the waterfall chart, it's still possible to see room for improvement. For example, *btn-search.png* is a single-use image for the search button, which could be consolidated into one of the existing sprites since the same styling is used for other buttons on the page. Any request for an image that's not associated with content should be treated with suspicion! Even when images are consolidated into sprites, consider whether it might be possible to replace them with typographic or CSS features instead.

 Follow along (*https://drupal.org/node/2031259*) with the issue we filed for this while writing this chapter.

While *webpagetest* was used for generating this example, you'll normally get richer information from local browsers using tools such as Firebug for Firefox, Chrome Developer Tools or Safari Developer Tools. These provide the ability to view all the HTTP headers for a request, as well as a timeline of the browser rendering layer itself, which can help to identify issues such as how many reflows and repaints happen on the page (i.e., due to images included in the page without dimensions).

Real User Monitoring

When testing frontend performance, a key point to bear in mind is that as a developer (or Jenkins job) running synthetic tests on a site that you're working on, you represent absolute best-case conditions for frontend performance in nearly all cases. Developers are most likely to be:

- On fast Internet connections
- Running powerful hardware
- Using recent operating system and browser versions
- From a location geographically close to the origin server

Whereas visitors to a site could be from multiple continents, running old hardware with out-of-date browser versions over public WiFi or 3G networks.

While an improvement made for the best-case scenario is usually an improvement for the worst-case scenario, too, particularly in the case of network latency and browser rendering speeds, differences in visitors' connections and hardware can mean extreme variation in results for the same page. A visitor with a slow 3G connection is likely to spend a much greater proportion of the page load time making upstream requests to the server (so watch those cookies!). A visitor with an older smartphone is much more likely to experience sluggish rendering performance due to poorly optimized markup,

CSS, and JavaScript, because that device will have significantly less CPU available than the average laptop.

In response to this, there is increased reliance on real user monitoring (RUM) to collect performance metrics from actual visits to sites in addition to "clean" tests.

RUM tends to be dominated by commercial Software as a Service (SaaS) solutions, since it requires capturing, storing, and presenting large volumes of information that many organizations do not have the ability to maintain in-house. However, there are open source alternatives, such as Jiffy (open sourced by Netflix) and Steve Souders' Web Episodes, and free commercial alternatives such as the page timing feature of Google Analytics (*http://bit.ly/18PMYZS*). There's also a Drupal contributed module (*https://drupal.org/project/navigation_timing*) for the navigation timing API that can be used to directly collect information from requests to the site within Drupal, although this is not suitable for production sites.

Regardless of the mechanism used, the end result is collecting real requests to the site by visitors, including timings such as time to first byte and page complete, via a snippet of JavaScript included in the web page. By recording this data for all requests made to a site, it's possible to generate reports that show overall trends for end user performance on the site—which pages are slow, whether particular browsers have a particularly slower experience than others, which countries are getting the best and worst response times, etc.

Depending on the tool used, it may be possible to collect diagnostic information as well. However, more often this information can be used to feed back into synthetic tests to make them better reflect reality, or to target them on specific areas of the site that need improvement or that experience the most traffic.

Analyzing Application Performance

Application performance is often the black sheep of site optimization, with efforts focused primarily on frontend performance and infrastructure. In our case, application performance means… Drupal! More specifically, we want to look at the PHP code and database queries that Drupal needs to run to serve a request. Application performance is not the same as the performance of your site overall. If 90% of requests are served from Varnish, then Drupal is only involved in the other 10%—but these 10% will be the slowest, and they may come all at once if the Varnish cache is cleared.

Measuring and understanding application performance is not at all the same thing as load testing. While load testing frameworks often include performance measurements, this is measuring the end-to-end performance, including infrastructure and network layers. Load tests are likely to only find the most glaring application performance issues, since there can be a high variation in response times between tests. See Chapter 20 for more discussion on how to run load tests and what to look for.

By contrast, understanding application performance means examining how the code that runs your application performs, more or less in isolation from external factors. This is done by profiling the code.

The Devel Module

The Devel (*http://drupal.org/project/devel*) module provides a number of debugging tools for developers. Amongst these are tools for monitoring page timing, memory consumption, and the query log, and for XHProf profiling. Most of the features discussed here apply across the Drupal 6, 7, and 8 versions of the module.

Page timing

Devel's own page timing uses microtime to measure the time from `drupal_boot strap_configuration()` to PHP shutdown and requires no PHP extensions to be enabled: just check the box on *admin/config/development/devel*. Microtime across a full page request can be extremely variable, so to ensure a like for like comparison, refresh the pages several times to ensure all application caches (as well as the opcode cache, MySQL query cache, etc.) have been primed, or expect very different results each time. There is one exception to this: when timing cache misses, you should ensure that all caches really are empty. The page timer can be used for a quick sanity check as to whether a page is taking dozens, hundreds, or thousands of milliseconds to load and is useful in situations where there is no opportunity to install lower-level tools, but usually it's better to go straight to one of the other techniques for measuring page execution time discussed in the following sections.

Memory usage

Memory usage in the Devel module is measured using `memory_get_usage()` and `memo ry_get_peak_usage()` during shutdown. As with page timings, no PHP extension is required, and the option can be enabled at *admin/config/development/devel*. Since this information is taken from PHP itself, it can be relied upon more than the page timings, but there are still some caveats. If you're trying to find out how much memory a page is going to use, ensure that other debugging tools like Xdebug, XHProf, and the query log are disabled, since these will increase memory usage. Also ensure that any opcode caches are enabled (unless specifically testing memory usage without an opcode cache), since these can impact memory usage by several megabytes. Finally, bear in mind that Drupal's memory usage varies widely depending on whether caches are primed or not. Often for memory usage, the worst case should be measured as opposed to the best case —an Apache process will always have a memory footprint of the worst PHP page it served from memory, not the best.

Query log

Devel's query log measures database queries from `devel_boot()` until PHP shutdown. Since it uses the APIs within Drupal's own database layer, it's able to present the exact queries that were triggered on the page in question. This makes it a very useful alternative to *mytop*.

 Drupal may execute some database queries before `hook_boot()` runs, depending on whether the database cache backend is used and which Drupal version is being tested.

Like the options for measuring page timing and memory usage, the query log option can be enabled at *admin/config/development/devel*. There are two options that allow customization of the query log display:

Sort Query Log
> The query log is sorted "by source" by default, showing the queries in the order they were executed. Changing this to "by duration" shows the queries in the order of execution time, slowest first. This is useful to quickly identify slow queries on the page, but bear in mind that query timings may change on each request due to the influence of the MySQL query cache, server load, or just margin of error, and this can make it difficult to identify the same query across different page requests since it may change position each time.

Slow Query Highlighting
> This defaults to 5 ms, and any query taking longer will be highlighted in red in the query log. Five milliseconds is not particularly slow, but most queries executed by Drupal should be well indexed, may be in the query cache, and are likely to have small result sets, so they should execute in well under 1 ms in most cases. Therefore even leaving this option at the default setting should not result in any highlighted queries on a stock install.

While not specific to the query log, there's one other Devel setting that affects the query log and other performance measurements taken by Devel: "Display redirection page." Drupal form submissions make a `$_POST` request to the same page as the form. Once the form has been processed, the page gets redirected. Since the query log only collects queries during the request, the redirect prevents the log from ever being rendered. "Display redirection page" provides an intermediary page that allows the output to be printed, along with a link to the page that was going to be redirected to. This is an invaluable option when trying to examine queries executed after submitted content or searches, which would otherwise be invisible except at the MySQL level.

Apart from these settings, note that the query log will only be displayed to users with the "Access developer information" permission. On a development site it should be fine to enable this for anonymous or authenticated users. The Devel module should never be enabled on a production site.

Once the option is enabled and permission granted, visiting any page will result in the queries being shown at the bottom. Figure 6-2 shows an example from the front page of a stock Drupal 7 install with no caches primed.

Executed 91 queries in 29.05 ms. Queries exceeding 5 ms are highlighted.

ms	#	where	ops	query
0.26	4	DrupalDatabaseCache::getMultiple	P A E	SELECT cid, data, created, expire, serialized FROM cache_bootstrap WH
0.2	3	_registry_check_code	P A E	SELECT filename FROM registry WHERE name = :name AND type = :type
0.24	4	DrupalDatabaseCache::getMultiple	P A E	SELECT cid, data, created, expire, serialized FROM cache_bootstrap WH
0.75	1	system_list	P A E	SELECT * FROM system WHERE type = 'theme' OR (type = 'module' AND sta
0.28	4	DrupalDatabaseCache::set	P A	SELECT 1 AS expression FROM cache_bootstrap cache_bootstrap WHERE (
1.6	4	DrupalDatabaseCache::set	P A	INSERT INTO cache_bootstrap (cid, serialized, created, expire, data) :db_insert_placeholder_4)
0.27	4	DrupalDatabaseCache::getMultiple	P A E	SELECT cid, data, created, expire, serialized FROM cache_bootstrap WH
0.19	4	DrupalDatabaseCache::getMultiple	P A E	SELECT cid, data, created, expire, serialized FROM cache_bootstrap WH
0.14	4	DrupalDatabaseCache::set	P A	SELECT 1 AS expression FROM cache_bootstrap cache_bootstrap WHERE (
0.18	4	DrupalDatabaseCache::set	P A	INSERT INTO cache_bootstrap (cid, serialized, created, expire, data) :db_insert_placeholder_4)
0.23	1	menu_get_item	P A E	SELECT * FROM menu_router WHERE path IN (:ancestors_0) ORDER BY fit [
0.2	3	_registry_check_code	P A E	SELECT filename FROM registry WHERE name = :name AND type = :type
0.2	3	_registry_check_code	P A E	SELECT filename FROM registry WHERE name = :name AND type = :type
0.21	1	PagerDefault::execute	P A E	SELECT COUNT(*) AS expression FROM (SELECT 1 AS expression FROM node
0.14	1	PagerDefault::execute	P A E	SELECT n.nid AS nid, n.sticky AS sticky, n.created AS created FROM nc DESC LIMIT 10 OFFSET 0
0.1	5	DrupalDatabaseCache::getMultiple	P A E	SELECT cid, data, created, expire, serialized FROM cache WHERE cid IN
0.14	1	_node_types_build	P A E	SELECT nt.* FROM node_type nt WHERE (disabled = :db_condition_placehc
0.09	4	DrupalDatabaseCache::set	P A	SELECT 1 AS expression FROM cache cache WHERE ((cid = :db_condition_

Figure 6-2. Devel query log with an empty cache

Figure 6-3 shows the same page load, now with a warm cache.

Executed 33 queries in 10.26 ms. Queries exceeding 5 ms are highlighted.

ns	#	where	ops	query
).32	3	DrupalDatabaseCache::getMultiple	P A E	SELECT cid, data, created, expire, serialized FROM cache_bootstrap WHER
).52	3	DrupalDatabaseCache::getMultiple	P A E	SELECT cid, data, created, expire, serialized FROM cache_bootstrap WHER
).24	3	DrupalDatabaseCache::getMultiple	P A E	SELECT cid, data, created, expire, serialized FROM cache_bootstrap WHER
).22	1	menu_get_item	P A E	SELECT * FROM menu_router WHERE path IN (:ancestors_0) ORDER BY fit DES
).35	1	PagerDefault::execute	P A E	SELECT COUNT(*) AS expression FROM (SELECT 1 AS expression FROM node n '
).3	1	PagerDefault::execute	P A E	SELECT n.nid AS nid, n.sticky AS sticky, n.created AS created FROM node DESC LIMIT 10 OFFSET 0
).27	2	DrupalDatabaseCache::getMultiple	P A E	SELECT cid, data, created, expire, serialized FROM cache WHERE cid IN (
).18	2	DrupalDatabaseCache::getMultiple	P A E	SELECT cid, data, created, expire, serialized FROM cache WHERE cid IN (
).29	1	_block_load_blocks	P A E	SELECT b.* FROM block b WHERE (b.theme = :db_condition_placeholder_0) A
).1	1	block_block_list_alter	P A E	SELECT module, delta, rid FROM block_role
).09	1	node_block_list_alter	P A E	SELECT module, delta, type FROM block_node_type
).21	1	menu_local_tasks	P A E	SELECT menu_router.* FROM menu_router menu_router WHERE (tab_root = :db
).23	10	DrupalDatabaseCache::getMultiple	P A E	SELECT cid, data, created, expire, serialized FROM cache_menu WHERE cid
).28	10	DrupalDatabaseCache::getMultiple	P A E	SELECT cid, data, created, expire, serialized FROM cache_menu WHERE cid
).2	10	DrupalDatabaseCache::getMultiple	P A E	SELECT cid, data, created, expire, serialized FROM cache_menu WHERE cid
).21	10	DrupalDatabaseCache::getMultiple	P A E	SELECT cid, data, created, expire, serialized FROM cache_menu WHERE cid
).18	10	DrupalDatabaseCache::getMultiple	P A E	SELECT cid, data, created, expire, serialized FROM cache_menu WHERE cid
).12	10	DrupalDatabaseCache::getMultiple	P A E	SELECT cid, data, created, expire, serialized FROM cache_menu WHERE cid
).14	1	shortcut_current_displayed_set	P A E	SELECT s.set_name AS set_name FROM shortcut_set s INNER JOIN shortcut_s
).11	1	shortcut_set_load	P A E	SELECT ss.* FROM shortcut_set ss WHERE (set_name = :db_condition_placeh
).24	1	menu_load_links	P A E	SELECT ml.* FROM menu_links ml WHERE (ml.menu_name = :db_condition_plac

Figure 6-3. Devel query log with a warm cache

At the top of the first query log is the summary:

```
Executed 91 queries in 29.05 ms. Queries exceeding 5 ms are highlighted.
```

And the second query log has the summary:

```
Executed 33 queries in 10.27ms. Queries exceeding 5 ms are highlighted.
```

While brief, this summary provides two fundamental pieces of information that indicate what problems might be present on the page:

Total time

This is the combined time taken for all queries on the page. In this example, the time is approximately 10 ms with a warm cache, which is likely to be a relatively small percentage of the overall time taken for the page request. An unindexed query with filesorts and table scans on a large data set could take hundreds of milliseconds or several seconds, so a high number here should be an immediate red flag.

Number of queries

Depending on the contributed and custom modules installed on a site, and the complexity of the page being rendered, the number of database queries executed on a Drupal page can vary from under 10 to several hundred or even thousands. A slow query taking seconds is more likely to be making a website hard to scale, but having to make hundreds of round trips to the database is likely to be a major contributor to slow page-building performance and will increase the overall load on the database server.

By dividing the number of queries by the total time spent executing queries on these pages, we can see that each query took approximately 0.3 ms on average. This kind of performance is expected with a stock core install and a very small data set.

After the summary, each query is listed in a table with the following columns:

ms

The number of milliseconds taken to execute the query.

#

The number of times the query was executed during the request. Note that from Drupal 7, the Devel module ignores placeholder values when counting queries, so two queries with different placeholder values are treated as the same query. Therefore, this may not show actual duplicates, but it will indicate when lots of queries are running that are very similar.

where

The caller that executed the query. This links to *api.drupal.org* by default but can be set up to link to a custom API site if desired.

ops and query

Added in Drupal 7, the ops column provides three ways to view the query itself, shown in the neighboring (query) column. The default is *P*, meaning PHP Data Object (PDO) placeholders (for example, :cids) are displayed:

```
SELECT cid, data, created, expire, serialized FROM cache WHERE cid IN (:cids_0)
```

 A query run via db_query() will have named placeholders as written in the code calling db_query(). When queries are run via db_se lect(), Drupal's query builder generates the placeholders dynamically, so they end up being called db_condition_placeholder.

Selecting the A link

> Shows the actual query executed, with placeholders replaced. This is ideal for copying and pasting into a MySQL client to check the result set or to try different variations:
>
> ```
> SELECT cid, data, created, expire, serialized FROM cache_bootstrap WHERE cid IN
> ('foo')
> ```

Selecting the E link

> Shows an EXPLAIN for the query, saving you the step of copying and pasting the query into a MySQL client in order to get this information. EXPLAIN shows the steps that MySQL goes through to solve a given query and can be very useful to track down why a query may suffer from performance issues. Table 6-1 shows Devel's EXPLAIN output for a query.

Table 6-1. Devel module query EXPLAIN

id	select_type	table	type	possible_keys	key	key_len	ref	rows	Extra
1	SIMPLE	cache_bootstrap	const	PRIMARY	PRIMARY	767	const	1	

Target

> This is the database target for the query, which could either be the primary database or a separate database being accessed via the database API.

Xdebug

Xdebug is a PHP profiling and debugging extension authored by Derick Rethans. It's very stable and as a debugger is more or less required for developing in PHP. Xdebug profiling generates *cachegrind* files, which can then be viewed in an interface such as KCacheGrind, which is available for most operating systems; or webgrind, which is written in PHP and has a web interface, as the name suggests.

Enabling profiling with Xdebug is done via one of two methods. This enables profiling for every request:

```
xdebug.profiler_enable =1
```

This allows profiling to be triggered via an XDEBUG_PROFILE cookie or a $_GET or $_POST parameter:

```
xdebug.profiler_enable_trigger =1
```

Xdebug will then write cachegrind files to xdebug.profiler_output_dir.

There are two more *php.ini* settings to be aware of:

xdebug.profiler_output_name

> configures the filename to be written to. By default this is the process ID, which means a single Apache process will write to the same filename with every request.

`xdebug.profiler_append`
> configures whether cachegrind files written to the same location will be appended to the existing content or overwrite it.

The combination of these two configuration options is very important to bear in mind the first time you try profiling. Since the default configuration is to write with the process ID and overwrite files each time, visiting a Drupal page that triggers an AJAX request (which several Drupal core modules do) is likely to result in the cachegrind file holding the profile of the AJAX request rather than the initial one you intended to profile. Including `%r` (random string) as part of `xdebug.profile_output_name` guarantees a unique file each time, and `%R` (`$_SERVER['request_uri']`) means that page requests can easily be associated to the profile output. See this page (*http://xdebug.org/docs/all_settings#trace_output_name*) for more filename options.

Profiling with Xdebug carries a lot of overhead, so it's important to only leave it enabled when profiling. Also, just having the Xdebug extension enabled (without profiling) has a performance impact, so ensure you disable it entirely before doing other kinds of performance testing.

XHProf

XHProf isa profiler for PHP, developed and open sourced by Facebook. XHProf does not contain a debugger and exists solely as a profiler. As a profiler, XHProf has several advantages over Xdebug and is our preferred profiling tool for Drupal. These include:

- The ability to collect data on memory usage as well as CPU usage and wall time while profiling. Xdebug has the capability to collect memory usage data via function traces, but this is less convenient since it's a separate mechanism to collecting cachegrind, and there is not the range of UIs available for examining the output.

- Less overhead from being enabled. Unlike Xdebug, XHProf does not add significant overhead simply by being enabled, allowing it to be installed on production web servers.

- Considerably less overhead when profiling. In addition, `xhprof_enable()` has `XHPROF_FLAGS_CPU` and `XHPROF_FLAGS_MEMORY` options that determine whether CPU and memory usage data will be collected, allowing a custom balance between the amount of data collected and performance overhead. While profiling does have a measurable overhead, this is low enough that XHProf can be considered for profiling a sample of requests on production sites if desired.

XHProf is available via PECL, so assuming you have PECL available already, it can be installed with:

```
$ sudo pecl install xhprof
```

Or, if you have PECL set to stable releases only:

```
$ sudo pecl install channel://pecl.php.net/xhprof-0.9.3
```

 Many resources on the Internet recommend compiling XHProf from source because the previous 0.9.2 release would not install from PECL successfully. However, this was fixed with version 0.9.3, released in May 2013, so compiling manually is no longer necessary.

You may also need to enable the *xhprof* extension yourself in *php.ini*:

```
extension=xhprof.so
```

XHProf ships with a web interface built in PHP. This is found in the *xhprof_html* folder (usually found in */usr/share* or */usr/local/share*). To use this, set up a virtual host and */etc/hosts* entry so that it's available at *http://xhprof.localhost* or similar. There are also third-party user interfaces available, but we'll focus on the default interface for the purposes of this discussion.

XHProf profiling is enabled via the xhprof_enable() and xhprof_disable() functions. This allows profiling to be conditionally enabled or disabled in runtime code— for example, if you were trying to sample requests in a QA or production environment, profiling could be restricted to a particular Drupal user or path, or to a 1/1,000 sample. This also allows profiling to be restricted to a particular section of code if desired.

Most commonly, however, when profiling a website, you'll want to profile the entire request each time, in order to put the numbers in context. There are several ways to do this:

- The Devel module provides an xhprof setting at *admin/config/development/devel*. Enabling XHProf profiling, adding the path to xhprof_lib, and adding the URL to the web interface is all that's necessary to begin profiling requests. The Devel module uses hook_boot(), so it will not profile code that runs prior to that. Once profiling is enabled, all pages will have a link to "XHProf Output" at the bottom.

- The XHProf module (*https://drupal.org/project/xhprof*) is similar to Devel in that it allows XHProf profiling to be enabled via configuration; however, it also provides a Drupal interface for examining the output.

- auto_prepend_file and auto_append_file allow arbitrary PHP files to be included at the beginning and end of each request via *.htaccess* when using mod_php. This allows the entire Drupal request to be profiled, since XHProf is enabled before any Drupal code runs.

The last method requires some manual steps compared to use of the Devel and XHProf modules, so we'll detail those here. Two files are required:

```php
<?php
  include '/path/to/xhprof/xhprof_lib/utils/xhprof_lib.php';
  include '/path/to/xhprof/xhprof_lib/utils/xhprof_runs.php';
  xhprof_enable(XHPROF_FLAGS_CPU + XHPROF_FLAGS_MEMORY);
?>

<?php
  $host = $_SERVER['HTTP_HOST'];
  $xhprof_data = xhprof_disable();
  $xhprof_runs = new XHProfRuns_Default();
  $run_id = $xhprof_runs->save_run($xhprof_data, $host);
  $source = urlencode($host);
  $url = "http://xhprof.localhost/index.php?run=$run_id&source=$source";
  echo '<a href="'. $url .'" target="_blank">Profiler output</a>';
?>
```

Then, in the *.htaccess* file at the root of your Drupal install, add these two lines:

```
php_value auto_prepend_file 'var/www/xhprof/header.php'
php_value auto_append_file '/var/www/xhprof/footer.php'
```

When you request a page in your Drupal installation, you should now see the text "Profiler output" at the bottom of the page.

Now that XHProf is up and running, you can profile a request, look for issues, then evaluate a way to fix them.

Starting with an 8.x install, with the standard profile, create a single node, then visit *node/1* as an anonymous user. Drupal has several caches to build on that page, so ensure you visit it two to three times before looking at the profiler output (unless you're explicitly looking to see what happens on a cache miss).

When viewing the default XHProf UI, the first thing you'll see is a summary like the one in Table 6-2.

Table 6-2. XHProf overall summary

Total Incl. Wall Time (microsec):	257,290 microsecs
Total Incl. CPU (microsecs):	233,884 microsecs
Total Incl. MemUse (bytes):	19,927,040 bytes
Total Incl. PeakMemUse (bytes):	20,004,696 bytes
Number of Function Calls:	51,151

Each category is worth looking at:

Total Incl. Wall Time
>   This is the actual elapsed time (i.e., time on the clock, which might be on the wall).

Total Incl. CPU
>   This represents time spent by the CPU. Time not spent by the CPU would include network round trips—external requests, database and cache queries, etc.

Total Incl. MemUse
>   This is the total memory used by the script by the time XHProf profiling ends. It includes the impact of loading files as well as any objects, static caches, etc. created during the request.

Total Incl. PeakMemUse
>   Roughly equivalent to `memory_get_peak_usage()`; this is the peak memory allocated at any time during the request.

Number of Function Calls
>   The total number of function and method calls recorded by XHProf.

Just the summary gives us quite a bit of information to work with. Total wall time is 257 ms, and total CPU time is 233 ms. That shows us that the vast majority of time is spent executing PHP. The remaining time is likely to be spent in the database, in the cache system, or on HTTP requests, since those external calls are not counted as PHP execution. Since this site is using the database cache layer, that only leaves two options.

To verify this, we can jump ahead a bit to check an individual function. Searching the page for "PDO" finds `PDOStatement::execute()`, the lowest-level function in Drupal 8 that executes database queries. Table 6-3 shows a truncated version of the results displayed on the metrics page.

Table 6-3. XHProf results for the PDOStatement::execute() method

Function Name	Calls	Calls%	Incl. Wall Time (microsec)	IWall%	Incl. CPU (microsecs)	ICpu%	Incl.MemUse (bytes)	IMemUse%
PDOState ment::execute	119	94.4%	29,269	11.4%	6,400	2.7%	728,144	3.7%

As you can see, 29 ms was spent overall, of which 6 ms was CPU time, leaving approximately 23 ms remaining. This confirms that the 23 ms of "missing" time was actually spent on the round trip to the MySQL server, which XHProf doesn't count as CPU time.

Note that these numbers are quite optimistic for the database, because the database server is local and is not under load. Longer network round trip times or a server under load could dramatically increase the impact of those database queries, as well as larger table sizes once the site has some content, due to slower queries. Also remember that while it's easy to add additional web servers, scaling MySQL is considerably more complicated, so the sheer number of queries executed per second could end up being an issue on a high-traffic site.

However, in terms of performance, more than 90% of the time spent serving this request was in PHP, so we need to keep looking to find the main source of slowness.

The default XHProf ordering by inclusive wall time shows which functions take the most time. XHProf and Xdebug both make a distinction between inclusive time (time spent in the function and any functions it calls) and exclusive time (time spent only in the function itself). A function that has a high inclusive wall time may not do anything particularly expensive, but may just call functions that do. However, once you're familiar with Drupal's bootstrap and rendering process, it gets easier to spot anomalies.

Let's look at the top few functions for inclusive wall time for this request. Table 6-4 shows what the table on the metrics page looks like, again truncated to fit the width of the page.

Table 6-4. Functions with the highest inclusive wall time for our request

Function Name	Calls	Calls %	Incl. Wall Time (microsec)	IWall%	Incl. CPU (microsecs)	ICpu %	Incl.MemUse (bytes)	IMemUse %
main()	1	0.0%	257,290	100.0%	105	0.0%	233,884	100.0%
drupal_handle_request	1	0.0%	257,012	99.9%	67	0.0%	233,605	99.9%
Drupal\Core\DrupalKernel::handle	1	0.0%	219,670	85.4%	17	0.0%	201,148	86.0%
Drupal\Core\HttpKernel::handle	1	0.0%	218,776	85.0%	32	0.0%	200,254	85.6%
Symfony\Component\HttpKernel\HttpKernel::handle	1	0.0%	218,640	85.0%	6	0.0%	200,118	85.6%
Symfony\Component\HttpKernel\HttpKernel::handleRaw	1	0.0%	218,634	85.0%	131	0.1%	200,111	85.6%
Symfony\Component\EventDispatcher\ContainerAwareEventDispatcher::dispatch	34	0.1%	193,842	75.3%	230	0.1%	176,492	75.5%
call_user_func	46	0.1%	181,808	70.7%	241	0.1%	163,983	70.1%
Symfony\Component\EventDispatcher\EventDispatcher::dispatch	34	0.1%	178,259	69.3%	360	0.1%	161,182	68.9%

Function Name	Calls	Calls %	Incl. Wall Time (microsec)	IWall%	Incl. CPU (microsecs)	ICpu %	Incl.MemUse (bytes)	IMemUse %
Symfony\Component\EventDis patcher\EventDispatcher::doDis patch	19	0.0%	177,054	68.8%	238	0.1%	159,968	68.4%
Drupal\Core\EventSubscriber \ViewSubscriber::onView	1	0.0%	133,762	52.0%	30	0.0%	124,379	53.2%
Drupal\Core\EventSubscriber \ViewSubscriber::onHtml	1	0.0%	133,667	52.0%	21	0.0%	124,283	53.1%
drupal_render_page	1	0.0%	133,135	51.7%	130	0.1%	123,751	52.9%
call_user_func_array	81	0.2%	72,108	28.0%	406	0.2%	65,780	28.1%
drupal_render	2	0.0%	67,728	26.3%	55	0.0%	62,663	26.8%
theme	4	0.0%	67,318	26.2%	332	0.1%	62,258	26.6%
block_page_build	1	0.0%	64,377	25.0%	63	0.0%	59,428	25.4%
block_get_blocks_by_region	17	0.0%	63,782	24.8%	56	0.0%	58,844	25.2%
Symfony\Component\ClassLoader \ClassLoader::loadClass	242	0.5%	59,264	23.0%	2,878	1.1%	59,593	25.5%
_block_get_renderable_region	4	0.0%	51,872	20.2%	190	0.1%	48,477	20.7%
entity_view	6	0.0%	47,140	18.3%	80	0.0%	43,696	18.7%

 This profiling was done with a Drupal 8.x alpha relese; exact profiling results will differ for later releases.

Looking down the list, we can see that most of the functions are called only one or two
times. While no guarantee, this usually suggests that they're high-level functions that
have a deep call stack, and may not be easy to optimize or may need caching added.
However, also in the list is `Symfony\Component\ClassLoader\ClassLoader::load`
`Class`, called 242 times and taking 59 ms. Clicking on the function name will show all
the parent functions/callers of this function, as well as all the child functions/callees.

Drupal 8 (as of Alpha 2) provides two options for class loading: `Symfony\Component`
`\ClassLoader\ClassLoader` and `Symfony\Component\ClassLoader\ApcClassLoad`
`er`.

Let's see what happens when we swap in `ApcClassLoader` and compare the results. Open
up *setting.php* and uncomment the following line:

```php
<?php
$settings['class_loader'] = 'apc';
?>
```

Then visit *node/1* again (twice, to allow the APC cache to be populated).

Searching the page for "loadClass" reveals that it's dropped down nearly to the bottom of the top 100 functions, nested between `node_access()` and `_menu_translate()`, and has taken only 21 ms this time (as illustrated in Table 6-5). That's nearly a two-thirds reduction in the time spent on this function.

Table 6-5. Results for the loadClass() method with the APC class loader enabled

Function Name	Calls	Calls%	Incl. Wall Time (microsec)	IWall%	Incl. CPU (microsecs)	ICpu%	Incl.MemUse (bytes)	IMemUse%
node_access	7	0.0%	21,506	10.0%	107	0.0%	20,736	10.9%
Symfony\Component\ClassLoader\ApcClassLoader::loadClass	242	0.6%	21,443	9.9%	2,957	1.4%	21,845	11.4%
_menu_translate	6	0.0%	21,318	9.9%	218	0.1%	18,549	9.7%

To see where the remaining time is spent, click on `loadClass` and scroll down to the "Child functions" section. Table 6-6 shows the top few.

Table 6-6. loadClass() child functions

Function Name	Calls	Calls%	Incl. Wall Time (microsec)	IWall%	Incl. CPU (microsecs)	ICpu%	Incl. MemUse (bytes)	IMemUse%
Symfony\Component\ClassLoader\ApcClassLoader::findFile	242	33.8%	2,026	9.4%	2,253	10.3%	54,312	0.7%
run_init::Entity/Role.php	1	0.1%	562	2.6%	563	2.6%	263,016	3.5%
run_init::mysql/Select.php	1	0.1%	411	1.9%	412	1.9%	193,624	2.6%
run_init::Entity/EntityDisplay.php	1	0.1%	337	1.6%	339	1.6%	176,624	2.4%
run_init::Entity/Node.php	1	0.1%	317	1.5%	320	1.5%	185,192	2.5%
run_init::Field/Field.php	1	0.1%	250	1.2%	251	1.1%	90,368	1.2%
run_init::user/RoleStorageController.php	1	0.1%	242	1.1%	243	1.1%	97,360	1.3%
run_init::formatter/TextDefaultFormatter.php	1	0.1%	229	1.1%	231	1.1%	72,272	1.0%
run_init::Entity/EntityManager.php	1	0.1%	222	1.0%	223	1.0%	51,416	0.7%

The top function is `findFile()`, also with 242 calls and taking 2 ms. `findFile()` looks like this in the code base:

```php
<?php
/**
 * Finds a file by class name while caching lookups to APC.
 *
 * @param string $class A class name to resolve to file
 *
 * @return string|null
 */
public function findFile($class)
{
    if (false === $file = apc_fetch($this->prefix.$class)) {
        apc_store($this->prefix.$class,
                            $file = $this->decorated->findFile($class));
    }

    return $file;
}
?>
```

Clicking on findFile() confirms that it only calls apc_fetch(). Comparing before/
after, in Table 6-7 we can see that there were 429 calls to file_exists(), 12,164 to
strpos(), 838 to str_replace(), 834 to substr(), and 428 to strrpos() using Class
Loader, all of which have been replaced with 428 calls to apc_fetch() with the Apc
ClassLoader, with a reduction of 41 ms down to 3 ms (see Table 6-8).

Table 6-7. findFile() details with ClassLoader

Function Name	Calls	Calls%	Incl. Wall Time (microsec)	IWall%	Incl. CPU (microsecs)	ICpu%	Incl. MemUse (bytes)	IMemUse%
Symfony\Component \ClassLoader\ClassLoad er::findFile	428	2.8%	41,274	16.0%	41,662	17.8%	108,000	0.5%
Exclusive Metrics for Cur rent Function			35,456	85.9%	22,436	53.9%	-83,256	-77.1%
Child functions								
file_exists	429	2.9%	2,571	6.2%	2,918	7.0%	1,128	1.0%
strpos	12,164	82.9%	1,448	3.5%	13,131	31.5%	1,120	1.0%
str_replace	838	5.7%	918	2.2%	1,378	3.3%	126,648	117.3%
substr	820	5.6%	506	1.2%	1,162	2.8%	61,240	56.7%
strrpos	428	2.9%	375	0.9%	637	1.5%	1,120	1.0%

Table 6-8. findFile() details with ApcClassLoader

Function Name	Calls	Calls%	Incl. Wall Time (microsec)	IWall%	Incl. CPU (microsecs)	ICpu%	Incl. MemUse (bytes)	IMemUse%
Symfony\Component\Class Loader\ApcClassLoad er::findFile	428	49.6%	3,164	1.5%	3,572	1.9%	100,936	0.5%
Exclusive Metrics for Cur rent Function	1,908	60.3%	1,965	55.0%	41,776	41.4%		
Child function								
apc_fetch	428	100.0%	1,256	39.7%	1,607	45.0%	59,160	58.6%

The remaining records are all for file execution (run_init), which can't be optimized within the application itself.

strace

Sometimes it's necessary to go to the system level to understand what's happening with your application. This is particularly true for system calls made by PHP, which won't show up in Xdebug or XHProf at all. *strace* is a great tool for looking at what happens here, and we'll use it as an example to examine how Drupal includes module files.

 In Drupal 7, file existence is checked before the module is loaded in drupal_load(), via a file_exists() check in drupal_get_file name(). This avoids errors being thrown when a module is moved in the filesystem without the module list being updated in the database. Drupal 8's \Drupal\Core\Extension\ModuleHandlerInter face::load() assumes that the module list is correct, and attempts to load the file with include_once() regardless (a PHP warning will be triggered if the file doesn't exist, but this is an error condition so is considered valid).

PHP's documentation states that file_exists() (*http://php.net/file_exists*) is cached when the file is present on the file system, but not cached when it's missing. A file_ex ists() will show up in XHProf whether it caches internally or not, so *strace* is an ideal tool to test the behavior at a lower level.

First, we need to attach *strace* to Apache. *strace* can be attached to an individual process ID or to Apache itself when it's started. On a local machine the only traffic should be your own testing, and restarting Apache isn't going to cause a site outage, so this is the simplest mechanism to get *strace* output:

```
$ sudo /etc/init.d/apache2 stop
$ sudo strace -f -o /tmp/strace.txt /etc/init.d/apache2 start
```

Creating the following test file in the root of a Drupal 8 directory covers the three variations:

```
<?php
define('DRUPAL_ROOT', getcwd());

// Just include_once
include_once DRUPAL_ROOT . '/core/modules/system/system.module';

// A file_exists() where the file is present on the file system:
if (file_exists(DRUPAL_ROOT . '/core/modules/tracker/tracker.module')) {
  include_once DRUPAL_ROOT . '/core/modules/tracker/tracker.module';
}

// A file exists where the file is not present on the file system:
file_exists(DRUPAL_ROOT . '/core/modules/foo/foo.module');
?>
```

Once Apache is restarted, visiting the page in the browser should lead to some *strace* output in */tmp/strace.txt*, which you can then open up in your browser.

Let's first of all focus on the request to *system.module* via include_once(), with no file_exists() check. Since this is the first request to Apache after a restart, the realpath cache is empty, meaning there are some additional lstat calls to be made:

```
26378 lstat("/var/www/8/core/modules/system/system.module",
           {st_mode=S_IFREG|0664, st_size=12685, ...}) = 0
26378 lstat("/var/www/8/core/modules/system",
           {st_mode=S_IFDIR|0755, st_size=4096, ...}) = 0
26378 lstat("/var/www/8/core/modules",
           {st_mode=S_IFDIR|0755, st_size=4096, ...}) = 0
26378 open("/var/www/8/core/modules/system/system.module", O_RDONLY) = 12
26378 fstat(12, {st_mode=S_IFREG|0664, st_size=12685, ...}) = 0
26378 fstat(12, {st_mode=S_IFREG|0664, st_size=12685, ...}) = 0
26378 fstat(12, {st_mode=S_IFREG|0664, st_size=12685, ...}) = 0
26378 fstat(12, {st_mode=S_IFREG|0664, st_size=12685, ...}) = 0
26378 mmap(NULL, 12685, PROT_READ, MAP_SHARED, 12, 0) = 0x7f31caf9e000
26378 stat("/var/www/8/core/modules/system/system.module",
           {st_mode=S_IFREG|0664, st_size=12685, ...}) = 0
```

Hitting the page again, those lstat calls disappear:

```
26606 open("/var/www/8/core/modules/system/system.module", O_RDONLY) = 12
26606 fstat(12, {st_mode=S_IFREG|0664, st_size=12685, ...}) = 0
26606 fstat(12, {st_mode=S_IFREG|0664, st_size=12685, ...}) = 0
26606 fstat(12, {st_mode=S_IFREG|0664, st_size=12685, ...}) = 0
26606 fstat(12, {st_mode=S_IFREG|0664, st_size=12685, ...}) = 0
26606 mmap(NULL, 12685, PROT_READ, MAP_SHARED, 12, 0) = 0x7fc6b917d000
26606 stat("/var/www/8/core/modules/system/system.module",
           {st_mode=S_IFREG|0664, st_size=12685, ...}) = 0
```

With the realpath cache warmed, let's take a look at the existing *tracker.module* file wrapped in a file_exists():

```
26606 access("/var/www/8/core/modules/tracker/tracker.module", F_OK) = 0
26606 open("/var/www/8/core/modules/tracker/tracker.module", O_RDONLY) = 12
26606 fstat(12, {st_mode=S_IFREG|0664, st_size=12685, ...}) = 0
26606 fstat(12, {st_mode=S_IFREG|0664, st_size=12685, ...}) = 0
26606 fstat(12, {st_mode=S_IFREG|0664, st_size=12685, ...}) = 0
26606 fstat(12, {st_mode=S_IFREG|0664, st_size=12685, ...}) = 0
26606 mmap(NULL, 12685, PROT_READ, MAP_SHARED, 12, 0) = 0x7fc6b917d000
26606 stat("/var/www/8/core/modules/tracker/tracker.module",
          {st_mode=S_IFREG|0664, st_size=12685, ...}) = 0
```

The file_exists() is represented by this line:

```
26606 access("/var/www/8/core/modules/tracker/tracker.module", F_OK) = 0
```

Remember, the PHP documentation for file_exists() states that the results of file_exists() are cached in the stat cache when the file is present on the file system. What it doesn't mention is that the stat cache is per-request, meaning each request to Drupal starts with an empty cache. This differs from the realpath cache, which is per-process.

When the file_exists() fails, no inclusion happens, so the only line in the *strace* output is the access call. Note that the return value changes from 0 to -1 ENOENT (No such file or directory):

```
26378 access("/var/www/8/core/modules/foo/foo.module", F_OK) =
                                        -1 ENOENT (No such file or directory)
```

As a further example, enable apc.stat = 0 in *php.ini*, then test the include_once() again.

Without apc.stat = 0, notice the stat call at the end:

```
26606 open("/var/www/8/core/modules/system/system.module", O_RDONLY) = 12
26606 fstat(12, {st_mode=S_IFREG|0664, st_size=12685, ...}) = 0
26606 fstat(12, {st_mode=S_IFREG|0664, st_size=12685, ...}) = 0
26606 fstat(12, {st_mode=S_IFREG|0664, st_size=12685, ...}) = 0
26606 fstat(12, {st_mode=S_IFREG|0664, st_size=12685, ...}) = 0
26606 mmap(NULL, 12685, PROT_READ, MAP_SHARED, 12, 0) = 0x7fc6b917d000
26606 stat("/var/www/8/core/modules/system/system.module",
          {st_mode=S_IFREG|0664, st_size=12685, ...}) = 0
```

With apc.stat = 0, that stat call disappears, as you'd expect:

```
26606 open("/var/www/8/core/modules/system/system.module", O_RDONLY) = 12
26606 fstat(12, {st_mode=S_IFREG|0664, st_size=12685, ...}) = 0
26606 fstat(12, {st_mode=S_IFREG|0664, st_size=12685, ...}) = 0
26606 fstat(12, {st_mode=S_IFREG|0664, st_size=12685, ...}) = 0
26606 fstat(12, {st_mode=S_IFREG|0664, st_size=12685, ...}) = 0
26606 mmap(NULL, 12685, PROT_READ, MAP_SHARED, 12, 0) = 0x7fc6b917d000
```

Note that `apc.stat` has some administrative overhead—you'll need to be able to clear the APC cache when code is deployed, for example. See Chapter 18 for more information on opcode caches.

Use of the tools in this chapter allows you to see exactly what's happening when code is executed, and therefore to verify accurately whether changes made for performance purposes are successfully reducing the amount of work being done at different levels of the application. While we cover load testing in Chapter 20, load testing tools should almost never be used for before/after performance testing of specific changes, since they're unable to provide the accuracy, detail, or introspection necessary to verify the impact of what are often quite small individual changes.

## CHAPTER 7

Infrastructure Design and Planning

Whether you are beginning to plan for the launch of a large website or managing the growing pains of an existing site, you will quickly come to the point where one server is not enough to handle the traffic to your site, or you need more reliability than a single server can provide. However, the leap from a single server to a multiserver infrastructure is a large one. There are a number of ways to architect your environment to ensure fast response times to your visitors and allow you the potential to further scale in the future.

Your infrastructure design will vary greatly based on your website's requirements. What kind of high availability do you require? What response times will your users or your management consider acceptable? Does your site require any "extra" services or applications, outside of a standard LAMP stack? All of these considerations and (of course, expected traffic to the site) will need to be taken into account when designing, building, and maintaining a multiserver hosting environment. There is no silver bullet solution for everyone, but we can provide some guidelines that should make it easy to find the right solution for your particular needs.

Horizontal and Vertical Scaling

There are two approaches to scaling out an infrastructure to add additional resources: horizontal scaling ("scaling out") and vertical scaling ("scaling up"). Horizontal scaling involves adding additional servers while vertical scaling involves adding more resources to existing servers. A good infrastructure plan will take both of these scaling approaches into account, as there are times when one may be more appropriate than the other. Initially, this consideration may be used to consider when to migrate from one server to multiple servers. For larger infrastructures, the same logic can be applied at a larger scale. As an example, let's consider a single-server infrastructure like that shown in Figure 7-1.

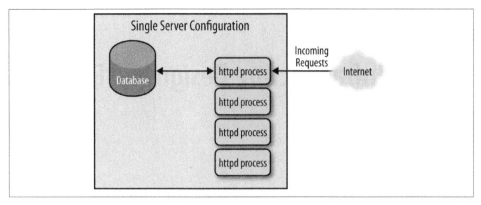

Figure 7-1. Single server running web and database services

Not all site admins have the resources to launch a site with multiple servers. This is not necessarily a bad thing—many sites can get away with using only one server, which gives a cost savings over hosting multiple servers as well as keeping system administration overhead to a minimum. With today's multicore CPUs and inexpensive RAM, it's easy and relatively cheap to host your site on a machine with enough power to run all the required services. But how do you know when one server is no longer enough?

There are a number of factors to consider when trying to answer the question of whether it's time to add another server:

Resources

As your resource usage increases due to additional site features or an increase in traffic to the site, you may start to see resource contention on the server. For example, two processes both needing a lot of disk I/O can dramatically slow each other down. Can your current server be allocated more resources (RAM, CPU, etc.)? This is generally easier to do for virtual machines than for physical servers. For example, you may be able to solve an issue by adding more RAM to a server. However, it is also important to consider if adding more RAM to a server might mean that you are now limited by CPU, network, or I/O resources on the server—and you may not have the ability to increase those resources quite as easily.

Costs

This doesn't just mean additional hosting costs, but may also mean more systems management overhead. As your infrastructure grows to include multiple servers, adding one more server should not mean a huge increase in systems management overhead (read up on configuration management in Chapter 9); however, making the initial jump from one server to multiple servers likely means you will need to step back and reanalyze your management plan, potentially starting to use a configuration management system for the first time.

High availability (HA)

If your entire site is hosted on a single server, it just takes that one server going offline for your site to go down. If this situation is unacceptable to clients or business owners, you will likely need multiple servers to offer better reliability. In essence, services will be offered by several servers, and any data will be synchronized across them.

Generally, outside of HA considerations, it's fairly common to scale vertically to the extent that is cost effective to do so—once you reach the point that scaling vertically is going to be more expensive than scaling horizontally, it is time to start adding more servers. However, this doesn't always hold true in practice, for a couple of reasons:

1. Adding resources to a server can be more difficult and time-consuming than simply adding an additional server to your infrastructure. It also can involve bringing the server offline, which is not ideal.

2. As sites grow to the point where they need additional resources, usually by that point there are business requirements in place that necessitate some form of high availability.

3. As a single server becomes larger and more important, the ability to take it down for security and feature updates starts to disappear. Eventually you end up with a single outdated and complex server, which is very problematic from a systems perspective.

Therefore, most infrastructure managers figure out a general server specification that will work for them and provide some room for growth—usually this server specification will differ between different services (e.g., one spec for web servers, one spec for DB servers). When a new server is needed, it is deployed with those predetermined specifications. This may be a more powerful server than is necessary for the short term, but it will give the service room for growth and ensures you have some standardization in servers (making them easier to manage).

Many times, knowing when to scale horizontally is more difficult than knowing how to scale horizontally. The world is filled with infrastructures where there are many web servers, all bottlenecking on a shared Memcache instance. To this end, we will now discuss methodologies for categorizing services and knowing when (and where) to add more servers.

Service Categorization

A basic Drupal site can be separated into two distinct services: web frontend, and database backend. The web service is responsible for handling incoming requests, processing Drupal's PHP code, and returning the results back to the requesting client. The database back end is queried during Drupal's PHP execution in order to pull out settings and data for the site. Every Drupal website will need infrastructure to support at least these two services. However, there are many more services that are often required to add features or enhance performance and scalability. These services can be grouped roughly into the following categories (starting with the web and database services we already mentioned):

Web
> Apache, Nginx, or another web server of your choice, plus PHP

Database
> Most commonly MySQL, though Drupal core supports many other databases to a lesser degree, including PostgreSQL, Microsoft SQL Server, Oracle, and SQLite

Frontend proxies
> Varnish, CDN, Nginx, or other proxy caches

Other caches and data stores
> Memcache, Redis, MongoDB, etc.

Search backends
> Apache Solr, Elasticsearch, Sphinx, etc.

Load balancers
> HAProxy, Nginx, IPVS, etc.

This generally categorizes most services that would be run as part of a Drupal website. The next step, once you've categorized your services, is to figure out which services may require their own server (or servers), and which services can safely coexist on the same server. Separating services into the different categories will give you the opportunity to scale out each service as it becomes a bottleneck for your site. As a visualization tool, we can represent each service category as a layer of the overall infrastructure, as illustrated in Figure 7-2—each layer can be expanded out horizontally by adding additional servers.

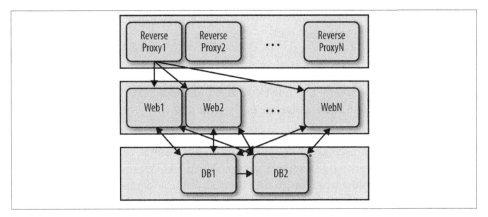

Figure 7-2. Infrastructure layers

Working Well Together

It's important to analyze your services to figure out which may or may not work well together on a server. Some services require substantial memory, CPU, or disk I/O resources. Those may run fine on a server with another service that requires minimal resources, but you most likely won't want to combine two I/O-intensive services on the same server, since they would be competing for resources. As services are split onto separate servers, network traffic also becomes a significant factor. Let's take a look at a few common services and what their typical resource consumption is like. The following examples are intended to give a general idea of resource requirements, but your requirements may be very different depending on your site's specifics:

Web services

> Web services will consume a moderate amount of CPU for PHP processing. You will also need enough RAM to support large numbers of web server processes as your traffic spikes. While this is a general rule for any website, Drupal in particular and many PHP CMSs in general have fairly high I/O latency requirements due to how many PHP files are loaded to serve each request. While opcode caches such as APC can help with this, you don't necessarily want to put an I/O-bound service on your web nodes since performance will deteriorate as it competes with the Drupal PHP processes.

Database

> Databases typically will consume large amounts of RAM and can require moderate CPU resources. A well-tuned database will not touch the system disk often, except if it is write-heavy. However, you want the disk I/O to be as fast as possible when it is required. Because databases can require so many resources and for optimal performance may need to "hog" disk or CPU resources in spikes, the database is gen-

erally the first thing to be separated onto its own server, where it can be finely tuned and guaranteed its own resources.

Reverse proxy

Varnish is a common example of a reverse proxy used as a frontend cache sitting in front of your web server. While Varnish should be allocated a moderate amount of RAM, its CPU and disk usage are fairly minimal.

Alternate Drupal cache

Memcache, often used as an alternative cache for Drupal, can be used to offload cache queries from your database server. Much like Varnish, Memcached (the Memcache daemon) will require RAM—a small to moderate amount depending on your site's needs—but will not consume a lot of CPU or disk resources.

Additional services

Of course, additional services will vary greatly in their resource utilization, so you will need to analyze each service independently. Solr, for example, can be memory- and I/O-heavy, depending on its usage.

Once you understand the resource requirements for the services you will be using, it will be easier to see which services can coexist on the same server without competing for resources.

Example Two-Layer Configuration

As mentioned previously, one of the most common ways to split services for a Drupal site is to use two servers, with the first server dedicated to web services and the second dedicated to the database. If high availability is a requirement for your site, then this would become four servers: two web nodes and two database servers, all with some form of load balancing and/or failover mechanisms. For the sake of a simple example, we'll assume no HA requirements in this setup and start with only two servers.

Let's assume that we want to run Varnish as a reverse proxy and Memcache as an alternate Drupal cache (these configurations are covered in depth in Chapters 19 and 16, respectively). Considering that we are working with two servers, it makes the most sense to run those services on the web server, along with Apache, httpd, Nginx, or whichever web server you have selected.

In most environments, we will isolate the database service on its own server if at all possible. As we went over earlier, this is so that it can be guaranteed resources and won't impact other services with its I/O and memory demands. Both Varnish and Memcache are able to run on the web node without stealing too much CPU time away from httpd —they will both have a memory limit, so that httpd is sure to have enough to deal with traffic spikes when it may need to spin up a lot of processes. Figure 7-3 shows which services are running on which server in this setup.

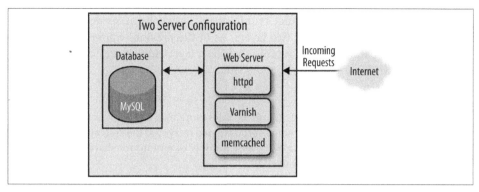

Figure 7-3. Two server configuration

As your site grows in complexity and traffic, you are likely to see performance bottle-necks in either the web layer or the database layer, or sometimes both. An example bottleneck in the web layer would be if you are consistently serving a high number of clients and the web node is not able to handle them all. An example bottleneck in the database layer would be if you have a large number of queries or a few large queries that are slowing down the database response time.

In order to deal with the increased demands of the site, you can scale each of the layers horizontally by adding more servers. Most services are pretty trivial to scale in this manner, and growing the infrastructure in this way allows you to specifically scale up each service layer as it becomes a priority. (The database layer requires a bit more thought and strategy to scale beyond one server; we'll go into more detail in Chapter 13 on scaling strategies specific to the database layer.)

This "two-layer" approach can work for some time, though eventually you may want to reassess your layer definitions and potentially separate things even further. For example, if you want to add Solr search to your site, that may not fit well on your current web nodes, and it's not typically something that you would want to run on the database servers due to I/O and RAM contention. Thus, we often add an additional layer for the Solr service. Another example would be if Varnish needs more RAM than is available for it on the web servers: in that case, you could separate it into its own layer of servers that sit in front of the web nodes. The benefit here is that you can then scale out either the frontend caching layer or the web layer separately, as needed. Our next example will show a larger infrastructure with such a setup.

Example Larger-Scale Infrastructure

The majority of websites will get along quite well following the preceding example of a two-layer setup separating web services (and some additional caching services) into one layer of servers and databases into a second layer. But for larger sites, or those that have specific HA, security, or performance requirements, it may be necessary to implement an infrastructure with more than two layers. As in the previous example, in this case, we will strive to separate services out into their own layers so that they can be managed and scaled separately.

> As soon as your infrastructure includes more than one web server, you will need to configure some sort of shared or synced file system for the Drupal *files/* directory. We cover a number of options for sharing files between servers in Chapter 10.

For this example, we'll assume that the requirements for a frontend cache (we'll use Varnish in this example) are large enough that it warrants having its own dedicated layer of servers. We'll also assume that the site will use Solr heavily enough that the Solr service should be separated off into its own layer. Add to that the web and database layers, and we end up with the service layers shown in Figure 7-4.

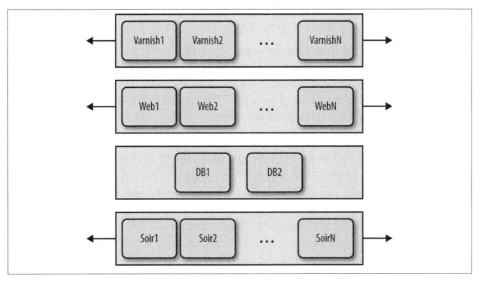

Figure 7-4. Example multilayer configuration

One benefit of separating Varnish onto its own servers is that it can then provide load balancing and fault tolerance for your web nodes. Given a pool of web servers, Varnish can distribute the load between them during normal service, and if one of the web servers goes offline, Varnish will notice the failing server and stop using it for backend web requests. While some larger infrastructures will have their own dedicated load balancing devices, for many people, using Varnish to provide basic load balancing works well and is cost-effective.

Going into such an infrastructure design, it's likely that you will want some form of high availability for the site, so we'll assume you're starting with at least two servers per layer in order to avoid a single point of failure.

Each service layer here starts with two servers, and the servers within a layer have replication or shared data between them such that if one server in a layer goes away, the other server is able to serve requests in its place. During times that all servers are online, load is shared between all servers in a layer in order to improve performance. Refer to Chapter 19 (Varnish), Chapter 18 (httpd), Chapter 13 (MySQL), and Chapter 17 (Solr) for specific setup and configuration settings for a similar infrastructure design.

Development and Staging Environments

Once you have designed your production infrastructure, an important next step is to allocate resources for development and staging environments. As the complexity and availability requirements of your site grow, it becomes even more critical to have a separate staging environment to test out code changes, module updates, and configuration changes.

For a staging environment to provide the most benefit, it should mimic the production environment as closely as possible, complete with load balancers, database replication, and any other configuration found in the production environment. Obviously this can become quite expensive if you are literally doubling your infrastructure to provide a staging environment. There are a number of ways to cut costs for the staging environment, but it's important to keep in mind the trade-offs you are making when you don't have an exact replica of the production environment. Some frequently used methods for cutting costs when setting up a staging environment include:

Reducing the number of redundant servers
>For example, the production environment may have five or six different web servers. For staging, you could likely get by with only two servers set up in a similar fashion. While this doesn't mimic production 100%, the configuration should be close enough to catch most bugs triggered by having multiple web nodes.

Virtualizing resources
>Even if your production environment is mostly or entirely run on physical servers, it's possible that you could run a staging environment using some or all virtual servers. It's important to remember, though that this—like any difference between the two environments—means that you may run into bugs in production that you don't hit in the staging (or vice versa).

Using lower-end servers

It is possible to use less expensive servers to host your staging environment. However, this can lead to a couple of issues. First of all, as with the previous examples, this can lead to bugs or performance issues in the production environment that are not repeatable in the staging environment. Secondly, if the staging servers are so underpowered that they don't perform well at all, it could lead to developers totally ignoring the staging environment because "it's too much of a pain," which in turn could lead to untested or poorly tested code making its way to production.

The staging environment should be used not only to test code and database updates, but also to test software and OS updates. Because these servers closely mimic your production servers, testing software updates on staging servers can help prevent downtime in the production environment when an update has unexpected consequences.

Providing a stable environment for your developers is another important consideration when designing an infrastructure. As mentioned previously, one way to implement a development environment is to share the staging server resources—for example, setting up separate development virtual hosts and databases on the same servers used for staging. Another option would be to use virtualized resources (or a lower-cost virtualized server if your other servers are already virtualized). In order to cut costs, sites with lower development activity could get away with only spinning up the development virtualized environment occasionally, when needed, instead of leaving it running all the time. A third option is to distribute the development environment so that it can be run locally by your developers on their workstations or laptops. Most developers can't or won't want to deal with setting up the system-level applications such as httpd or *mysqld*; however, by providing a virtual machine image (or using a tool such as Vagrant to build one on the fly using Puppet or Chef configuration management scripts), developers can pretty easily run a virtual machine that pretty closely mimics the production and staging configuration. We cover Vagrant in more depth in Chapter 9.

Internal Network Layout

If you are in a hosted environment, you may not have much choice about how the network is configured. However, if possible, it's preferable to set up a separate backend network for your devices to communicate on instead of using their public network interfaces. It's best that most servers not even be accessible on a public IP address — only those with user-facing services need to have a public IP.

Setting up a backend network not only can improve performance, but also can increase security. In almost every case, there is no reason for your database servers or other not-public-facing services to be open to the Internet. In order to access the servers, you can connect through one of your public-facing services or, even better, create a dedicated "jump host" that is accessible to the outside world and is used specifically to access your internal hosts (see Figure 7-5). Don't overlook the importance of securing your jump host; it does no good to segregate your hosts onto a separate network if it's easy for an attacker to gain access through your jump host.

When your frontend web nodes are experiencing high traffic, if they also had to communicate with the database over the same network interface you would start to see slower database response times as well. Using a separate network for backend requests such as database traffic, as shown in Figure 7-6, means that you won't be competing with network traffic from external sources when trying to communicate with your internal hosts. By offloading this traffic onto its own internal network, you can also avoid potential traffic charges with your hosting company and avoid possibly congesting the public-facing firewall or router with additional traffic.

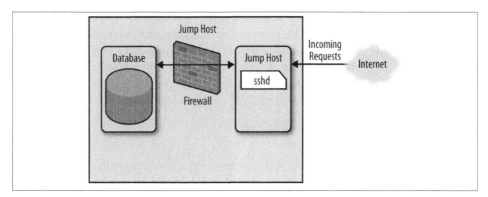

Figure 7-5. Jump host

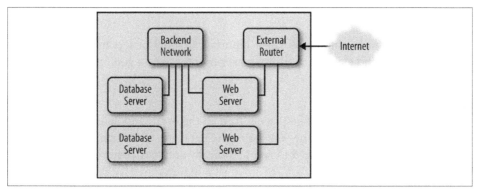

Figure 7-6. Backend network traffic

Be sure to ask your provider about the availability of its "backend network." While providers spend a lot of money on redundant networking equipment for the public network, the backend network sometimes doesn't get as much attention. If a backend switch going down can take down your website, it doesn't matter how many redundant switches are on the public network.

Utility Servers

As your site and infrastructure grow, you may end up with a number of services that don't directly power your website, but are used to manage the servers, monitor services, or host code repositories. In many situations, infrastructures are deployed without a utility server and all of these "side" services end up littered across various servers without much thought being given to where they should reside. This is not a very good solution and can lead to problems as you scale. As you are planning your infrastructure, you may want to consider a utility server that is built specifically for these sorts of supporting services, or a VM host to create dedicated VMs for "one-off" services.

Here are some common uses for a utility server:

Continuous integration

Depending on your workflow, you may be using a continuous integration server such as Jenkins in order to test and deploy code between environments.

Code revision control

The utility server provides a place to host your revision control system, such as Git or Subversion.

Monitoring

As discussed earlier in this book, it's important to monitor servers and services for performance and stability. A utility server is potentially a good place to run such monitoring services.

Periodic jobs

A utility server can provide a place to run all the "odds and ends" scripts that do something against either the website or the database—for example, Drupal cron and queue workers that need to run perodically and may require more resources than a typical web request.

Configuration management

As the number of servers you are managing increases, you'll benefit immensely by using a configuration management system (popular options include Puppet, Chef, and CFEngine). The utility server would be an ideal choice to run as the central configuration management server.

There are, of course, other things that you could run on a utility server; the main idea is to have a secure, internal server that can be used to run jobs and services that may require trusted access to other servers. In general, this should *not* include any services that are publicly accessible from the Internet, because this host typically ends up being trusted to some degree on all of your other hosts—and that makes it an ideal target for attackers.

High Availability and Failover

For many sites, being offline for any significant amount of time is unacceptable. For those situations, it is necessary to set up redundant servers and a method for detecting failures and automatically switching over to the secondary server.

At the very least, for a Drupal site to remain online during downtime for a server, you will need to plan failover for web and database services. If you have additional services that are used by your Drupal site, you may consider it acceptable for those to be offline for some period of time as long as the core website is functioning.

There are different ways to approach high availability, and your approach may depend on a number of factors:

- Business requirements set for acceptable downtime
- Whether or not failover needs to be completely automated
- Whether certain failures could put the site in a "read-only" mode (for database access and/or file uploads)
- Whether you have a budget for hardware and staff time to implement high availability

In subsequent chapters, we cover specific configurations to accomplish high availability with various services. At this point, it's important to figure out if HA is something you require (or may require in the future) for your website, and to look at the various services, servers, and network equipment you will be hosting to get an idea of all the single points of failure you may have in your infrastructure.

Hosting Considerations

Some websites end up being hosted internally if there are sufficient hosting resources; other situations call for paying for an external server (or service) host. If you are looking for an external hosting provider, there are many important aspects to consider, including:

Cost

Analyze the cost for hosting your planned infrastructure. Include additional bandwidth costs that you may incur. Also, look at how cost will increase should you need to grow your infrastructure by adding additional servers or dealing with increased bandwidth requirements.

Uptime

What kind of uptime does the host guarantee, and what is its average uptime for services, etc.? Consider reading through public customer forums or hosting "status" sites, if it has such a thing. What kind of redundancy does it have in place for power, network, and cooling?

Support

What type of support is offered, and how does this correspond to your support needs? For example, do you want a host who will support only its own equipment, leaving you to handle all OS and application support? Or would you rather have a host who manages the servers for you, so you only have to deal with Drupal specifically? Does support cost extra, or is it included with your hosting plan (and to what extent)?

Backups

Are servers backed up, and if so, on what schedule? Is backup size limited? How long are backups kept? Does the backup service cost extra? Where are the backups stored, and are they mirrored to another location?

Security

What kind of physical and network/server-based security is provided?

Failover and geographic distribution

Does the host offer servers at different geographic locations that could be used for failover in the event of a disaster at one data center?

Virtualized Versus physical servers

Are you looking to host physical servers (owned by you, or rented from the host), or virtualized resources? How will this decision affect your ability to scale in the future and to deal with estimated traffic loads now? Does the host offer the ability to mix physical hosts and virtualized hosts as part of the same hosting plan?

 We'll cover specific details about virtualized and cloud hosting in Chapter 11.

With the sheer number of hosting providers out there, it's often very easy to find one that appears to fit all of your needs, but it can be very difficult to find one that actually delivers. Be sure to ask around and do some due diligence research before committing to any hosting provider. If possible, don't jump into a long-term contract before you're able to test out its service and support for at least a couple of months to be sure you are happy.

Summary

Scaling an infrastructure can be difficult, but when you take the time to plan out your infrastructure design in advance, it becomes a lot easier. Your infrastructure plan doesn't need to be set in stone, but it should be clear and forward-thinking enough to be used as your infrastructure grows and changes during the lifetime of your site. Going through the process of categorizing potential service layers and plans for horizontal and vertical growth will ensure that you are much better equipped to deal with any infrastructure change requirements you may be presented with in the future—either growth due to performance requirements, or coping with adding or removing services to support your site.

It's important to plan not only for a production infrastructure to directly support your site, but also for dedicated development and staging environments (some sites also add a separate QA or demo environment). In addition, it's best to have at least one dedicated utility server to host your central and supporting services that help the site and infrastructure run, but don't directly power the site itself.

Decide whether or not you need high availability for your site, and plan your infrastructure resources accordingly. Supporting high availability for services generally means you are doubling the number of server resources in your infrastructure and increasing your management overhead.

There are a number of things to consider when selecting a provider to host your website. Be sure to consider your options carefully and select a host that meets all of your needs —hopefully without breaking the bank.

## CHAPTER 8

Service Monitoring

Running a website without service monitoring is an exercise in flying blind. Nobody cares about monitoring when everything is going well, but as soon as something goes wrong, the additional information and warnings provided can be instrumental in quickly and correctly diagnosing the problem.

There are different types of service monitoring. Tools like Icinga and Nagios are designed to watch hosts and services, sending alerts when a service check falls outside an acceptable range. Other tools, such as Cacti and Munin, provide a graphical look at server and service information in order to give historical context to performance and usage statistics. Still other applications, such as Zabbix, aim to combine these two types of monitoring. Throughout this chapter, we'll take a look at the various types of monitoring systems and give examples of how they can be used to ensure your site is stable and performing optimally.

The Importance of Monitoring Services

Imagine a situation where you are using an alternate cache backend for Drupal, such as Memcache—we'll provide details on how to implement this in Chapter 16. Your cache items are now only accessible if the Memcached service is running. Imagine if the service stopped responding, unexpectedly causing your entire Drupal cache to disappear. This would force a great deal more load on your database server. Without service monitoring in place, it may take some time to figure out what the problem is; all you know for sure is that the site feels slower than normal. You might not realize what's wrong until you start going through recent Drupal log entries.

If you had a monitoring server that was configured to run periodic tests to ensure the Memcached service was responding as expected, you would receive an email or text message alerting you as soon as the service failed to respond. You would know exactly what was happening before you even logged into the server. Being able to respond to issues immediately, or even be warned as services start to deteriorate, is extremely important—especially if things can be fixed before users realize something is wrong.

Another important aspect of monitoring is collecting data over time. Having a strong grasp of the baseline usage of your servers and services makes it easy to see when something out of the ordinary is occurring. One example is tracking general things such as server load going up during times of increased traffic on the site. Going beyond that, monitoring could be used to track specific service information, like if and when your APC opcode cache (see Chapter 18) fills up. By setting up a thorough and reliable monitoring system, you will be able to stay ahead of problems with your site as well as providing yourself with an indispensable troubleshooting tool.

Monitoring Alerts with Icinga

Nagios (*http://www.nagios.org/*) is a very popular open source monitoring system that was initially released in 1999. It gained popularity in the following years, though there were complaints in the development community about bugs going unfixed and general lack of transparency within the core of Nagios. In 2009 this led to a core group of Nagios developers (who felt that their efforts to contribute to Nagios core were being ignored) to fork off a new project, which they named Icinga (*https://www.icinga.org*).

Since forking, the Icinga project has grown substantially in both developers and users; it includes many bug fixes (*https://wiki.icinga.org/display/Dev/Bug+and+Feature+Comparison*) and feature improvements (*https://www.icinga.org/nagios/feature-comparison*) that are not found in Nagios while remaining compatible with all external plug-ins. One of these improvements is a new web interface that was designed to be more modern and configurable than that provided by Nagios. If you don't have much of a preference of which system to use, then our opinion is that the new web interface alone should be enough to encourage you to adopt Icinga over Nagios, unless you are paying for the Enterprise version of Nagios.

There are other open source and commercial monitoring options as well: these include OpenNMS, Sensu, Zabbix, and ZenOSS, to name just a few open source options. However, our past experiences have kept us coming back to Icinga when we need to set up a monitoring system. For that reason, we will be using Icinga-specific examples here, but we encourage you to review other options and pick the one that works best for you.

What to Monitor

Deciding what to monitor and with what failure conditions should be viewed as an iterative task, where you continually improve the monitoring configuration in response to false positives, or lack of alerts when expected. On the one hand, you want to monitor as many different aspects of your infrastructure as possible; but on the other hand, if too many alerts are being generated (or worse, false positives), they will be ignored and important alerts may go unseen. We recommend striving for the middle ground—monitoring as much as possible without becoming the monitoring system that cries wolf.

There are actually two things to consider when choosing what to monitor: first is which services and information to monitor, and second is how to set your thresholds. We'll start with "what to monitor," and then discuss how to select and refine threshold values.

It's obvious that you would want to monitor all of your core servers and services. This generally means starting with simple checks such as *ping* or *ssh* checks against servers, and overall health checks against services—for example, checking that your website returns a *200 OK* status code, or that the MySQL server accepts connections. Beyond those simple checks, there is a virtually unlimited number of things that you can monitor within each server or service. For example, server monitoring might include:

- RAM and swap usage
- Disk usage
- CPU usage
- Network connection count

And service monitoring might include things like web server response time to serve a request or a whole wealth of MySQL information, such as:

- MySQL thread and connection counts
- MySQL replication status
- MySQL query activity
- InnoDB buffer usage

It's advisable to start with at least a set of "simple" checks for the various server resources (RAM, CPU, disk, network). Service-specific checks are more subjective and depend on what is important in your environment. You'll definitely want some simple up/down checks for services such as web and MySQL services (plus any others running in your environment). Beyond that, review some of the common checks for MySQL to see what you feel is important. For example, if you know your InnoDB buffer pool is relatively full, it would be prudent to monitor its usage in order to have a warning before it completely fills up.

How to Tune Monitoring

Most prepackaged and third-party checks for Icinga will come with suggested threshold values when needed for warnings and errors. If you are creating your own checks, you will need to set those thresholds yourself. In that case, it's important to set them low enough that you are sure they will trigger before or during a problem. A monitoring check does no good if it is configured to such a high value that the site can become unusably slow or go offline completely without the alert actually catching anything. For new sites and infrastructures, this can be a bit of a guessing game until you have established some baseline data. Remember, you can always increase the alert thresholds if you are receiving too many false positives.

All plug-ins include options for setting warning and critical thresholds. When defining a check in Icinga, these command-line flags are passed either in the *service* or the *command* configuration file as part of the check_command option. Icinga will automatically configure the hostname for the check command based on the host_name value set in the *service* configuration file.

A service definition for checking the HTTP response time of your website might look something like the following to warn if the page takes longer than three seconds to respond, or send a critical alert if the HTTP response time is longer than five seconds:

```
define service{
        host_name               www1
        service_description     WEB_RESPONSE_TIME
        check_command           check_http!3!5
        }
```

Graphing Monitoring Data

In addition to setting up an active monitoring system to send alerts, it's also very useful to be able to view historic data for your servers and services. Building on the preceding example, it's great to receive an alert when the website begins to load slowly, but in order to troubleshoot what might be causing the slowdown, it would be ideal to be able to view information like the number of Apache processes over the last hour, how loaded the database has been over the last day, etc. By implementing a monitoring tool to track resources over time, you can have this and other important graphs at your fingertips, whether for urgently debugging a problem or just for a periodic review of how services are performing.

Two systems that we use the most for this capability are Cacti (*http://www.cacti.net/*) and Munin (*http://munin-monitoring.org/*). Both are very capable applications, and the choice between them (or one of the many other options) can often boil down to personal preference. In the case of Munin and Cacti, both use RRDTool (*http://oss.oetiker.ch/rrdtool/*) to graph their data and make it available from a web interface, and both have a plug-in system for monitoring various applications and server resources (generally, people find Munin plug-ins easier to implement). Figure 8-1 shows a sample Munin load graph.

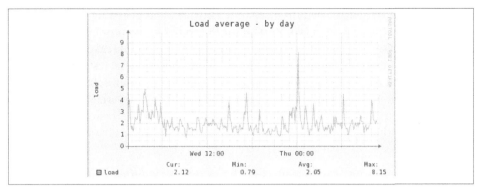

Figure 8-1. Munin load graph

There are many plug-ins available for Munin, Cacti, and other monitoring systems. We generally try to graph as much data as possible, because even if something isn't a problem today, it might end up being important at some point in the future. When considering what to monitor, we recommend looking through the default and popular plug-ins for whatever system you select. However, here is a list of things that we generally monitor:

System data
This includes disk I/O, disk usage, network traffic and errors for all network interfaces, network connections, email activity/queues, CPU load, memory usage, total swap usage, and swap activity.

Web server data
This can include the number of Apache processes; APC memory usage and evictions; Varnish requests, hit rates, and evictions; Memcache (or other external cache) memory usage, hit rates, and evictions.

Database data
MySQL has a ton of data, most of which is worth tracking: this includes slave lag; command types and counts; connections; InnoDB information such as buffer pool size, activity, and I/O; query cache information such as memory usage and hits/inserts/prunes; slow query counts; table locks; and temp table types and counts.

Internal Versus Remote Monitoring

The location—internal or external to the rest of your server and network infrastructure—of your monitoring server(s) is very important. There is a case to be made for either location, and generally those that want to be very thorough in their monitoring will end up with both an internal and an external monitoring system in order to benefit from each. In fact, the services can and should be set up to complement each other instead of duplicating all monitoring in both locations.

The use of an external (hosted on a separate network, and generally geographically dispersed) monitoring system is important for the ability to monitor externally facing services. The reason for externally monitoring those services is quite easy to understand: you want to see the same thing your users are seeing. For example, testing a web page load over a local network won't see any delays introduced on your outbound network (or worse, if that network goes down). If you are testing from a separate network, however, the monitoring system will see those faults and delays. For this reason, we generally recommend setting up an external monitoring server to do at least basic ping and web page load checks.

An internal monitoring system is much better suited to monitoring backend services (MySQL, Memcached, Solr, etc.) and server resources. Keeping that monitoring internal means you don't need to worry about external network bandwidth or the security implications of allowing an external host to connect to your internal services. As you add more servers and service checks to your monitoring system, having it on a low-latency local connection can help improve monitoring performance.

## CHAPTER 9

"DevOps": Breaking Down Barriers Between Development and Operations

Historically, there has been a strict separation between development and infrastructure. In recent years, the "DevOps" methodology has become very popular, stressing the integration of development and infrastructure operations in order to improve the code deployment process. There are many aspects to DevOps, including close collaboration between development and infrastructure teams, easing the deployment process with automation, and standardizing development and QA environments. This methodology becomes even more important as infrastructure demands increase with new technologies, as development teams move toward rapid-release models (agile/iterative development), and when dealing with distributed teams.

While you may not feel that you need to fully embrace DevOps for your environment, there are still many ideas that stem from DevOps culture that can prove beneficial. For example, ideas that are commonly used in DevOps environments that can help simplify deployments and reduce the chances of regressions when deploying to the production environment include having the ability to track changes to both code and infrastructure and roll back should something not work; maintaining separate (but nearly identical) environments for development, testing, and staging for code and infrastructure changes; and the use of revision control systems and continuous integration systems for code deployment.

This chapter shouldn't be considered a set of instructions on "how to do DevOps"; instead, it will focus on some of the underlying ideas and technologies that we hit on throughout the rest of the book.

Revision Control Systems

Revision control systems have a bit of an upfront learning curve, but once you get over that, you will never go back to not using one. Generally these days, the argument is not over whether or not to use a revision control system for your code, but which revision control system to use. We'll stay out of the "which revision control system is best" holy war here, and just stick with Git for our examples since Git is used for Drupal.org and all projects hosted there. If you're not already sold on a particular revision control system, here are some of the features you should consider when selecting one:

Distributed system versus central system
> Distributed systems have become much more popular of late, and with good reason —every copy of the repository stores all files and history locally, which not only speeds up many commands, but allows developers to work offline.

Branching model
> Depending on your development workflow and team size, having a revision control system with a powerful branching model can be very useful (even mandatory). This makes collaboration and testing changes very easy.

Performance
> Is the system you've chosen fast enough for your common tasks?

That said, it's not especially important which revision control system you use, just that you use one at all! While the trend has been toward distributed systems recently, and those do provide some definite benefits, what's important is that you choose something that fits in with your workflow and the technical skill level of your team.

Locally Hosted or External Service

One of the first decisions you'll need to make when implementing a revision control system is whether to host it on a local server or to use an external service (potentially a paid service). There are many services, such as BitBucket and GitHub, that provide hosting for code repositories. Some people prefer to use these services, not only for the ease of use (and setup) they offer, but for the additional features, such as user management and, in the case of GitHub, the easy forking and pull request model, which makes it simple for developers to review and discuss proposed changes. That said, any modern revision control system can be set up locally with just a few commands, so if you don't want or need the additional features offered by the hosted services, it's cheap and relatively easy to host yourself.

Not Just for Code

Generally, your actual website code will be the first thing you think about when implementing a revision control system. However, it's also very useful for other things, such as keeping your system configuration management scripts in a code repository. By storing configuration management or other scripts in a revision control system, you get an automatic log of system changes, the ability to easily collaborate with other developers and/or system administrators, and an easy way to roll back changes.

Configuration Management Systems

Like revision control systems, configuration management systems are something that people generally are reluctant to use at first, but once they get comfortable with them, there is no turning back (in a good way). Configuration management systems allow you to write code (in various languages, depending on the underlying system) to define how a system is configured. This has many benefits; for example, it provides a sort of "live documentation" for your servers, and it means you won't have 50 manually copied configuration files on a server (*httpd.conf.bak, httpd.conf.old, httpd.conf.not.working…* don't pretend you've never seen something like that before!). An example of what you can do with a configuration management system is store your custom PHP and Apache configuration files on a web server, and ensure that Apache is running and configured to start on boot. While this may seem like a very simple example, think of what happens when you have multiple servers and you suddenly need to make a configuration change or bring up a new service. What if there are some special commands you use when deploying something manually? It is much better to keep those commands in a configuration management system so that they are documented and not forgotten. Likewise, what happens if one of your servers crashes and needs to be rebuilt? With a configuration management system that becomes a simple task, and you can ensure that everything will be configured as it was before.

Which System to Use

There are many popular configuration management systems. The most widely used are CFEngine, Chef, and Puppet. A relative newcomer is Ansible (*http://www.ansible works.com/*), which aims to keep configuration management as simple as possible. While these all have the common goal of allowing you to write configuration to define a system, they go about it in slightly different ways, using different languages for their configuration and different underlying programming languages. All of these systems have active communities and development and are fairly well supported by most Linux distributions. We suggest trying them each out and selecting the system that you are most comfortable with.

Pulling It Together: In-Depth Example with Puppet and Git

We mentioned the usefulness of keeping your configuration management scripts in revision control, but what does that look like exactly? For this example, we'll use Puppet and Git, though it is just as applicable to other configuration management and revision control systems. There are a few pieces involved:

1. A master repository to which changes will be pushed.

2. A mechanism to update the scripts on the master server (*puppetmasterd*) when changes are pushed to the master repository. This could be a post-receive Git hook, or something external such as a Jenkins job.

3. Local clones of the repository where each developer/administrator can do work and then push it back to the master repository for review and/or implemenation.

For this example, let's assume we have a utility server that will serve as both the Puppet master server and the host of the master Git repository.

First, we'll set up a Git repository. This could be at any path you choose, but we'll go with something under */srv*:

```
# mkdir -p /srv/git/infrastructure.git
# cd /srv/git/infrastructure.git
# git --bare init
```

The `git init` command creates an empty Git repository for us. In this case, the `--bare` flag is used in order to skip creating a working directory; since this is on a server, that's exactly what we want.

That's all that's needed to start an empty Git repository, but we'll also run a couple of commands to configure the git repository for a shared environment (multiple people contributing to the same repository). Here we assume that you've set up an "infrastructure" Linux group—anyone with membership in that group will have read and write access to the repository:

```
# git config core.sharedrepository 1
# git config receive.denyNonFastforwards true
# chgrp -R infrastructure .
# find . -type d -exec chmod 2770 {} \;
```

The `find`/`chmod` command will set the `sgid` bit on directories in order to retain group ownership on new files created there—this will help keep permissions correct as people push to the repository.

The Git repo can now be cloned by any user with SSH access to that machine who belongs to the *infrastructure* group:

```
$ git clone util.example.com:/srv/git/infrastructure.git
```

Now that you have a local clone of the repository, you can add some files and push them back to the central repository. For this example we'll assume we have a Puppet directory tree something like that in Figure 9-1.

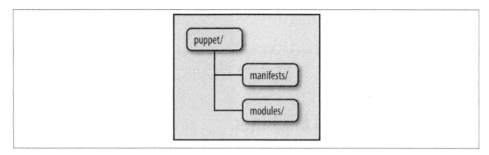

Figure 9-1. Puppet directory structure

When setting up the Pupppet master server, we will use a Git clone of this repository to populate the Puppet *manifests/* and *modules/* directories. In this case, we'll configure Puppet to look in */srv/puppet* for those files:

```
# mkdir /srv/puppet
# git clone /srv/git/infrastructure.git /srv/puppet
```

You'll need to edit your *puppet.conf* to point to that directory.

Next, for the automation bit. You don't want to have to log in to the server, change directories, and do a *git pull* every time you push changes to the configuration management scripts! Instead, we'll use a *hook* in order to update the Puppet master scripts each time new changes are pushed to the repository.

 Most revision control systems have the idea of hooks. A hook in this case is a script that gets run before or after a specified action (e.g., before a code push is accepted, or after a code push). Each revision control system has slightly different hooks and names, but the basic idea is the same across them all.

In this case we'll use the git *post-receive* hook, which is run after new code is pushed into the repository. To implement this, we need to create the post-receive script in the *hooks/* directory inside the git repository (on the server). The file we'll put there needs to be named *post-receive* and be an executable script. We'll use the following script:

```
#!/bin/sh
cd /srv/puppet
```

```
/bin/echo "`/usr/bin/whoami` is updating puppet master config @ `/bin/pwd`"
/usr/bin/git pull
```

Simply name that file *post-receive*, copy it into */srv/git/infrastructure.git/hooks/*, and ensure that it has executable permissions. Of course, the destination directory needs to have permissions set such that anyone pushing to the git repository can update files there. Following the same permissions as used for the git repository in */srv/git* would work well.

To test the new hook, commit some changes to your local Git clone and then push it back to the central repository. You should see the script output informing you that the directory is being updated.

Development Virtual Machines

It can be difficult for developers if they are working in a development environment (think a local laptop) that is set up completely differently than the staging and production environments. There are various ways to work around this—some people choose to set up a development server with Apache virtual hosts for each developer and let them develop on that server directly. However, this has the downside that developers aren't able to test certain (infrastructure) changes without affecting other developers. What if it were possible to give each developer a local (virtual) environment that closely matched production, and gave the developers the power to test any code and/or infrastructure changes locally? There are a number of ways to do this, but if you already have a configuration management system in place, a tool called Vagrant will provide a very easy solution for creating just such a virtual machine (VM) environment.

 Vagrant provides an easy way to create development VMs. It ships with support for VirtualBox, but also has a plug-in system that allows you to use Vagrant with other virtualization providers, such as VMware or AWS. More documentation is available at the official project website (*http://www.vagrantup.com*).

Typical Vagrant usage is to start with a bare-bones "base box," which is a virtual machine image with minimal packages and services installed. Vagrant provides support for multiple provisioners, which are the scripts run against the base box in order to configure it to meet your needs. In the most simple form, you could use a set of shell scripts to do the provisioning; however, Vagrant really shines when used with a configuration management system (currently support is provided for Ansible, Chef, and Puppet). If you are already using a configuration management system with your production infrastructure, it is very easy to integrate it into Vagrant in order to create an easily reproducible development environment that closely matches the production server configuration.

Distributing a small base box image and then doing all configuration with a configuration management system provides a few benefits:

- Initial download of the VM image is faster, since it isn't very large.
- Although the initial provisioning step may take a while (and transfer many packages from the Internet), future changes to the VM can be made by updating the configuration management scripts instead of having developers download a full VM image simply to make a few small changes.
- Infrastructure and configuration management changes can be easily tested on a local Vagrant VM in order to give some assurance that things will work similarly in other (test, staging, production) environments.

How to Distribute Development VMs with Vagrant

Generally, you will want to start with a small base box image, and it should match the operating system you are using on your production infrastructure. You can either create your own (instructions are provided in the Vagrant documentation), or use one of the many base boxes that are publicly available on sites such as *http://vagrantbox.es*. One important thing to look out for is that you use a base box that includes support for whichever configuration management provider you will use. This simply means that, for example, Puppet is installed on the VM image if you are going to be using Puppet for provisioning.

Once you've settled on a base box, you can start integrating your existing configuration management system. Most things will just work if you've done a good job of writing your configuration management scripts; however, since the Vagrant image is starting out mostly unconfigured, it's very important that your dependency order is set correctly for everything so that all services will work correctly after one run of the provisioning scripts. Depending on how you are doing code and database deployments in your production environment, you may need to create additional scripts for deploying the site code onto the VM—for example, a "sitedeploy" Puppet module that gets a copy of the site code from your configuration management system, imports initial data into the database, and ensures that the Drupal database user is granted correct permissions.

Now, distributing the system to all developers and admins becomes a matter of distributing a copy of your Vagrantfile (Vagrant configuration directives) and the configuration management scripts. The Vagrantfile can automate the downloading of a standard base box image. Generally we keep all the configuration in a revision control system so that it's easy to make updates and everyone can pick them up with a *git pull* or similar.

Deployment Workflow

Now that your developers can quickly provision local virtual machines that closely match the production configuration, it's time to take advantage of them to test changes to Drupal. We've mentioned the importance of a revision control system for managing your site's code, but it doesn't stop there. Once you have a revision control system in place, you will also need a well-defined workflow in place for your developers, as well as for code deployments to individual environments. A well-defined workflow will improve site stability (you are testing code first and not editing directly on your production site) and should allow developers to easily collaborate on changes for upcoming releases, while still giving the ability to make quick "hotfixes" when a bug is found that requires immediate attention. There are a number of widely used and accepted workflows, and generally there is no wrong way as long as you find something that works for you and everyone on your team agrees to stick to it.

Example Workflow with Git

As we mentioned, there are almost endless options for how to approach your development and deployment workflow. We'll give an example consisting of three environments: development, staging, and production. This is a standard setup that we strongly recommend. The Git branching model described here is based on a workflow initially written about by Vincent Driessen (*http://nvie.com/posts/a-successful-git-branching-model/*) and referred to as "Git Flow," which is also the name of the set of optional Git plug-ins used to easily work in the model. For the sake of simplicity, we won't use so-called release branches; however, some people will find those very useful and should read Vincent's full article for more information.

There are a couple of things to consider here: the Git branching workflow, and the deployment workflow. The deployment workflow is easy to understand from a high level—we want new code to start in the development environment, then be pushed to staging for testing before finally being pushed to production when it's deemed ready. Figure 9-2 illustrates this workflow.

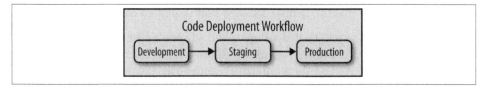

Figure 9-2. Code deployment workflow

We'll get more in depth into the code deployment process in the next section. For now, it's only important to understand that code changes flow in only one direction, except in the case of hotfixes, and that code is never edited directly on the servers, but is instead

---

always pushed through the revision control system (although some sites make an exception for this rule when working in the development environment, with the caveat that developers clean up after themselves so that the automated deployment tools continue to work as expected).

There are a number rules and guidelines that shape the development workflow and Git branching model:

- Production is run from the *master* branch (specifically, from a Git tag pointing to a commit on the *master* branch).
- Staging is run from tags created from the *develop* branch.
- Development is run from the *HEAD* of the *develop* branch.
- Developers create branches off of the *develop* branch to do their work, and those are merged back into *develop* once they've been reviewed.
- If a hotfix is ever needed, a hotfix branch is created off of *master* and then merged into *develop* for testing (and inclusion in the next full release). After testing, it is merged back into *master* for deployment to production.

This gives us three distinct environments, with active development happening in the development environment, testing and QA happening in the staging environment, and code being pushed to the production environment once QA is complete in the staging environment.

To see exactly how this all works together, we can look at a specific developer branch as it makes its way through the workflow and eventually is deployed to the production environment:

1. The developer creates a branch (we'll call the branch "feature-go-faster") off of the current *develop* branch.
2. Code is committed to the developer's branch, *feature-go-faster*, and the branch is pushed to the central repository for review.
3. The *feature-go-faster* branch is reviewed, and once it passes review it is merged into the main *develop* branch.
4. Code on the development web server is updated with the latest code in the *develop* branch. This may also involve syncing the current database and files from staging or production back into the development environment.
5. Basic (or extensive, if that's your thing) testing is performed in the development environment. At some schedule—which could be weekly, biweekly, monthly, or just "when there are enough changes to warrant a new release"—a release tag is created pointing to the current state of the *develop* branch.

6. The new release tag is deployed to the staging environment. In many cases, this also involves syncing the current database and files from the production environment into the staging environment.

7. Testing is performed in the staging environment.

8. Once testing is complete, the code from that tag is merged into the master branch and a new release tag is generated.

9. The new release tag is deployed to the production environment and any final QA testing is performed there.

This design can be considered a starting point that can be adapted to fit your specific needs. Smaller sites may choose to combine the development and staging environments since they have fewer developers and changes, or potentially fewer testing requirements. Other sites may add additional testing or maintenance environments.

Deployment with Jenkins CI

As demonstrated in the preceding workflow example, there are a few interactions between the various environments that need to happen during deployment. This includes the actual code deployment (usually some sort of git pull or git checkout command); syncing files and the database back from production or staging; and potentially some additional tasks such as running database updates, clearing the cache, taking a database snapshot, or even rebuilding Solr search indexes. There are many ways that these tasks can be run, but one popular option is to use Jenkins, which can connect over SSH (or with Jenkins "slaves") to the various server environments and run shell scripts, *drush* commands, etc. on each server as needed. Using a continuous integration (CI) server such as Jenkins provides a number of benefits, such as job health and history tracking, job scheduling (time- or event-based), a fine-grained permissions system, and a web user interface for those that aren't comfortable running scripts from the command line.

 Other popular deployment options include Capistrano or, if using Chef, the built-in Chef *deploy* resource.

It's advisable to run Jenkins from an internal utility server if you have one. It's important that access to Jenkins is limited as much as possible because once it's configured, it will have access to make changes to all of your site environments, including the production site. Access can be restricted with the Jenkins users/permissions system; in addition, access can be controlled with a firewall, or Jenkins can be configured to listen only on the local interface, requiring users to use SSH port forwarding in order to connect to the Jenkins web interface.

SSH port forwarding is a useful trick for connecting to Jenkins, as well as other services that may be protected behind a firewall. Forwarding ports over SSH can be done with the -L flag. For example, if Jenkins is listening on port 8080 only on the local interface on the server, you could use ssh -L 8080:localhost:8080 servername.com and then access Jenkins by pointing your browser to *http://localhost:8080*.

In a simple setup, the *jenkins* user on the server running the Jenkins service can be given an SSH key pair. Then, on each server that Jenkins needs to access (generally this would be limited to only your web servers, but it depends on exactly what you are configuring Jenkins to do), a local user can be created granting login access with the *jenkins* user's public key. In this manner, jobs can be configured to use *drush* (with a properly configured *drush* aliases file), or by calling SSH directly:

```
'ssh deploy@webhost /usr/local/bin/deploy_script.sh'
```

The *deploy* user on the web servers can be given any username you like. In some cases, the account may need access to run scripts as another user—for example, running a cache clear as the *apache* (or *www-data*) user so that it has access to remove files from the Drupal *files/* directory. Those commands should be configured in *sudo* as needed. The following is an example file that can be placed in */etc/sudoers.d/deploy*:

```
Defaults:deploy !requiretty
Defaults:deploy !env_reset
deploy ALL=(apache) NOPASSWD: /usr/local/bin/site_cache_clear.sh
```

Note that the *requiretty* option must be disabled for the user that Jenkins is connecting as, since it will not be running from a valid terminal.

There are a number of different types of scripts that are typically run from Jenkins:

Code deployment
> These are scripts that connect to a revision control system to update/deploy code onto the web servers.

Deployment helpers
> These scripts are for handling tasks related to a deployment—for example, taking a database snapshot before an update, putting the site into maintenance mode, performing a cache clear, performing database updates, etc.

Environment synchronization
> These scripts are for syncing the Drupal *files/* directory and the database between environments. While code is deployed from development to staging to production, database and *files/* sync happens in reverse: the production database and *files/* are synchronized to staging, and then from there to development.

Site management

These are periodic scripts that support the site—for example, running Drupal cron, daily database backups, etc.

## CHAPTER 10

File Storage for Multiple Web Servers

In this chapter, we will discuss the options for file storage in infrastructures with multiple web nodes. Ensuring your file storage is coherent and synchronized between your web nodes is often the redheaded stepchild of infrastructure design—most everyone is aware that you need all your web nodes to agree on database information, and quite a few know that your object cache needs to be coherent. However, the complication of ensuring your static files are synchronized between web nodes is often overlooked.

Why is this important? Imagine that a user goes to your site and uploads an avatar. That user's avatar is written to disk on *webnode1*. If there is a delay in that file becoming available on *webnode2*—or worse, if its not synchronized at all—users will start seeing broken image links for that file. Even if your site doesn't accept user uploads, Drupal creates its own JS/CSS aggregate files on disk, and if those don't exist on both web nodes, you will quickly hit issues on the web node without them. Keep this in mind while debugging "strange issues" that may come up on your infrastructure (certain users not seeing CSS correctly, 404s on only certain web nodes, etc.). It is easy to forget how important coherent file storage is to a functional website.

Now that we understand why this is important, we can cover a few different methods of maintaining this consistency when using multiple web nodes. In this chapter, we will discuss some of the more popular methods for Drupal deployments and their various advantages and disadvantages.

rsync

The first option we should consider is, at first glance, the simplest. In this configuration, you would simply set up rsync (*http://rsync.samba.org/*) processes between your web nodes to ensure that every file on *webnode1* is also on *webnode2*, *webnode3*, and so on. This setup has a few problems, though. First, there will always be some sort of delay in file syncing. It must be acceptable to have broken links on pages during this sync delay.

Additionally, this configuration virtually requires session affinity. Having a missing user avatar during the sync delay for some users is a problem, but having the user who uploaded that avatar not able to see it on his own profile page is a critical problem. Because of this, session affinity is usually a requirement as it "resolves" the issue by ensuring that a user who uploads an avatar remains on the webnode he uploaded it on.

Even if you are entirely fine with having session affinity enabled and with the synchronization delay, there are other complications. For example, there is no clear method for removing files from web nodes where the file removal did not originally take place. During an rsync from point A to point B, how do you differentiate between a file having not yet been synced and a file having been deleted? Issues like this are why "just using rsync" is becoming less of an answer to this problem.

GlusterFS

Gluster is one of the most popular options for file storage, and in particular file storage in cloud deployments (discussed in the next chapter). It is popular for good reason— Gluster is simple to set up, does not create a single point of failure, and works extremely well for many types of deployments. It is in essence a clustering filesystem, but one designed for standard deployments and not necessarily an enterprise configuration (meaning it doesn't assume you have access to high-quality disk backends, etc.).

GlusterFS (*http://www.gluster.org/*) works as follows. First, you define storage "bricks," the servers and mount points where the actual data will be stored. Note that these can be the web nodes themselves; all that matters is that they exist, are relatively stable, and have a low-latency network connection. You then can "combine" these bricks together using GlusterFS "translators." This sounds complicated, but the default configuration is fairly good and largely just creates a redundant array of these bricks with locking, caching, prefetching, and other performance and feature translators layered on top. You can then mount the Gluster volume on each web node, and the Gluster translators will do the work of ensuring both that files are kept in sync and that there are replicas of the files across the brick cluster. Figure 10-1 illustrates a Gluster mount across two servers and the underlying Gluster brick on each server.

There are multiple ways to mount the Gluster volume: you can mount it via Gluster's native protocol, using the FUSE (File Systems in User Space) driver, or you can mount the volume over NFS (Gluster has an NFS emulation layer). There are mixed reports as to which is better, with many people agreeing that NFS is somewhat less stable, but better for high concurrency. Most people tend to use the native FUSE driver.

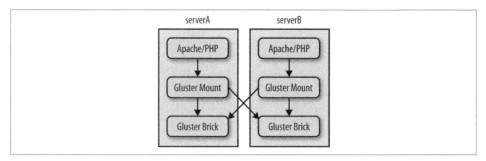

Figure 10-1. GlusterFS overview

Example Configuration

Recent versions of Gluster have made it quite easy to get up and running with a simple setup. Assuming you have at least two servers with available disk space for the bricks and Gluster is installed on all of the servers, you can get started by typing something like the following in the terminal (let's assume you have two servers, *serverA* and *serverB*, and that on each server you're going to store data in */var/gluster/data*):

```
(On serverA): gluster peer probe serverB
(On serverA): gluster volume create testVolume replica 2 \
             serverA:/var/gluster/data serverB:/var/gluster/data
(On serverA): gluster volume start testVolume
```

You can now check on the status of your volume with:

```
(On serverA or serverB): gluster volume info
```

And you can now mount your new volume by executing the following on any server you want it mounted on:

```
# mount -t glusterfs serverA:/testVolume /mnt/gluster_volume
```

The hostname used in the mount command could be either of the *glusterfs* hosts (that is, serverA could be replaced with serverB to access the same volume, only mounted directly from *serverB*). Thus, if you had two web nodes, you could have a brick on each and then mount from the local server on each. This is often the easiest way to get a replicated files directory between web nodes, without inserting a single point of failure.

Single NFS Server

A decreasingly common practice is to set up an NFS share somewhere on your cluster and just hope for the best. The advantage of this practice is simplicity. The disadvantage is that if that one NFS server goes down, needs a reboot for updates, or has a hardware failure, the entire site will go down. You should really only use this method (illustrated in Figure 10-2) if you have single points of failure everywhere else in your infrastructure as well and one more won't bother you.

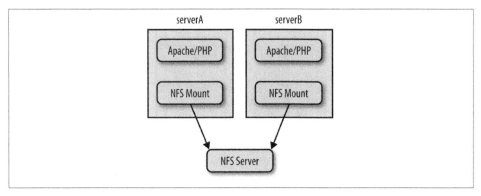

Figure 10-2. Single NFS server

HA NFS Cluster

While a single NFS server is usually a poor idea, there are other configurations that are quite useful and still use NFS as the protocol of choice. One such setup is to use DRBD (a kernel-level distributed remote block device) to replicate the actual block device NFS is hosted on. This allows you (with some significant configuration) to successfully fail over an NFS mount without having stale file handles on the client side. This configuration (shown in Figure 10-3) is somewhat difficult to get correct, but is one of the few ways to have truly highly available NFS.

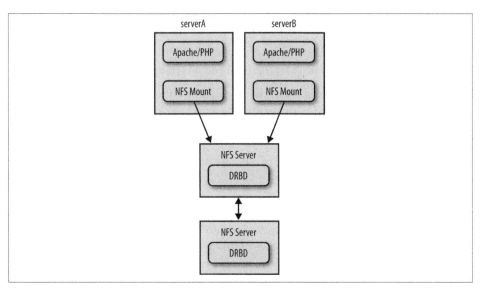

Figure 10-3. HA NFS cluster

Example Configuration

The configuration of HA-NFS actually has very little to do with NFS and more to do with having a truly (and absolutely) replicated block device. NFSv3 has no concept of failover, so when you do actually failover between two servers, the challenge is convincing it to "look over there" during the failover and then pretend like nothing happened. Heartbeat and DRBD are surprisingly good at this.

This whole system depends on two things. Firstly, NFS file handles on the client side not only depend on the IP address and NFS *statd* hostname, but also on the inode on the server itself. DRBD allows you to have these inodes be the same between two servers, which is a core requirement, since if all the inodes suddenly changed, everything would break. Secondly, NFS has a directory where it stores state information, and DRBD is accurate enough that you can synchronize this directory between the two servers, as well as the data itself. Once you have the data and this state information perfectly replicated between the two servers, failover becomes much more possible, as the event itself looks like just a momentary network failure to the NFS clients.

Setting Up DRBD

The first step in setting up DRBD is to create two identical partitions on two servers. They must literally be exactly the same size. You must then install DRBD—this will include the userland utilities and a kernel module. Start the DRBD service and you can begin with the standard setup procedure.

 We assume DRBD version 8.4 in the following discussion, if you are using 8.3, we recommend following the instructions on the DRBD website (*http://www.drbd.org*).

Edit */etc/drbd.conf* (or *global.conf* and *r0.res* in */etc/drbd.d*, depending on your distribution). There are two sections in the *drbd.conf* file: the global/common section and the resource section. (These two sections map to the two different files in some distributions.) The global/common section is very simple and should contain something like this:

```
global {
  usage-count yes;
}
common {
  net {
    protocol C;
  }
}
```

The resource section is where you define your volume and should have something like this in it:

```
resource resourceName {
  on server1 {
    device    /dev/drbd0;
    disk      /dev/sdb1;
    address   192.168.1.2:7789;
    meta-disk internal;
  }
  on server2 {
    device    /dev/drbd0;
    disk      /dev/sdb1;
    address   192.168.1.3:7789;
    meta-disk internal;
  }
}
```

Once you have this file in place and exactly the same on both servers, start the DRBD service and proceed to set up the volume. The following commands will need to be run on *both* servers:

```
# drbdadm create-md resourceName
# drbdadm up resourceName
```

At this point, you should be able to run `cat /proc/drbd` and see the state of the volume. It should list the two servers as both up, in the "Secondary/Secondary" state, and "Inconsistent." This means that the two physical devices are not synchronized and that neither server considers itself the "primary" (the server receiving reads/writes with the volume mounted). Now let's perform our first synchronization. Run the following command on the server you want to be the primary:

```
# drbdadm primary --force resourceName
```

Note that this will copy every bit of data on the physical device on this server to the secondary server. This is important if there is actual "legitimate" data on one of these devices—in that case, you would run this command on the server with legitimate data. This is an important consideration when resynchronizing a cluster or replacing a DRBD node.

You can monitor the process of the synchronization via `cat /proc/drbd`. Once the sync is complete, you can format and mount this new DRBD resource on your primary server. The device name will be */dev/drbd0*, and it can be treated exactly like a new partition (i.e., you format and mount it the same way).

This is a very general description of how to set up DRBD; you really should go to the DRBD website and read the detailed documentation there before ever attempting to use it in production. It is a complicated system, but exceptionally useful in many situations.

Setting Up Heartbeat

The part of this configuration that actually detects failure and then takes action on that failure is Heartbeat. This software is packaged in most distributions and should be easy to install. There are two ways to configure Heartbeat: the "v1" way and the "pacemaker" way. We recommend the v1 method for most people as it's quite simple, and for a NFS-DRBD cluster, you don't need anything more complicated. Heartbeat is used repeatedly in many sections of this book (and many infrastructures), and most of Chapter 12 is dedicated to it.

Setting Up NFS

The NFS setup is mostly normal, with a few exceptions (they are weird exceptions, though!):

1. Stop *nfs*.
2. Set the *statd* hostname to the same thing on both servers. On Red Hat-based systems, this is located in */etc/sysconfig/nfs*.
3. Unmount *rpc_pipefs*. This may be difficult, and you may have to force the umount. This is a virtual file system used for NFS4, and it's mounted into the NFS state directory. We want to move this directory, so we need to unmount it.
4. Copy */var/lib/nfs* to the DRBD mount and then delete the original */var/lib/nfs* and symlink the directory from the DRBD mount back to */var/lib/nfs*.
5. Remount *rpc_pipefs*.
6. Finally, on the other server, ensure that the *statd* hostname is changed, unmount *rpc_pipefs*, and symlink */var/lib/nfs* to the path where the NFS state directory would be if the DRBD volume was mounted. (The same symlink command you ran on the primary server will work here. This directory will only actually exist on this server when the DRBD volume is failed over. This is important, as this state directory must be synchronized between the two machines.)

Testing

We recommend starting Heartbeat (*drbd*, *nfs*, etc.) on the primary, mounting NFS on another server, and either attempting a failover via the Heartbeat utilities or just shutting down the server you're testing. For example (given *heartbeat/drbd/nfs* running on *serverA* and *serverB*):

```
(on serverA): cat /proc/drbd
# verify that you are master
(on serverA): /etc/init.d/heartbeat stop
(on serverA): tail -f /var/log/messages
# watch it failing over and ensure there are no errors
```

```
(on serverB): cat /proc/drbd
#verify that it is master
(on serverA): /etc/init.d/heartbeat start
(on serverA): tail -f /var/log/messages
# watch it failing back and ensure there are no errors
(on serverA): cat /proc/drbd
# ensure that serverA is now master--there may be a resync period shown
```

During all of the above, your test website should never go down. (There may be brief stalls in service, but it shouldn't go down completely.) If your website does become unavailable for a few minutes at a time around a failover event, consider mounting the NFS volume over UDP and not TCP. Some additional information and tips on this method of HA-NFS is available here (*http://wiki.linux-ha.org/HaNFS*).

Storage Area Networks (SANs)

It is difficult to really discuss a SAN device (an enterprise appliance specifically designed to provide highly available shared storage) while comparing it to these other options. Very few people have the money or inclination to buy a SAN device for a single website. If you do have both the money and the inclination, you also probably have a very large site (or, more likely, several). The summary here is that every option presented so far in this chapter is designed to get you partially to the feature set and reliability of a real SAN device. If a SAN is an option for you, then it is the obvious choice. However, it is a rarity that it is a realistic option.

 If you rent space on a SAN from a provider, get details on exactly what type of SAN it is (i.e., what brand it is) and how much it is provisioned (how saturated it is). Providers have a tendency to oversaturate SANs or call a regular file server a "SAN."

## CHAPTER 11

Drupal and Cloud Deployments

You've probably heard one of two things about "the Cloud":

1. Cloud deployments are the future and the present; the be all and end all of flexible, dynamic, enterprise-grade, and agile infrastructure design.

2. Cloud deployments are entirely a marketing innovation and are championed by people who probably should be in the PR department, but somehow wandered into the wrong meetings too many times and are now on the technical staff.

You can easily hear both of these arguments at any major conference (usually in the same conversation and at high volume). You might say there is some disagreement in the community on the merits of the cloud. We will try to clear up some of the confusion in this chapter.

What Is the Cloud?

That this question must be asked is one reason some people find the concept of "the cloud" annoying. The term is used so often that it now means basically nothing (a phenomenon now known as "cloud washing"). For our purposes, we will be defining the cloud as a virtualized hosting solution, where VMs can be created and destroyed on demand via an API with no human interaction. This is a very common definition and fits clouds such as Amazon EC2 (*http://aws.amazon.com/ec2/*) and Rackspace Cloud (*http://www.rackspace.com/cloud/*). Just to be absolutely clear, by "API" we mean a client-visible API that allows you to script automatic growth and shrinking of an array of servers.

Why Use the Cloud?

The major advantage of a cloud deployment is flexibility. If you need 10 web nodes today, 30 tomorrow, and 5 the next day, that's something the cloud can give you that a typical hosting environment struggles with. This makes cloud deployments incredibly good for startups and any venture where traffic varies greatly. They can also be excellent for testing, as you often only need a VM for a matter of hours.

This flexibility is definitely revolutionary and is why the cloud is such a big deal right now. The ability to design a system that actively scales itself up (i.e., increases VM counts) as load increases allows for infrastructures that used to be impossible without a huge investment. Some clouds even allow you to integrate into an existing hardware infrastructure; for example, having a web node array to supplement your hardware web nodes during times of high load.

This ability to dynamically adjust your infrastructure, and to treat hardware as a service, opens up huge possibilities and is very exciting.

Infrastructure Overhead

One of the reasons that, despite all of these exciting aspects, some people are still annoyed with "the cloud" is that there is a significant cost to building up the automation required for using it well. This cost (technical overhead) is glossed over by many, and as a result, people end up with virtualized infrastructures that are not doing them any good (and may in fact be doing them significant damage). Let's discuss an example.

Suppose you are currently testing your site with two web nodes and a database server, and you decide to move to a cloud deployment. You start the two web nodes and DB server on this cloud deployment. You don't have any automation, so you must configure each of the web nodes by hand (at least partially—let's say you have part of your web stack automated, but not all of it). What are you gaining at this point? Your new VMs are likely less powerful than the hardware you had before and they are certainly less reliable—remember that these clouds are designed for automation, and a VM "disappearing" is not unexpected. At least you can scale automatically though, right? No. Unless your automation is complete (meaning able to go from an "empty" VM or a saved image to a working web node without interaction), your response to a load increase will be very limited. You can manually start and set up new VMs, but that's not going to be exceptionally effective. This is the big issue: to leverage the cloud, you *must* have fully working automation. There is a very real cost for this, and it's a cost that is often ignored.

Prepackaged Clouds

There are other options besides trying to build this automation entirely yourself. There are providers that have built "managed clouds," allowing you you to input your code and database on one side and have your site hosted on their reliable, autoscaling infrastructure on the other. The tools you are given are somewhat more detailed than this, but the idea of a black box for the infrastructure component is valid. Acquia Cloud (*http://www.acquia.com/products-services/acquia-cloud*) and Pantheon (*https://www.getpantheon.com/*) are examples of providers offering prepackaged cloud services for Drupal.

The advantages to this are: you get some of the autoscaling benefits of cloud deployments, without the large investment in infrastructure building. The disadvantage here is flexibility. If your site doesn't fit the provider's expectations for build or usage, you will not have a good experience.

There is also a middle ground where you get to manage your own infrastructure, but many tools and scripts are provided to help you automate it. An example of this is RightScale (*http://www.rightscale.com/*). There is still a lot of infrastructure investment required for this option, but less than if you were to start from scratch, and they give you a significant amount of documentation.

Common Issues with Cloud Deployments and Their Mitigations

Obviously this isn't a book on virtualization, and your issues with cloud deployments will vary widely by what type of site you are hosting, its usage, and what technologies you are using. However, we can go over some common issues and how to mitigate them:

Slow IO

> This varies by provider, depending on what type of IO backend they use. Many cloud hosting providers have very slow IO backends when compared to a typical hardware-based RAID host. This often impacts database servers the most, but it can also slow down web requests depending on how many PHP files are touched during Drupal's bootstrap. Mitigating this concern involves ensuring that you tune the real-path cache, possibly turning off `apc.stat`, and ensuring that your DB server has enough memory and is configured to fully cache your data. These topics are covered in Chapters 13 and 18.

Disappearing or failing VMs

> Virtual machines on most cloud providers are treated as a variable resource. This isn't a failure of clouds at all; it's by design. Hardware as a service cuts both ways. When designing your infrastructure, you need to be able to both take advantage of this (increase resources when needed, reduce when not) and prevent the negative aspects from taking your site down. Test your high availability plan to ensure that it will really work, as it will eventually need to be used.

Limited IP failover

A common method of building high availability into a system is to have a floating IP address that moves between two servers in the event of a failure. This method is not supported (or not supported well) by most clouds—for example, some clouds have the ability to fail over IPs, but with a variable delay to the failover. Thus, alternate solutions are often required. Many providers have these solutions built into their clouds; if not, you may need application layer failover or DNS failover. We discuss this to some degree in Chapter 12.

In summary, there are very real advantages to cloud hosting and hardware as a service. It is very exciting to be able to handle load and build infrastructures that would never have been possible for smaller companies before. However, the hype around cloud hosting needs to be managed carefully. There should be a real reason for you to use cloud hosting, and you must actually plan for its use and the automation it requires.

## CHAPTER 12

Failover Configuration

A few chapters earlier in this book, we mentioned that we would cover how to actually direct traffic in a failover situation in a later chapter. Congratulations, this is that chapter! Your patience has paid off. Sadly, the wait may not be entirely worth it. Being able to consistently direct traffic between two servers, depending on which one is marked "active," is tremendously important for high availability in general and many services that back Drupal sites specifically. Having an HA MySQL cluster, NFS cluster, Solr cluster, and load balancing cluster all depend on this. However, it's not the most exciting thing in the world. The general concept is very simple: you run a daemon on two servers, and those two daemons ping each other fairly constantly. When *serverA's* daemon doesn't get a response from *serverB's* daemon within a certain failure criterion, *serverB* is marked down and traffic is directed to *serverA*. The interesting issues with failover configurations are:

- What are the failure conditions?
- Can we insert other conditions besides just a full host down? Service-level failure conditions, perhaps?
- How do you direct traffic consistently?
- How do you deal with split-brain?
- Wait, what is split-brain?
- It is not a problem with my brain specifically, is it?
- This seems scary; can't we just take a downtime?

We will cover some of these issues here, starting with traffic direction.

In most cases, we are assuming that whatever service you are failing over is already prepared for failover (i.e., set up to be synchronized between the two servers in question).

IP Failover Versus DNS Failover

There are two types of failover that are commonly deployed: IP-based failover and DNS-based failover. In essence, these two methodologies only differ in what "resource" is changed in order to direct traffic. IP-based failover, not surprisingly, directs traffic via moving an IP between two machines. Its major advantages are simplicity and very "immediate" results. However, it is problematic to use in most cloud environments (usually you cannot get an extra IP assigned for the failover IP, also called the virtual IP or VIP) and can be somewhat difficult to manage for those not used to it. This is as compared to DNS failover, which involves changing a DNS record to point to the "new" server in order to direct traffic.

DNS failover is a fairly common method of implementing HA in cloud environments and can be easier to set up, especially with some specific DNS services designed for it. However, the failover is definitely not as immediate or dependable as IP-based methods. DNS names have some implied caching in many cases, and services such as the Name Service Cache Daemon (NSCD) can cause issues with failover lag. Due to this, you must plan for the possibility of a "slow" failover, where some traffic continues to hit the "old master" before the "new master" fully takes over.

In most cases, this decision will be heavily influenced, if not entirely decided, by how open your provider is to IP failover/moving IP addresses between your servers. Some providers won't allow you to have an additional IP address assigned to your server to use for failover, and others are nervous about IP failover confusing their switches. However, these issues are fairly rare for dedicated server providers.

Service-Level Issues

One might note that much of our discussion so far has centered on host-level issues. We have discussed directing network traffic between two full hosts and checking whether hosts are up from a network and OS perspective. This is nice, but it is fairly rare (or at least it should be) for an entire host to fail. More commonly a service will fail or start responding slowly. In cases like this, an HA cluster must detect this and start a failover. Likewise, simply moving traffic from *serverA* to *serverB* sometimes isn't enough to actually failover a service. Many times there are other actions that need to be taken, such as setting `read_only` to `false` on a MySQL slave.

The failover system we introduce here doesn't really handle service-level detection and failover in and of itself, but instead uses external services and scripts. For example, to failover a MySQL service using Heartbeat, you could write a "mysql resource" script. This script would perform the failover and would be triggered in the event of a MySQL failover scenario. As far as monitoring is concerned, the system we will cover here can easily be triggered by an external source (i.e., it can be told to "failover this host"). Thus, you can use another monitoring system for services and have it trigger failovers. A common choice for this is Mon (*http://sourceforge.net/projects/mon/*) (not to be confused with Monit (*http://mmonit.com/monit/*)), a very simple framework that can check for service health and then trigger Heartbeat upon a detected failure.

Heartbeat

Heartbeat has been the de facto Linux failover tool for a very long time. It is quite stable, very well supported, and decently documented. However, it comes in two "versions," and the difference between the two can be quite confusing. Heartbeat by itself (sometimes called Heartbeat v1) is a simple failover tool that moves resources and IP addresses between two services. It only supports two servers and is quite simple to set up and use. Heartbeat+Pacemaker (formerly called Heartbeat v2 or Heartbeat+CRM) is a full clustering suite that is quite complicated to set up and use but supports complex configurations and more than two servers. This level of complication is simply not needed for the services that back most Drupal deployments. Because of this, we will only be covering Heartbeat v1 (henceforth just called Heartbeat).

 Discussion of v1 versus v2 doesn't imply actual software changes, but just different types of configuration. The Heartbeat package and actual software are the same in both versions.

Installation

Most Linux distributions and *BSDs will have a Heartbeat package. It may also install Pacemaker, but you can mostly just ignore that unless you really need advanced clustering. Thus, to install Heartbeat you can just use one of the following commands:

```
# *yum install heartbeat*
# *apt-get install heartbeat*
```

Configuration

There are three important configuration files for Heartbeat:

authkeys
> This sets the type of authentication for the cluster and the hash to use for authentication.

ha.cf

This is the general configuration file, defining the two nodes of the cluster, failure timeouts, failback settings, and other major configuration options.

haresources

This defines the resources Heartbeat will be controlling. Usually this means IP resources and various services to be started/stopped during resource acquisition and failover.

We'll look at some examples of these files next. In these examples, we have two servers that are load balancing MySQL, named *node1* and *node2*.

 The *authkeys* file needs to be the same on both servers—they both need to have the same key to successfully be a cluster. Likewise, this file needs to be secured (not group or "other" readable/writeable).

Here's an example *authkeys* configuration:

```
auth 1
1 sha1 your_secret_key_here
```

 You can generate a secret key like this: dd if=/dev/urandom count=4 2>/dev/null | md5sum | cut -c1-32.

And here's an example *ha.cf* configuration:

```
ucast eth1 _<the IP of the other node>_
node node1
node node2
auto_failback on
```

The *ha.cf* file can become very complicated, but for some situations, it is as simple as this. There are a few very important lines here. First, the ucast line is telling Heartbeat the IP address of the other node and the interface on which to ping that node. This file differs on each node (as the IP listed in each case will be the IP of the "other" one). If this IP is incorrect, the interface is incorrect, or there is a firewall preventing this ping, Heartbeat will not work correctly (both nodes will believe themselves to be the master as they cannot communicate, this is often called split-brain). Equally importantly, the node lines identifying the members of the cluster must contain hostnames that actually match the return of "hostname" on each node.

The auto_failback line is actually quite important, too. If you set this to on, resources will be failed back to their "home" node whenever that node comes back from a failure. If it is set to off, you will have to fail them back manually. Having this option off is generally safer, as you can decide when you are ready to fail back to the "home" node and you avoid the possibility of resources "ping-ponging" back and forth between nodes.

Finally, here's an example *haresources* configuration:

```
node1 192.168.1.3/32/eth1 httpd mysqld _<resource4> <resource5>_
```

This file is very simple: you just list the resources that Heartbeat will be managing and which node each resource "belongs" to by default. A "resource" is either a Heartbeat-specific resource, such as IPaddr or Filesystem (file system mounts), or just an *init* script. So, you can manage system-level resources such as IPs and mounts, as well as services such as *apache*, *mysql*, and *memcache* (via their *init* scripts).

So what IPs might you put in *haresources* for failover? You should never put the main IP address for a server in this file and have it managed for failover. This would render the server unreachable upon failover. Instead, you should always assign an *extra* IP (often called the *virtual IP* or VIP) to be managed by Heartbeat. This IP will then be the one used by whatever service you want to failover. For example, if you were trying to failover HTTP traffic between two servers, you'd request an extra IP from your provider, set up Heartbeat with it managed between the two servers, and then use that IP in your DNS records. When it was failed over, traffic would then move transparently.

Usage

Once configured, using Heartbeat is quite easy. You start it via the *init* script (*/etc/init.d/heartbeat* in many cases) and can watch its progress in the system log. Once it's fully started, you can failover resources by either fully shutting down Heartbeat on one of the nodes or using *hb_takeover* or *hb_standby*, two small tools that either set resources into standby mode (i.e., fail them over to the other server) or take over resources from the other server. These utilities have three main options:

all
  Failover all resources.

foreign
  Failover just those resources not "owned" by the current node (this goes back to the *haresources* file).

local
  Failover only those resources "owned" by the current node.

These small utilities are also how you integrate Heartbeat with an external monitoring system—you have it call them when a failure is detected.

## CHAPTER 13

MySQL

One could easily write an entire book on MySQL configuration, monitoring, and query optimization. Actually, many people have, and getting one of these books would be an excellent idea. We will cover some facets of configuration and optimization here (those that directly relate to Drupal). This is a very large subject, and one any Drupal developer should be well versed in. Any content management system is in essence a very advanced database frontend, and not knowing the underlying technology of your site and/or business is asking for trouble.

Drupal and MySQL Engines

MySQL includes support for pluggable storage backends, putting data storage and retrieval entirely in their hands. There is even a CSV storage engine that literally stores tables as comma-separated values (CSV) files. While pluggable engines is an interesting feature and makes it possible for MySQL to be surprisingly flexible, in practice, InnoDB and MyISAM are the only engines you are likely to use.

MyISAM is an older-style engine with very limited data durability, simplistic caching, and very few advanced features of any kind. It excels in low-memory situations and on some very poorly optimized queries. These days it is considered dangerous to actually use MyISAM for production data, due to it not being crash safe and it lacking row-level locking. However, it is important to keep in mind that MyISAM is used for temporary tables written to disk. So, while it shouldn't be used for actually storing data, it is still going to be used during query execution.

InnoDB is the flagship MySQL storage engine. It has been around for a long time, but has recently seen a lot of advancement. It is very stable, and is now scaling across multicore CPUs considerably better than it has in the past. Some versions of InnoDB even support tuning parameters to make it use the full IO capacity of solid-state drives. As of Drupal 7, InnoDB is the default for new installations. If there is one thing to take away from this chapter, it is this: *use InnoDB.*

There are other engines that could be worth looking at that specialize in integrating other technologies or in data archiving. If you have a very specialized task, some of these can be useful; however, they are beyond the scope of this book and most Drupal deployments.

Versions of MySQL

It has been an exciting few years for MySQL. While you could argue that development had been stagnating, the purchase of MySQL AB and the immediate forks thereafter have really accelerated development across the board. While many were concerned about the MySQL ecosystem around the time of these forks, they have turned out to be very positive for users. The one downside is that it's now quite difficult to figure out which version of MySQL to use. To be clear, we will not be recommending one here. However, we will be covering the differences and pointing out that in most cases, whatever version "fits" best in your infrastructure (i.e., is easiest to install/update) is likely going to be fine for you.

Oracle MySQL

Oracle's MySQL is what everyone thinks of as "MySQL." There was definitely a period where this fork was significantly lagging in scalability features, but that time is long past. If you have a recent version of Oracle's MySQL and don't need a specialized feature in another distribution, you are likely to be fine with this version.

MariaDB

MariaDB is a fork of MySQL by one of the project's founder, Monty Widenus. The original goal of this project was to create a better version of MyISAM, but the project quickly grew into a fork of the entire server as more developers joined the project. MariaDB has gotten a lot of traction recently, including being integrated into Fedora and RHEL7 instead of Oracle's MySQL. Some of the highlights that you may notice are:

Aria storage engine
This is the result of the original goal of the project, creating a crash-safe version of MyISAM. While it's still not something you should use for your main database, it definitely is more generally usable and has some decent advantages for temporary tables (e.g., better buffering of data).

XtraDB
XtraDB is a fork of InnoDB that includes some advanced instrumentation, hooks for online binary backups, and many scalability changes. This version of InnoDB

is the default in MariaDB. You can optionally enable the mainline InnoDB, but most people using MariaDB enjoy the "Xtra" features of XtraDB.

"Enterprise" features

There are some features, such as threading changes, that Oracle's MySQL doesn't include in the community (free) version. MariaDB ships with these in all versions.

If you look at the feature comparison charts available online, you can see many other differences; however, concurrent development happens fast enough that many of these lists quickly become outdated or are somewhat debatable. We are fans of MariaDB in general, but it's fairly rare that you see a Drupal site that really needs any of these features.

Percona Server

Percona Server is a fork of MySQL that is developed by one of the leading MySQL performance firms. In general, if you need one of the specific features in this version, you are going to be well aware of that fact. It is somewhat of a niche MySQL distribution for those with extensive scalability requirements. However, many of the features developed by Percona in this MySQL distribution make it into other versions—XtraDB is an example of this.

General Configuration

There are many books on MySQL configuration and many sources for template configuration files. Due to this, we are not going to cover every configuration option, but instead will focus on those that are most important for Drupal.

MySQL configuration can generally be split into global configuration, per-thread configuration, and storage engine configuration. Let's take a look at some of the important settings for each.

Global Configuration

Drupal doesn't require tuning of many nonstandard global options. Those you may want to consider include:

`max_connections`

This configuration option is pretty self-explanatory, but it's often set far too high. This is because when `max_connection` errors are seen on the frontend, the problem is often assumed to be that `max_connections` is set too low. Usually, however, the problem actually is that there are a massive number of slow queries running. In many cases, increasing `max_connections` only allows a server to thrash itself to death more effectively. This limit should be seen as a safety maximum and should be adjusted based on the amount of memory available. You can calculate memory usage with a formula like the following to get something that is "close enough to accurate":

```
(global buffers) + ((per-thread buffers + tmp_table_size) * max_connections)
```

key_buffer

This is a very important buffer for MyISAM, which you should keep in mind is still being used for temporary tables. Any sane default is likely fine (30–50 MB for a dedicated server is not a bad starting point), but if you use a statistics script such as *mysqlreport* and the buffer is constantly full, make sure you increase it.

query_cache_size

It is remarkably easy to talk about the MySQL query cache for a long, long time. It is both a really effective cache that can increase performance dramatically and a terrible global lock that can destroy performance completely. For most Drupal sites, it is definitely worth enabling, but it's best to not set this above 100 MB, and we tend to set it at 60 MB as a default.

Per-Thread Configuration

Per-thread options are generally related to either temporary tables or the various buffers used in the execution of a single query. Many of the quality configuration templates, such as those from the IUS RHEL/CentOS repositories (*http://iuscommunity.org/*) or Percona Tools for MySQL (*https://tools.percona.com/wizard*) have good defaults for these values. You can spend a lot of time tweaking and testing the various buffers to very slightly increase performance for your specific query load. However, the benefit is often fairly negligible. In almost every case, the defaults are fine, and that time is better spent on query optimization. The only per-thread settings we often recommend tweaking for a Drupal website are those affecting temporary tables:

tmp_table_size/max_heap_table_size

These two variables control the maximum size of in-memory temporary tables. When a temp table exceeds this limit (or if a table contains TEXT/BLOB columns), it is copied to disk. In general you want to avoid this, while not increasing these settings to a size that is not sustainable for your server. Finding what is sustainable is the issue. In general, you could just take your maximum temporary table size and multiply it by max_connections to ensure you have enough memory to support every connection with a temporary table. However, this isn't a perfect method, as many people do intentionally run with temporary table sizes that are "too large" for their server. These people tend to have historical knowledge of their database server's usage to allow them to feel comfortable running "overcommitted" from a memory perspective.

These variables should be set to the same value, and *both* need to be set or the smallest value will be used.

Storage Engine Configuration

Unlike most of the per-thread configuration, correctly configuring InnoDB is extremely important. In particular, the InnoDB buffer size and transaction flush method are possibly the most important tunables for a Drupal installation. MyISAM has few important tunables for a Drupal installation other than the generic `key_buffer`, so we will focus on InnoDB here:

innodb_buffer_size

> This configuration option defines the size of the global InnoDB buffer. It's difficult to overstate how important this buffer is. The InnoDB buffer holds data cached here for reading, the insert buffer, as well as any hash indexes the engine builds for optimization. Not only do you want a large enough buffer to hold your entire dataset, but you want it large enough to have free space for the insert buffer and hash indexes. The usual recommendation is to set this to two-thirds of your memory space, but we tend to start at around half and then monitor it from there. Drupal sites specifically tend to have some fairly high `tmp_table` requirements, and that can eat into your available memory.

innodb_flush_log_at_trx_commit

> This option defines exactly how careful InnoDB is with your data. Possible settings are:

0

> Write out and flush the log to disk every second, no matter when a COMMIT is triggered.

1

> Write out and flush the log to disk at every COMMIT.

2

> Write out the log at every COMMIT, but only flush every second.

InnoDB defaults to 1, which is fully durable and in theory will lead to no data loss even on full power loss (this is very dependent on the backend IO device). This setting is exceptionally slow for Drupal, though, as it COMMITs quite a lot. Most people end up setting this to either 0 or 2, as the risk is the possibility of losing up to one second of data. In most infrastructures, not only is that not a huge issue, but there are more likely ways to lose one second of data.

While losing one second of data isn't that scary, what is sometimes an issue is the InnoDB transactional state getting out of sync with the binary log. There are deployments where this is a significant problem, either because it's difficult to resync the slave or because the slaves are very important to the correct operation of the site. In cases like this, you will have to run InnoDB with more data protection and likely should ensure that you have a new enough version of MySQL with group commit (this combines COMMIT operations, reducing disk flushes).

`innodb_log_file_size/innodb_log_files`

These settings can be important if you have a very frequently updated site. If you have a lot of updates, it's quite possible to fill up your log file space, which will force InnoDB to process its log files immediately and can cause both IO spikes and queries stacking up. The default log file size for InnoDB is actually quite low. Increasing this to something like 256 MB is usually not a bad idea, but be aware it will increase the time it takes InnoDB to recover from a crash (more logs to traverse).

 The InnoDB log file size is one of the few settings that not only requires a restart to load in, but also requires some work to move the old log files away. When you change the log file size, InnoDB will see the old logs and then throw an error because they are the wrong size. It will simply refuse to start. Because of this, you must fully shut down MySQL and move the *ib_logfile* files out of the way before starting MySQL with the new setting. It is *extremely* important that InnoDB shuts down fully and purges out the log files before you move them out of the way. Because of this, you must ensure that `innodb_fast_shutdown` is *not* set to 2. Having it set to 1 is fine, but 2 will not perform a clean shutdown.

Replication

Most every production deployment will need a replicated slave, at the very least for failover during crashes and/or updates. Again, there are many books and tutorials on setting up replication, and thus we are not going to cover this topic in detail. However, there are some Drupal-specific considerations:

Replication type

There are three types of replication: statement, row, and mixed. Statement replication simply sends the SQL statements themselves to the slave, which then runs them. It is the oldest style of replication in MySQL. Row-level replication replicates the actual binary delta and applies it to the tables on the slave. Mixed replication is, not shockingly, a mix of these two modes. Where Drupal comes into this is for contrib modules, which can have some poorly written SQL queries that don't always comply with the requirements for statement-level replication. When a query like this is run on a recent version of MySQL that has statement-level logging enabled, a warning will be put in the error log. You should watch for these warnings and consider row-level or mixed replication if it becomes a problem for you.

> There are quite a few exceptions to the rules for which queries can be perfectly replicated with statement replication and which cannot. In general, the issues center around repeatability. For example, UPDATE statements with a LIMIT clause tend to be the biggest offenders for statement replication.

Slave lag

MySQL replication is currently single threaded. This can be a problem, because Drupal has historically had a habit of running some longish DELETE queries to maintain its various logging and metrics tables. Contrib modules are also guilty of this. Most of these issues have been fixed in core and many of the popular contrib modules, but if you ever use your MySQL slave for read queries, this is something you need to actively monitor. Your slave server falling several minutes behind during cron runs can lead to some very difficult-to-debug issues if you are not monitoring slave lag actively.

Read-only queries

Pressflow 6, Drupal 7, and Drupal 8 have the ability to register a slave server and mark certain read-only queries to be sent to the slave. Pager queries (queries that show listings of information across several pages), for example, are often slave-safe.

> There are modules that automate the splitting of queries between the master and the slave, but they are not 100% accurate and we do not recommend them. It is usually safer to manage this yourself via the slave options to Drupal Views or the _slave versions of Drupal's db_query routines.

Virtualized Deployments

Configuring MySQL for virtualized deployments usually involves making absolutely sure your dataset fits in RAM and then configuring InnoDB to be a bit less durable (using the flush_log_at_trx_commit configuration option described earlier). This is due to most cloud systems having really below average IO throughput, which is something that is very important to most database systems and thus is an issue that must be mitigated.

Some other options for increasing IO throughput are:

- Configure a shared memory (SHM) mount/ramdisk and point the `tmpdir` configuration directive at it. This will write all temp tables to the memory mount and remove that IO from the disk backend.

 This reduces the data durability of temp tables, and if your memory mount fills up, queries will start failing.

- Use striped volumes (RAID-0). This is mainly useful for Amazon EC2, and some templated server configuration packages, such as RightScale, even offer an automated way to stripe EBS volumes for use as MySQL volumes. These volume stripes tend to increase performance somewhat, but are more useful in evening out performance. EBS volumes tend to have very volatile IO throughput, and striping them together helps to alleviate this volatility.

## CHAPTER 14

Tools for Managing and Monitoring MySQL

The last few years have been tremendously exciting when it comes to third-party tools for MySQL. We have gone from a few little tools here and there to professionally maintained packages of tools, with many of the utilities in these packages solving issues that have been problematic for MySQL DBAs for a very long time. We will be covering a few of our favorite packages in this chapter. We will not be covering any commercial (for-pay) utilities. There are many great ones, of course, but we will limit this chapter to either open source or "free as in beer" utilities.

Percona Toolkit

The Percona Toolkit (*http://www.percona.com/software/percona-toolkit*) actually used to be called Maatkit, before its adventures in rebranding. It was a must-have toolkit before the rename and has only gotten more so since. It contains over 30 tools, varying from hugely complicated and impactful utilities to glorified output reformatters. Some of the most important tools include:

pt-query-digest
> There once was a tool called *mysqlsla*, which basically everyone used to read the MySQL slow query log and output reports showing the top slow queries in the log. This was very useful, but *mysqlsla* didn't really progress much. *pt-query-digest* is a replacement that allows for running EXPLAINs automatically, monitoring process lists, and even generating ASCII graphs. Is it an overengineered tool for its purpose? Probably. Is it awesome enough that we don't care about that? Absolutely.

pt-table-checksum
> We recommend this tool for every replication cluster that uses statement-based or mixed binary logging (It is somewhat less needed for, and more importantly not supported with, row-based replication). *pt-table-checksum* allows you to run a replicated checksum across your cluster to ensure that the two (or more) servers are

actually consistent. MySQL itself doesn't have checksums or validation built into the replication engine, and this tool fills a critical gap. (Note that some MySQL forks, such as MariaDB, are now integrating checksums into the binary log.)

pt-online-schema-change

This tool is very dangerous to use, but quite cool to think about using. This script automates the somewhat common practice of ALTERing a large table by creating a new table with a new table definition and then filling that table from the old table, while triggers are inserted to update the new table in real time while the fill is executed. At the end of all of this, you switch the two tables. It's a complicated procedure that is fully automated by *pt-online-schema-change*.

pt-index-usage

This tool can take a slow log (or general log), EXPLAIN the queries, and generate reports on index usage. It is a useful companion to *pt-query-digest*, more specific to index usage.

There are many more tools in this package, and we recommend taking a look at all of them. They generally make your life far easier when managing a DB server and examining query performance.

Openark Kit

The openark kit (*http://code.openark.org/forge/openark-kit*) gets less attention than Percona Toolkit, but it has some equally useful tools. While Percona Toolkit tends to be slightly more focused on performance optimization and replication, openark is more focused on operational tools. These are a few of the tools we have found most useful:

oak-chunk-update

This tool takes a large UPDATE/DELETE statement and automatically splits it into chunks to prevent it from locking a large segment of an often-used table.

oak-kill-slow-queries

In a perfect world, this script wouldn't need to exist. However, perfection is sadly lacking in most database clusters. For those times when perfection is escaping you, we have this script. It connects to your DB and kills queries that take longer than a configurable time period. This is useful when you have a site with a known "bad" query that hasn't been fixed yet and could possibly harm your database server's performance if left unchecked (for example, a query that only causes problem when run many times concurrently).

oak-purge-master-logs

This script can connect to your entire replication chain and then purge the master logs on a server (leaving a configurable number of logs). What is useful about this is that it will check every slave server and won't purge a log that a slave still needs. Thus, it is a safe way to purge master logs.

oak-security-audit

This tool runs a quick audit of some standard security settings, accounts, and privileges.

oak-show-limits

This script is really only useful for large installations, but it's very useful for those —it shows the "space" you have left in AUTO_INCREMENT columns. This doesn't sound critical, right up until it's incredibly critical.

mysqlreport

mysqlreport (*http://hackmysql.com/mysqlreport*) has been the standard in "general MySQL statistics" for as long as we can remember. It should be run on every MySQL server at least once. This utility will print out current usage information for the query cache, key buffer, and InnoDB buffer pool, as well as detailed InnoDB statistics and much more. If you only install one of these utilities, this should be the one. A guide for understanding its output is available here (*http://hackmysql.com/mysqlreportguide*). We mentioned a few variables that are important to tune correctly for a Drupal/InnoDB MySQL instance in the previous chapter—this tool is how you would track those variables and validate your configuration. Let's look at some example output, with comments describing each section.

The first section of mysqlreport's output describes the MyISAM key buffer cache: for most deployments, you are mainly interested in whether it's 100% used or not. If it is 100% used, it should likely be increased in size (note that even with an InnoDB server, the key buffer will be used for temporary and internal tables):

```
__ Key _____
Buffer used    14.00k of  30.00M  %Used:     0.05
   Current      5.50M           %Usage:   18.33
Write hit       0.00%
Read hit       70.21%
```

The next section describes the breakdown by query type: in most cases, you will have far more SELECTs than the volatile UPDATE/INSERT/DELETE/REPLACE options, but if that's ever not true, this will allow you to discover that and track it. If you suddenly see a huge spike in volatile statements, you may need to investigate why that is (a cache table being refreshed repeatedly, a spam network registering new users, etc.) and take action:

```
__ Questions _____
Total         1.81G    2.3k/s
  QC Hits   920.26M    1.2k/s  %Total:  50.78
  DMS       831.76M    1.0k/s           45.90
  Com_       39.21M    49.5/s            2.16
```

```
       COM_QUIT      21.09M     26.6/s             1.16
        -Unknown     91.11k      0.1/s             0.01
       Slow 2 s      68.31k      0.1/s             0.00  %DMS:    0.01  Log:  ON
     DMS           831.76M       1.0k/s           45.90
        SELECT     809.20M       1.0k/s           44.65           97.29
        INSERT      11.49M      14.5/s             0.63            1.38
        UPDATE       9.07M      11.4/s             0.50            1.09
        DELETE       1.24M       1.6/s             0.07            0.15
        REPLACE    769.68k       1.0/s             0.04            0.09
     Com_          39.21M      49.5/s             2.16
        set_option  29.66M      37.4/s             1.64
        show_tables  9.49M      12.0/s             0.52
        begin       29.75k       0.0/s             0.00
```

The following section gives a breakdown of the types of sorts, scans, and joins you're performing. This section is usually a lot more useful when you have a huge amount of query control. Drupal deployments (especially multisite deployments), are not always a great fit for making this section useful. However, you should always monitor this for large changes and trends:

```
__ SELECT and Sort _____
Scan           15.80M      19.9/s %SELECT:   1.95
Range         234.83M     296.3/s            29.02
Full join      12.67k       0.0/s             0.00
Range check         0         0/s             0.00
Full rng join 201.66k       0.3/s             0.02
Sort scan     121.17M     152.9/s
Sort range     26.33M      33.2/s
Sort mrg pass   3.26M       4.1/s
```

The Query Cache section describes the query cache fill percentage and its usage: There are two important aspects to this part of the report. First, it allows you to monitor the hit to insert ratio and the prune ratio. The hit to insert ratio in particular is very important, as you're really looking for a case where this ratio is quite hit-heavy. This represents a stable query cache that is very effective. However, if this ratio is close to 1:1, the cache is not being very effective and may not be worth the extra locking. Secondly, this section allows you to monitor how full the query cache is and whether there are excessive amounts of prunes. Assuming your cache is effective, it being full and being pruned often could mean it needs to be bigger:

```
__ Query Cache _____
Memory usage   26.57M of  50.00M  %Used:   53.15
Block Fragmnt  16.39%
Hits          920.26M       1.2k/s
Inserts       807.94M       1.0k/s
Insrt:Prune     1.24:1     196.1/s
Hit:Insert      1.14:1
```

The next section is pretty simple: it just describes table locks. If you have a lot of waited table locks, you may have a MyISAM table that you need to convert to InnoDB:

```
__ Table Locks _____
Waited               0       0/s  %Total:   0.00
Immediate         1.21G    1.5k/s
```

The Tables section describes the table cache. The major concern here is whether it is 100% full or not. In this example, the table cache should likely be increased as it is full:

```
__ Tables _____
Open            1000 of 1000   %Cache: 100.00
Opened          1.55k    0.0/s
```

The next section allows you to monitor your peak connection count:

```
__ Connections _____
Max used         289 of  300   %Max:   96.33
Total           21.09M   26.6/s
```

The following section is largely useful for figuring out how many of your temporary tables are hitting disk and finding temporary table spikes. If you have a huge spike after a deployment, for example, there is likely an ill-behaved query in that code push and it should either be reverted or hot-fixed:

```
__ Created Temp _____
Disk table       4.59M     5.8/s
Table          129.73M   163.7/s   Size: 200.0M
File           859.24k     1.1/s
```

The Threads section of the report shows what proportion of your threads are coming off the thread cache (ideally, most of them). As you can see in this example, this server isn't doing well in this regard and should have the thread cache settings checked:

```
__ Threads _____
Running            4 of   19
Cached             0 of    0   %Hit:      0
Created         21.09M   26.6/s
Slow               0       0/s
```

The next section is often not a focus, but if you see large spikes in aborted clients and connections, it can indicate network issues:

```
__ Aborted _____
Clients           50      0.0/s
Connects        31.32k    0.0/s
```

The Bytes section gives a simple data transfer report:

```
__ Bytes _____
Sent            1.65T     2.1M/s
Received      240.05G   302.9k/s
```

The next section of the report covers the InnoDB buffer pool usage and fill rate; it is likely the most important section of the report for an InnoDB server. In this example, you can see that the buffer pool is 100% full and should be increased in size. However, it's not the end of the world, as the read hit rate is still quite high, if not 100%. This part of the report also includes information on the pages in the buffer pool, the number of pages free, the number of data pages, etc., and it covers the IO InnoDB is performing (pages read and written and flushes to disk performed). In general, you are reading this section to ensure that your buffer pool has a 100% read hit rate and has free pages:

```
__ InnoDB Buffer Pool _____
Usage          15.00G of  15.00G  %Used: 100.00
Read hit       99.97%
Pages
  Free              0                %Total:    0.00
  Data         828.94k                         84.32 %Drty:    3.37
  Misc          154101                         15.68
  Latched                                       0.00
Reads        411.66G  519.5k/s
  From file  129.71M   163.7/s                  0.03
  Ahead Rnd        0      0/s
  Ahead Sql             0/s
Writes       350.34M   442.1/s
Flushes       18.50M    23.3/s
Wait Free        222     0.0/s
```

The following section gives some introspection on InnoDB locking. The biggest things to watch for here are excessive waits (if it can actually compute a per-second value for this, it is a bad sign) and your average time for acquiring a lock. As you can see in this example, we actually have some slight locking issues on this server. At this point, we would want to review the slow log to look for queries with high lock times (note that only recent MySQL versions support InnoDB lock times in the slow log):

```
__ InnoDB Lock _____
Waits            16218     0.0/s
Current              0
Time acquiring
  Total        4370595 ms
  Average          269 ms
  Max            19367 ms
```

Finally, the last section describes InnoDB data and IO usage in detail. Unless you are doing fairly advanced tuning and configuration related to IO throughput, this section is likely not a focus for you:

```
__ InnoDB Data, Pages, Rows _____
Data
  Reads        130.65M   164.9/s
  Writes        15.47M    19.5/s
  fsync          2.09M     2.6/s
  Pending
    Reads            1
    Writes           0
    fsync            0

Pages
```

```
   Created       686.23k      0.9/s
   Read          140.26M    177.0/s
   Written        18.50M     23.3/s

Rows
   Deleted        12.93M     16.3/s
   Inserted       14.48M     18.3/s
   Read          178.26G   224.9k/s
   Updated         8.96M     11.3/s
```

Percona Monitoring Plug-Ins

Percona Monitoring Plug-Ins (*http://www.percona.com/software/percona-monitoring-plugins*) is a set of extensions for Nagios/Icinga and Cacti that make them far more useful for MySQL administrators. They are a very useful addition to most Nagios or Cacti installations.

## CHAPTER 15

MySQL Query Optimization

We noted in a previous chapter the importance of MySQL query optimization in relation to MySQL configuration tuning. While tuning is important, it often has nowhere near the impact of actually fixing a poorly performing query. Fixing queries is also a lot more fun. As in the other MySQL chapters, we need to note that this subject is massive and we cannot possibly cover it fully here. It is highly recommended that you get a book on this subject, as it is a very deep one and is well worth learning for any Drupal developer. As a web developer using a CMS, you are only slightly removed from the SQL layer. Not deeply knowing how to use this layer and how to optimize it is very limiting. To get you started, this chapter will cover some very basic optimization, index usage, and join optimization techniques.

Index Basics

Indexes are very important for database performance. But even though they have this level of importance, they are not completely understood by many developers. This often leads to problems that could easily have been avoided. The biggest issue is a belief that indexes are kind of magical and that the MySQL optimizer should be able to run a query quickly if an index even touches the columns in question. Sadly, indexes are not magic.

It is best to think of an index as a tree, largely because they are trees in most DB systems (B+Trees, specifically; there is a link to an excellent article on B+Trees and how InnoDB uses them at the end of Chapter 21). Thus, if you have an example index test that covers (columnA, columnB), you literally have a tree of columnA values, with columnB values in the leaves. If you have a query that has a WHERE condition on these two columns, MySQL will go through this tree looking for the correct columnA value first, and then go into the leaves of that object and find the correct columnB value.

Due to this tree organization, there are some limitations. For example, if you have a query with a WHERE condition on columnB and not columnA, it can't use the index on (columnA, columnB). Thinking about this, it makes a lot of sense. How would you get to the columnB values in this index? You must have a way to traverse the columnA branches to get to the columnB values. This leads to some interesting decisions. For example, if you have five queries that run against a table and three of them have WHERE conditions on columnB alone, that column should come first in the index so that it can be used.

 Range queries are a special case. A range query is one that is going to return a range of values in an index. A good example is a datetime query, such as SELECT * FROM table WHERE date > "SOMEDATE";. Sometimes you may want to put a particular column at the beginning of an index (henceforth called the *prefix* of the index), but if that column's condition is a range, you have to reconsider. MySQL cannot use any column of an index after a range query. So, if your index is (columnA, columnB) and your query is SELECT * FROM table WHERE columnA > 5 AND columnB = 2; you will not be using the index to satisfy the second condition (columnB = 2). In this situation, you must have columnB in the prefix of the index for it to be used.

Base Tables and Join Order

Now that you have a basic understanding of how indexes work, you need an equally basic understanding of joins. In keeping with our nature theme, we are going to visualize indexes as trees and tables as pools of water—specifically, you can think of a table as a large pool of water at the top of a hill, with smaller pools of water under it as you progress down the hill. Each pool has a little waterfall that flows from it into the pool below. The largest pool at the top of the hill is the *base table* for the join. The goal is to limit the size of the waterfalls and ensure that the resulting pool doesn't need water treatment (temporary tables used to service a GROUP BY, ORDER BY, or DISTINCT).

Let's consider an example. Our biggest pool is the Drupal node table. We then join against a taxonomy table (pool) and filter on a taxonomy type. So, we have no real filter on the node table, and our only real filter (the one that defines our dataset) is on the taxono my table. How do we limit the water flowing from the node pool into the taxonomy pool? We don't. This is going to be a big waterfall. The node table being the base table and all the filtering/conditions being on subtables is a very common problem in Drupal. The issue here is conceptually somewhat simple: to fulfill this query, we need to join every node against every taxonomy term, whereas in reality, it would be far better to start with the taxonomy table and only join the filtered rows that match our condition. You *always* want to have your major conditions (the ones that limit your returned data the most) in the base table. Drupal, in particular Views, makes this very difficult sometimes.

Let's consider another example. Again, we have node as our base pool, and we are going to join against taxonomy. This time our only filter is on node, so that's good, but then we are going to GROUP BY a column in taxonomy. Unfortunately, we have a problem. We can't execute this GROUP BY via an index when it's not in the base pool, and thus the resulting pool after the join will need some water treatment (a temporary table sort). Again, this is a very common problem with Drupal Views queries. It all goes back to ensuring that you actually have the right table as the base for your query.

The question now is, how do you determine the base table for a join? For Drupal, the answer usually comes down to making sure your relationships in Drupal Views are set correctly. It is quite easy to have a Views query with all LEFT JOINs. A query like this forces MySQL to treat the node table as the base table, which is almost always a problem. Other than this issue, you often have to just run EXPLAIN on the query in question and figure out why the base table is what it is, then edit your View or Views handlers to swap the tables or set the conditions differently. We will go over some common examples of issues with Drupal Views next.

Common Issues

We are now going to cover some examples of common problems that arise with Drupal Views, indexing, and joins.

First, let's discuss the debugging options available to you with Views. In the Views settings, there are a few very important options for tracking Views and Views performance:

"Show the SQL query" (live preview section)
> This allows you to see the SQL query Views is building for execution. Obviously, this is quite important.

"Show performance statistics" (live preview section)
> This allows you to easily track build and execution time.

"Show other queries run during render during live preview" (live preview section).
> It is quite possible that other queries are being called during the processing of a View, besides the main view query. This is a common point of confusion and this debug setting will help immensely.

"Add Views signature to all SQL queries" (advanced tab)
> This is arguably the most important option on this page, as it allows you to actually tell where a query is coming from. Back in "olden times" / "the good old days," you could just search for a query in an application to find it. These days, with the advent of Views and other dynamic query builders, this is basically impossible. Having the Views signature built into the query is hugely valuable.

Now that you have Views set up to assist you, or at least to not insist on making your job impossible, it's time to look at some common issues.

The ORDER BY on an Unrelated Table

This truly is a classic for Drupal Views. Because so much of the data in Drupal is heavily normalized (split into different tables), it's quite common to have your dataset defined by tableA (i.e., all your WHERE conditions are on this table) and then ORDER BY your data on a column in a totally different table. This is a problem, as the ORDER BY will have to be serviced by a temp table or filesort. The tracker query that ships with Views is a great example of this:

```
SELECT node.type AS node_type, node.title AS node_title, node.nid AS nid,
users_node.name AS users_node_name, users_node.uid AS users_node_uid,
node_comment_statistics.comment_count AS node_comment_statistics_comment_count,
node_comment_statistics.last_comment_timestamp AS
node_comment_statistics_last_comment_timestamp, history.timestamp AS
history_timestamp, node.created AS node_created, node.changed AS node_changed,
'tracker:default' AS view_name
FROM
{node} node
LEFT JOIN {users} users_node ON node.uid = users_node.uid
INNER JOIN {node_comment_statistics} node_comment_statistics ON
node.nid = node_comment_statistics.nid
LEFT JOIN {history} history ON node.nid = history.nid AND history.uid = '1'
WHERE (( (node.status = '1') ))
ORDER BY node_comment_statistics_last_comment_timestamp DESC
LIMIT 25 OFFSET 0
```

This query has a single filter on node.status, and then ORDER BYs on node_com ment_statistics. However, this query is better than most because at least node_com ment_statistics is a required relationship in this View, which means it's an INNER JOIN and not a LEFT JOIN. This means that if the optimizer decides that node.status as a filter is not very useful (i.e., all your nodes have the same status), it can "flip the join" and start with node_comment_statistics, making it possible to use an index for the ORDER BY. (You can only use an index for this when the table containing the column or columns in question is the base table.)

The Useless DISTINCT ("In Case of Accidents!")

Views allows you to just "throw in" a DISTINCT in the Query Settings of the View. The ease with which you can add a DISTINCT to a query to ensure it doesn't start returning duplicates is a big problem, much more so than you might think. Many times performance can be hugely improved by just removing these safety-net DISTINCTs. However, it takes a lot of work to differentiate between a useless DISTINCT and one that is actually needed. It's better to think about this from the beginning.

It is a good idea to always EXPLAIN a query after you add a DIS
TINCT. It's good to know if you should be thinking about structuring a
query a different way or if the DISTINCT is fine when you are still in
the development stage. Restructuring a query is far more difficult to
do in the testing stage.

Starfish Syndrome (All LEFT JOINS)

When you create a query, Drupal Views has you define relationships between the data.
When a relationship is not required, it's translated into a LEFT JOIN in most cases.
However, when it is required, it's just an INNER JOIN. The problem with this is the
amount of importance placed on a somewhat poorly worded checkbox. Quite often,
this checkbox is left unchecked even when a relationship is required.

For example, if you have a user table and another table that holds email addresses for
those users, there will always be at least one row per user, and this is a required relationship. However, it's tempting to not check that box, because it doesn't really impact
functionality and it seems more complicated. The impact of this decision will be to
greatly limit MySQL's optimizer, as it will only ever be able to use the user table as the
base table for the query.

We call this *starfish syndrome*, because if you diagram queries like this, you have the
base table in the center and all the joined tables around it (like the legs of a starfish).
The optimizer has no choice in JOINs. This is almost always bad for Views queries in
particular, because often the default base table is node. Not only is this a huge table in
most installations, but it often doesn't define the returned data very well (it doesn't
contain columns that define custom data).

Going back to our waterfall metaphor, you could think of this as a big
pool in the middle with all the smaller pools flowing into it. The
amount of water never gets smaller; the middle pool just gets bigger
and bigger.

Node Access

Node access is a problem. Having fine-grained permissions on a per-node basis is a nice
idea. However, it is terrible from a query performance perspective. It adds a set of filters
that are totally separate from anything defining the dataset for your query and that use
tables that have nothing to do with your dataset. While it is possible if you work really
hard to make this work quickly and have good queries, in general you can either have
node access or have good queries. It's an OR, not an AND, question.

There is work underway on refactoring `node_access` to work in a different way with better performance on new versions of MySQL. Hopefully this work will resolve this long-standing issue.

## CHAPTER 16

Alternative Storage and Cache Backends

Drupal uses MySQL as the default storage backend for all data on a site. This includes low-level APIs such as caching and queues, as well as site content.

MySQL provides a great database backend for Drupal, but there are certain issues that arise, especially as Drupal sites get larger. Drupal is very modular and flexible in terms of how data can be defined. Entity types such as nodes, users, and comments can be extended with configurable fields, and then the Views module allows those to be queried and presented—all without leaving the user interface. This is a very powerful set of features, but it can make getting great performance out of a traditional relational database quite difficult. The entity/field storage provided by core provides one or two tables for each core entity, then two tables for each individual field (one for the current or "live" revision and one for older revisions). Queries with a condition on one field that sort on another then have to join across multiple tables, which is very hard to optimize with a relational database.

Another common performance bottleneck that particularly affects higher-traffic Drupal sites is that cache and session data are stored in MySQL tables by default. While this is generally fine for smaller sites, as the number of cache and session objects grows, frequent actions such as cache invalidation put a high demand on the database layer. This can cause increased network traffic and ultimately increase the load on the database servers. There are multiple Drupal contributed projects that provide a way to pull cache entries out of MySQL and store them in an alternative storage backend, such as Memcached or Redis. Not only can these backends help to offload queries from MySQL, but they can be easily scaled out horizontally as your site grows.

 Drupal's default MySQL-based search can also be replaced with alternative backend solutions. This is covered in Chapter 17.

Cache, Lock, and Session Storage

As introduced in Chapter 3, Drupal's cache API stores data in MySQL by default, but it can be easily integrated with other technologies. Swapping out the cache backend can help improve both performance and scalability; however, we should look closely at exactly what changes when the cache storage is replaced. One incorrect assumption that many people make is that replacing the cache backend will automatically make each individual cache request faster. For cache gets, this is often not the case—a well-tuned MySQL server can perform as well as or better than Memcache in some cases, although Memcache should almost always outperform MySQL for cache sets.

The true benefit becomes clearer as traffic to the site increases. Key/value stores such as Memcached and Redis are great at dealing with large amounts of data, and Memcached in particular can be scaled horizontally simply by adding more servers. MySQL, on the other hand, is far more difficult to scale horizontally and is likely to also be being used as your primary data source. Having your caching layer impacting the speed of your primary data store is not really acceptable. By swapping out cache backends, we achieve two things:

1. Offloading queries from MySQL, allowing the server to perform better for other queries
2. Placing data into a key/value store, which will maintain performance as the data size increases to multiple gigabytes and allows for easy horizontal scaling

This is why even though replacing the cache backend may not improve speed for an individual request, it can actually make a dramatic difference for large or heavily loaded sites.

So far we have concentrated on two alternatives: Redis and Memcached. There are other cache storage options, such as the APC user cache (this allows you to use the APC cache for objects other than PHP opcode); however, Redis and Memcache are by far the most widely used options for large Drupal sites, as they perform well and are generally much easier to scale. APC in particular is unable to share its cache across multiple servers, which makes it unusable as a data cache for any site that uses more than one web server, and even on a single server the user cache suffers from fragmentation and does not implement the least recently used (LRU) eviction. (APC is obviously still very usable as an opcode cache, even when you have multiple servers.)

Redis and Memcached both provide a similar service: an in-memory key/value store. They are both designed to provide $O(1)$ performance for all GET and SET operations. What this means in practice is that GET and SET calls maintain a constant speed as your cache size grows (this is a very good thing!). While both are strictly in-memory caches for all queries, Redis also adds the option for on-disk persistence using one of two options: using periodic flushes to disk or an append-only file to store all commands.

The benefit to persistence in this situation is that if your caching servers are restarted or go offline for any reason, the cache will be prewarmed when the servers come back online—meaning a smaller dip in performance while the caches are rebuilt.

As far as the Drupal modules for Memcached (*https://drupal.org/project/memcache*) and Redis are concerned, Memcache has been around a lot longer and is more mature, with a wider user base. That said, the Redis (*https://drupal.org/project/redis*) module is quickly gaining popularity now that Redis technology has matured. For new sites, either option works; we suggest testing out both and seeing which you are more comfortable with. Both modules include their own lock implementations, and Redis can also be leveraged for a queue implementation (using the Redis Queue (*https://drupal.org/project/redis_queue*) module). While not specifically related to caching, this can be useful in situations where you require a job queue.

Memcache In Depth

With the Drupal Memcache module being a bit more mature and better tested, we'll focus on it for a more in-depth exploration. First, it's important to understand how things differ between Memcache and the default MySQL-backed cache API:

1. All data that was being stored in the *cache** tables in MySQL will instead be stored in Memcached. There is a way to override this for individual caches, covered in the next section.

2. Clearing Drupal caches does not explicitly delete things out of Memcached. Instead, the time of the last cache clear is tracked and retrieved items are compared to that timestamp (along with any item-specific expiry time) to see if they are still valid.

3. Since the maximum amount of memory the Memcached daemon can allocate is defined at startup, it's possible to fill up available memory, at which time Memcached will evict least-recently-used items—meaning you can lose your items out of the cache if it isn't large enough. Don't worry, we'll explain how to monitor and avoid this.

PHP Extensions for Memcache

In order to use the Memcache module, you'll need to add Memcache support to PHP. There are currently two PHP Memcache extensions available in PECL: *Memcache* and *Memcached*. The older and more stable of the two is Memcache (no *d*). Later, the Memcached extension was created as a rewrite and to leverage *libmemcached*, a lightweight library shared by several client implementations. Both are considered stable, and either will work with the Drupal Memcache module. In general, we recommend the Memcache extension, as it's consistently proven to be more stable. Though the Memcached extension enjoyed a surge of popularity, it's been linked to a number of bugs that have proven difficult to solve. All modern Memcache features are provided by both PECL extensions, though as of this writing, you will need to use a Beta 3.x version of the Memcache extension to access some newer features (this has been in Beta since 2008 and is widely considered stable). The Memcache PECL extension has been more heavily tested by the Drupal module's authors. That said, either one should work fine for most situations, and both are packaged on the majority of Linux distributions.

> The PHP Memcache extensions use different hashing algorithms, which will lead to cache inconsistencies if you have multiple web servers using different Memcache extensions. Be sure that whichever extension you choose is used by all of your servers.

Assigning Memcached Servers and Bins

The Memcache module supports splitting a single cache storage *bin* across multiple Memcached instances. The Memcached instances could be distributed across different servers, or multiple instances on the same server (or some combination). There are a lot of references online that suggest splitting up the various Drupal cache tables so that each has its own Memcached instance. This was required at one point due to the lack of wildcard flushes in the Memcache module. However, now that wildcard flushes are supported, there is generally no reason to split the caches into individual Memcached instances (sessions being a notable exception, as covered in the section "What to Store in Memcache" on page 158). The settings for this would look something like the following configuration, but for the latest documentation on how to configure the Memcache module, please see the module's *README.txt* file:

```
$conf['memcache_servers'] = array(
  '172.16.1.5:11211' => 'default',
  '172.16.1.6:11211' => 'default',
  '172.16.1.6:11212' => 'default'
);
```

> If you are connecting to a Memcached instance on a local server, it's also possible (and potentially better performing) to connect over a Unix socket. Simply use the syntax *unix:///path/to/socket* for the server definition in your *$conf[memcache_servers]* array.

It is useful and recommended to run multiple Memcached instances across servers for all cache bins. By splitting the cache across multiple servers, you ensure that if one of the servers goes offline, only that portion of your cache is lost. On the other hand, if you only have one Memcached instance, you will be left without any cache entries if that Memcached instance goes offline. In many cases, we find that creating a Memcached instance on each of the web servers is a good setup. Another alternative, if your web servers don't have memory to spare, is to create a group of servers specifically for Memcached. Whatever you decide, be sure that the Memcached port is not open to external traffic—this is covered below in the section "Configuring the Memcache Daemon" on page 159.

When using multiple Memcached instances for a single cache bin, the PHP Memcache(d) extension uses a hashing algorithm to create a key hash for each item, and then uses that hash to decide which Memcached instance to store/fetch the item on. If you are using multiple Memcached instances, it is important to use the *consistent* hashing algorithm, since it will minimize cache item reassignments if your Memcached instances ever change—for example, when adding or removing a server. The two PHP extensions have different settings for this value, and different packages or Linux distributions may override the default, so you should always verify that this is set correctly.

To enable consistent hashing in the PHP Memcache extension, use:

```
memcache.hash_strategy consistent
```

To enable consistent hashing in the PHP Memcached extension, use:

```
memcached.sess_consistent_hash 1
```

The default behavior of the PHP Memcache(d) extensions is to only store values in a single Memcached instance. Adding additional Memcached servers and grouping them into a single bin in your Drupal settings does not get you high availability for your cache data. Both of the extensions provide a configuration option that enables them to write items to multiple servers at the same time. However, this can lead to invalid cache items being served should a server go offline for a time and then come back. Generally, it's better to have a few cache misses if a server goes down instead of worrying about high availability for your cache data and then having to deal with potential cache corruption.

Memcache Locking and Stampede Protection

The Drupal Memcache module provides stampede protection, which helps minimize the overhead of rebuilding cache items during a cache rebuild. For example, if the cached version of a popular article on your website was invalidated by a visitor posting a comment, and then several other visitors requested that page at the same time, each Drupal process accessing the article would typically go through the following steps (unaware that other processors were doing the same thing):

1. Check for the item in Memcache.
2. See that the item is invalid/expired.
3. Regenerate the item (this step can involve many SQL queries, PHP processing, etc.).
4. Push the data into a cache item in Memcache.

This can be particularly problematic if step 3 is a large operation that could put heavy load onto your database. Enabling stampede protection, ensures that the module will create a lock for the cache item so that only one process will attempt to update it in Memcache. Other requests that come along while the lock is in place will serve stale content out of Memcache (or simply wait for a valid cache entry if the existing item is missing or invalid as opposed to expired) to prevent overloading of the database while the cache is being rebuilt.

As stampede protection relies on Drupal's locking layer, it's critical that you also move locks out of MySQL and into Memcache. If you enable stampede protection without also moving locks into Memcache, you can experience severe performance degradation. Enabling stampede protection and the Memcache lock implementation is done with the following settings in *settings.php*:

```
$conf['memcache_stampede_protection'] = TRUE;
$conf['lock_inc'] = 'sites/all/modules/memcache/memcache-lock.inc';
```

What to Store in Memcache

When you enable the Drupal Memcache module, by default, all cache tables will be stored in Memcache. In Drupal 8, form state information has been moved into a key/value store, but in previous versions, it was stored in a cache table (though not strictly a cache). For Drupal 7 sites using Memcache, it is important to keep the cache_form table in MySQL to ensure form data isn't lost if Memcached goes offline. If the form IDs are lost, then any form submissions will fail, and since Memcached is not persistent, there is the potential that this could happen. So, be sure to follow the instructions and always keep the cache_form table in MySQL. This override is done for Drupal 7 with the following setting in *settings.php*:

```
$conf['cache_class_cache_form'] = 'DrupalDatabaseCache';
```

The Memcache module also gives the option to store Drupal sessions in Memcached instead of MySQL. As of this writing, though the 6.x implementation is considered stable, the 7.x version has known bugs (tracked in *https://drupal.org/node/656838*). Some people see session storage in Memcache as a great feature, while others see it as a disaster waiting to happen. The nice part about moving sessions out of MySQL is it means a lot less read and write activity on the database. The downside is the potential to lose the session information out of Memcache in the event of a Memcached server going offline or because of an eviction should the Memcache bin fill up. We recommend doing two things to reduce the risk of sessions being evicted from Memcache: create a new bin dedicated to sessions with ample space so other caches can't cause session evictions, and spread the sessions bin across multiple servers so a failing Memcached server only invalidates a portion of live sessions.

Configuring the Memcache Daemon

As mentioned earlier in this chapter, it's very important to allocate enough space in Memcached that you aren't constantly running out of memory for cache storage and forcing Memcache to evict valid cache items in order to store new items. Most Linux distributions ship Memcached packages with a default bin size of 32–64 MB. Generally, this is way too small for Drupal sites, as many sites can end up with multiple gigabytes of cached content. When first setting up Memcached, you can guess your size requirements by looking at the size of your cache tables in MySQL—while this won't be an exact representation of the size required to store your cache items in Memcache, it can provide at least a ballpark figure to get you started. From there, you can watch the Memcache usage using the built-in `stats` command or the statistics section provided by the *Memcache_admin* module, or track it with something like Munin or Cacti. If you start to see space near full or a large number of evictions, then you should increase the memory allocation for Memcached.

It's possible that you'll start to see evictions happen before the Memcached instance is using 100% of its allocated memory. This is because Memcached allocates space in various *slabs*, where each slab is used to store items of a certain size range—for example, one slab will store items that need 1,000–2,000 bytes, another slab will store items that need 2,001–4,000 bytes, etc. So, if you have a lot of items with a similar size, then it's possible to fill up a slab while the overall Memcached instance still has free space in other slabs. While you can adjust the slab allocation size increments, it is generally not a good practice; except in very special cases, you're generally better off to simply allocate more memory to Memcached overall.

Beyond the memory allocation, you shouldn't need to customize much in the Memcached configuration. One important point, however, is to ensure that Memcached is locked down to prevent remote access. This can be done either with *iptables*, by hiding the Memcached server(s) behind a network address translated network, by using the -l flag to Memcached to specify which port to listen on, or using some combination of those options.

How to Break Your Site with Memcache

Although the Memcache module is in very wide use, its usage seems to be a source of confusion for many. There are a number of common problems we've come across related to Drupal Memcache configuration that we'll share here, in the hope that it will help others to implement Memcache correctly.

Inconsistent Caching

In infrastructures with multiple web nodes, it's important that the Drupal Memcache server and bin configuration is the same across all servers. The three most popular ways to break this rule are to:

- Configure one web server to list more or different Memcache bins than other servers. This will cause the hashing algorithm on each web server to assign different servers for the same cache item, leading to an inconsistent cache.

- Configure each web server to only connect to Memcached on *localhost*. A common variation of the previous example, this causes each web server to have its own separate cache, meaning you may see changes in content based on which web server the load balancer directs you to. Also, depending how your cache clears are done, you may only ever be clearing out the cache from one of the Memcached instances.

- Forget to enable *consistent* hashing in the PHP Memcache extension configuration. This causes the PHP extension to use the *standard* hashing strategy, which invalidates your entire cache on all servers any time a server is brought online or offline for any reason. You should be sure to always set this explicitly in your PHP configuration, because different packages on different Linux distributions will have different defaults for this setting.

Constant Evictions

As described previously, it's important to allocate enough memory to Memcached so that it can fit all of your active cache items. Failing to do this, or failure to watch the usage as your site grows, can cause it to run out of space and be forced to evict cache items before they expire. Avoid this by closely monitoring memory usage and evictions. You should keep in mind that some evictions in the statistics are not bad. Because Memcache uses an LRU algorithm and the Drupal Memcache module, by design, doesn't actually flush out data, some evictions are to be expected. What you don't want to have is a constant level of evictions, as that likely means you don't have enough memory to fit your full data set.

Vanishing Sessions

If you are storing Drupal sessions in Memcache, it's important to ensure two things:

- Your Memcached servers and your network connections between them and your web nodes are stable. If you lose even one of your Memcached servers, even for a small duration of time, you will lose session data for some number of active users.

- Sessions are being stored in a bin where they will not be evicted. Generally this means creating a separate bin exclusively to hold sessions, and ensuring that it has more than enough space for your active traffic.

Sessions are an area where Redis has an advantage over memcache: items are persisted to disk, and it's possible to have an instance with LRU disabled specifically for session storage, ensuring that sessions won't be evicted until they've expired.

Entity/Field Storage

Drupal 7 introduced the field API to Drupal core, providing functionality previously provided by the Content Construction Kit, or CCK. It's this API that allows for entity types such as nodes, users, and comments to be extended with configurable fields. Since fields may be added to or removed from entities at any time, each field is stored in its own set of database tables. One table stores the values for the current revision, and another stores the values for any historical revisions of the entity. Both are written to when entities are saved, but only one is queried at any one time.

Loading of field values happens via a single query, and the values are cached via Drupal's cache API, so in itself is not a significant performance issue, and the Entity Cache (*https://drupal.org/project/entitycache*) contributed module allows for caching of the entire entity object, including data from base tables and hook implementations. However, in certain cases, saving entities can require dozens or hundreds of writes to the various field tables. Where performance issues usually arise first are with queries generating lists of entities: a condition on one field and a sort on the other requires a JOIN, making it impossible for MySQL to effectively use indexes for those queries.

The vast majority of sites are able to deal with these issues by caching the results of listing queries (either using Drupal's cache API directly, or by enabling caching in the Views module) and using pregeneration or custom denormalization in SQL for particularly bad queries.

However, with large data sets and a highly dynamic site with lots of pages, cache hit rates may be too low, or queries may be unacceptably slow on a cache miss.

To allow sites to optimize for these cases, the field API also has the concept of pluggable storage. This allows the field_sql_storage module to be replaced entirely. Drupal 7 does not, however, allow the entity base tables to be replaced, so data is still written to those and core queries them directly. In practice, it was found that field storage implementations needed to store the entity base table information as well, requiring duplication between the hardcoded entity storage and the field storage.

As a result, Drupal 8 has the same default MySQL implementation, but storage is controlled at the entity level rather than for individual fields, allowing the base tables to be replaced as well as the field storage.

While entity/field storage is pluggable, changing the storage layer is unfortunately not as transparent (especially in Drupal 7) as it is with the cache or sessions. Many contributed modules query entity tables directly, and poorly written custom modules may directly query field tables. If considering using pluggable storage, there are several best practices to keep in mind in order to ensure the smoothest possible transition. If you have an existing site and are considering changing the entity storage, enforcing these best practices at the application level early on is a prerequisite to making the switch, and you should also be prepared to audit contributed modules as well as your own custom code.

EntityFieldQuery/EntityQuery

When querying entities, using `EntityQuery` as opposed to `db_select()` or `db_query()` on the tables directly ensures that the query will work regardless of the storage used.

When using Views, the EntityFieldQuery Views Backend (*https://drupal.org/project/efq_views*) module replaces Views's SQL query builder with an `EntityFieldQuery` builder, providing the same interoperability for exported views.

CRUD

Contributed and custom modules often attempt to avoid loading or saving full entities, opting instead to query individual values or to update via `db_update()`, especially when multiple entities are being loaded or updated. Bypassing the API like this can lead to inconsistent results due to caches not being invalidated correctly, alter hooks not firing on load, etc. It also makes it impossible to use those modules with an alternative storage backend, since the database table being queried directly may not even exist. And when loading, querying the table bypasses both static and persistent caches, so it's often slower anyway. Always use the proper CRUD (create, read, update, and delete) functions whenever dealing with entities.

MongoDB

While there are theoretically many potential options for entity storage, currently the only viable option is MongoDB. MongoDB is an open source document database that has so far proved extremely promising in solving many of the performance issues that affect Drupal's entity storage. Integration is provided via Prod: change text to the MongoDB (*http://drupal.org/project/mongodb*) module. MongoDB allows considerable improvements in both the performance and the scalability of sites with very large data sets, but it's still a relatively new technology both in terms of general adoption and Drupal specifically. You should carefully consider whether your project requires MongoDB entity/field storage before making the change, since it imposes development constraints (albeit good ones) as well as introducing an additional system to administer—one that holds all of your site's most important data! You'll need to set up replication and backups for MongoDB in addition to MySQL. Also ensure you're comfortable maintaining MongoDB long-term. Entity data cannot be regenerated in the same way as a cache entry if it gets lost, and migration from MySQL to MongoDB and back again is a manual process at the time of writing, so while it is possible, changing entity storage on a live site is a very complex process.

The main feature of MongoDB as a document database is that each entity is stored as a single record. MongoDB stores documents in BSON format (a variant of JSON), so the resulting entity storage is very similar to what you'd see running `json_encode(entity_load(1));`. It should look quite familiar to any Drupal developer who's ever looked at an entity structure with `var_export()` or via a web service. Queries against MongoDB are written in JSON syntax; while this is useful on the command line, at the Drupal level, you should only ever use `EntityFieldQuery` to avoid being locked into MongoDB at the application layer (much as using `db_query()` and `db_select()` enforces MySQL storage).

As opposed to potentially dozens of individual database tables, a single record is created with both the properties and configurable fields of the entity all in the same place. Since configurable fields can have multiple values, this is impossible to achieve in SQL in terms of a single database table with a column for each field. This allows complex entity queries, which might `JOIN` across 20 or more tables with the default MySQL field storage, to be executed against a single collection.

MongoDB is schemaless, in that it's not necessary to define the structure of a collection up front before documents can be saved. Therefore, adding new fields or field values does not require any Data Definition Language (DDL) operations on the storage. However, being schemaless doesn't mean no schema as such; it just means it's entirely up to the application to enforce it.

Indexes can be applied to collections in a similar way to how MySQL indexes are applied to tables. There is currently no automated way for the MongoDB module to create indexes for `EntityFieldQuery`, so sites planning to use the MongoDB module in production should expect to audit queries and add their own indexes.

One of the main limitations of MongoDB is the inability to join between collections. The MongoDB module stores entities in their own collections, meaning that it's not possible to query specific groups of nodes as easily as it would be with MySQL—for example, nodes created by users who live in Australia. There are workarounds for this —for example, adding an "author country" field to nodes and copying over the value from the user would allow that query to be run—but as with denormalization in MySQL, this requires maintaining both sets of data should the user record be updated.

## CHAPTER 17

Solr Search

Drupal's default search backend uses MySQL to implement some fairly advanced search capabilities. While this is fine for small sites and kind of impressive in its own right, it can prove quite a performance bottleneck for larger sites that contain many nodes and where the database may already be under moderate to heavy load. Luckily, Drupal's core search system can be enhanced or completely replaced by contrib modules. Not only does this provide a way to offload search queries from MySQL, but it can also bring additional features that aren't part of the traditional Drupal search. For example, searching with Solr provides faceted search functionality—a way to filter search results based on categories or groupings—and spellcheck, two widely used search features.

There are a number of popular open source search technologies, such as Elasticsearch, Solr, Sphinx, and Xapian. While all of these have Drupal modules, Solr is by far the most actively developed and widely used module, so we will focus exclusively on integrating Solr throughout this chapter. That is not to say that other search technologies aren't as good as Solr; they simply haven't been as well integrated into Drupal as Solr.

Performance and Scalability Considerations

On smaller Drupal sites, the search queries done by the default search module may not be particularly "heavy" SQL queries, but they do contribute to the overall load on the database server. On sites with a large enough data set, the queries can be downright performance killers. For this reason, Drupal's built-in search should not be used on anything but the smallest of sites; it does not scale well enough for large sites. Search is one place where we can not only offload a task from the database server, but improve performance and scalability at the same time.

As discussed in Chapter 7 and the chapters on MySQL, MySQL is not something that can easily be scaled horizontally simply by adding more servers. On the other hand, pretty much every search-specific application has been designed to be able to scale horizontally. While most sites won't have enough search traffic to necessitate a large search cluster, there certainly are sites that benefit from increased performance and easily scalable search.

Integrating Solr with Drupal

There are at least two modules that tie into Solr for search: *apachesolr* (*https://drupal.org/project/apachesolr*) and *search_api* (*https://drupal.org/project/search_api*). They provide a similar set of features, either directly or by tying into other modules. Some of the most commonly used Solr features are:

Spellcheck
> Solr can provide search results for words spelled similarly to those in the initial query.

More like this
> This feature allows you to find similar content to a particular result; this can be useful for displaying a block on a page to link to other similar pieces of content.

Faceted search
> This provides users with a way to filter search results—for example, limiting results to content updated within a certain time frame, or only by a particular author.

The main difference between the two modules is that *search_api* relies on the Drupal entity API, actually doing a full entity load for each result returned, whereas the *apachesolr* module retrieves more data from the index when doing a search, meaning that it can provide at least a title and teaser text without having to pull anything in from the database. There are some other small differences, but in general, the options are pretty similar. For our examples in this chapter, we'll be using the *apachesolr* module, but the majority of the Solr setup remains exactly the same for either module.

Solr Configuration

Solr has a number of configuration files, many of which define settings that both the server and the client need to be aware of. For that reason, both the *apachesolr* and *search_api* modules include a set of configuration files that need to be used on the Solr server. The configuration files included in the module may vary over time, but the most important files included there are:

solrconfig.xml
> This file includes Solr-specific configuration settings. You may need to tweak some of these values, but the provided config works well for the general case.

schema.xml

This file defines the schema used when storing documents. Since this defines which fields will be used for searching and storing, it's important that whatever is used on your server matches what the module expects.

protwords.txt

This file is a sort of "blacklist" for words and stops them from being "stemmed." In Solr parlance, this means that any word listed here won't be considered part of a larger word. For example, by default "test" would normally be stemmed into other words such as "tester," "testing," and "tested," but if it were listed here, that behavior would stop. The *apachesolr* module includes some HTML entities here in order to keep those from being stemmed.

Indexing Content

Solr contains its own search index that is totally separate from your site's main content stored in MySQL. This means that an indexing job is required in order to load content out of the database and push it into the Solr search index. The *apachesolr* module tracks information on which content needs to be indexed in its own SQL table, and by default it will index a small number (currently the default is 50) of those items each time that the site cron job runs. There are also admin options and *drush* commands used to run the indexing job outside of the main cron run, to mark content for reindexing, and even to fully delete the Solr index.

Be aware that if you have a large amount of content on your site, it can take a long time (from a few up to even dozens of hours) to index it all the first time. Once content is indexed initially, only new and updated content will be indexed, so it happens much faster. The bottleneck here is generally not Solr, but the fact that the *apachesolr* module needs to do a full node_load( ) on content in order to pull out the information needed for the index.

Most sites can support indexing of many more than the default 50 items at a time, and you can usually improve the indexing time by increasing *$conf[apachesolr_cron_limit]* to something higher. Depending on the database and network infrastructure specifics, we've found the sweet spot for this setting to be somewhere from 100 to 1,000 items. Try a few different values in that range and see which performs best in your environment.

 Solr indexing can be very resource intensive for a web node. Verify that your PHP memory limit and maximum execution time are high enough to avoid errors when indexing.

Infrastructure Considerations

Solr, as of version 1.4, has built-in replication that makes setting up multiple slave servers very easy. Because of that, there's really no excuse not to run at least two Solr servers in a master/slave setup. Since most sites don't need full high availability for Solr writes, usually they are fine with failing over to read-only on the slave as needed. Full HA with write failover is a bit harder to configure, though Solr 4.x attempts to address some of those shortcomings (leveraging Zookeeper).

Currently, Solr versions 3.x and 4.x are supported by the Apache Lucene project (and either will work with Drupal). A lot of sites are currently using 3.x versions because they don't need the new features from 4.x, and the 4.x releases are young enough that some bugs are still being worked out.

When you download Solr, it includes a "built-in" Jetty server (a Java servlet engine with a built-in web server). This works fine for testing, but it's not designed to be used in a production environment. The most popular options for a production-ready servlet engine are either using the full Jetty distribution, or using Tomcat. Either of those options will work fine with Solr, so it's really just a matter of preference which you choose.

Solr Replication

We recommend starting with at least two Solr servers set up as master/slave. This will allow you to support at least read-only failover in the case that the master goes offline. The reason for having two servers is more about providing a failover than it is about having the option to load balance search queries — however, there's no reason you can't benefit from each. There are various choices for a failover mechanism; often we use IP failover controlled with Heartbeat, and if you set up Varnish on the Solr servers to direct traffic, it can easily be configured to filter out "write" queries to only go to the master server:

```
sub vcl_recv {
  if (req.url ~ "^/solr/[^/]+/(select|admin/ping)") {
      set req.backend = solr_server_pool;
  } else {
      set req.backend = solr_master;
      if (req.request == "POST") {
        return(pipe);
      }
      return (pass);
  }

  // rest of vcl_recv...
```

In this example, we send Solr select queries and requests for *admin/ping* to a Varnish director containing a pool of all Solr servers. All other traffic is forced to go to the Solr master server only. In the case of POST requests (index updates), we use a pipe in order to avoid timeouts should the update queries take a long time.

Enabling the built-in replication in Solr is fairly straightforward. If you set a few variables in the file *solrconfig.properties* located within a Solr core's *conf/* directory, they can then be referenced in *solrconfig.xml* within each Solr core configuration. Handling the configuration with variables and conditionals makes it possible for both master and slave to share the same *solrconfig.xml* file.

The following replication snippet from *solrcore.properties* shows the settings for the master server:

```
solr.replication.master=true
solr.replication.slave=false
solr.replication.pollInterval=00:00:60
solr.replication.masterUrl=http://solr-master-hostname:8112/solr
```

For the slave, simply swap the true/false values for the master and slave settings. The replication interval can be adjusted if you need to ensure that the slave receives updates faster than once per minute.

With those settings in place, the default *solrconfig.xml* that ships with the *apachesolr* module will handle replication for you, using the solr.replication.master and solr.replication.slave variables to conditionally enable master or slave behavior on each of the servers.

Drupal Module Installation

Download and install the *apachesolr* (*https://drupal.org/project/apachesolr*) module. There are some additional modules listed there that may be desired for extra features. There's no need to enable the module just yet, since we need to get Solr set up first.

Inside the module, you'll find a directory, *solr-conf/* that contains Solr configuration files for different versions of Solr: *1.4*, *3.x*, and *4.x*. Any new installation should use 3.x or 4.x as 1.4 is already quite dated. Depending on which Solr version you decide to use, copy the configuration files from the corresponding directory here to your Solr server. They should be placed in */<path_to_solr>/<corename>/conf/*.

Once you've copied those in place, you'll need to (re)start your Solr service (e.g., Jetty or Tomcat) in order to recognize the configuration changes. Once that is running, you should be able to enable the *apachesolr* module and update its settings to point to your Solr URL. It will report if it's able to successfully connect to the Solr server, and from that point, you can start indexing your content in Solr.

With the Solr server successfully up and running, the remaining module setup and configuration is fairly easy. Instead of covering it here, where it may quickly go out of date, we recommend reading through the *apachesolr* module's project page and documentation, as well as the *README.txt* file that ships with the module.

## CHAPTER 18

PHP and httpd Configuration

Web server (httpd) and PHP configurations are often overlooked or trivialized. Many Drupal deployments make only small changes to the httpd or PHP configuration (raise your hand if your biggest change to *php.ini* has been to increase PHP's memory limit), and otherwise blindly accept most default configuration values. This is sometimes with good reason: using a default *httpd.conf* file will work fine in some cases, and generally sites can perform pretty well with little to no tweaking of the httpd configuration. On the flip side, it is very possible for a default httpd configuration to grind your server to a halt should you experience a large traffic spike. Not only that, but there are configuration options that can help improve performance, sometimes drastically.

This chapter will focus mainly on changes that can be made to improve performance in PHP and Apache's httpd daemon. We give Apache 2.2 more attention than other web servers because it is the most widely used web server; however, the chapter also contains a section on alternative web servers and PHP configurations (e.g., CGI versus running as an Apache module).

APC: PHP Opcode Cache

To understand what an opcode cache is and why it's important, you first need to understand how PHP works server-side. When a PHP script is run on your web server, the PHP source file is read and then compiled into byte code before being executed. If you add an opcode cache, the intermediary executable code gets compiled on the first access of a script but then is stored in the cache and used for subsequent requests of the same script. This saves a lot of overhead, which is especially noticeable on a busy server.

Although there are a number of PHP opcode caches available, we'll focus on APC, as it is the most widely used. However, with the release of PHP 5.5, the core PHP distribution now includes Zend Optimizer+, which after being open sourced has become the default opcode cache in PHP moving forward. PHP is now referring to Zend Optimizer+ as

"OPcache." APC currently ships as a PECL extension, meaning it can be installed via the PECL install tool, though most Linux distributions and add-on software repositories have prebuilt packages available. OPcache is built into PHP versions 5.5.0+ and is available as a PECL extension for versions 5.2, 5.3, and 5.4. An alternative to APC is most welcome, and we imagine most sites will soon migrate from APC to OPcache. In the meantime, however, the vast majority of sites are running on APC, so we will focus on APC throughout this chapter.

Once installed, the APC extension needs to be enabled either in *php.ini* or in its own apc.ini file. For servers hosting a single Drupal site, most of the default settings for APC will work fine; however, it is very important to set an appropriate memory size. For most sites, using a single shared memory segment with a size of 128 MB is a good starting point. Once set, restart Apache to pick up the change, then load your website and repeatedly load a few different pages. Then visit *apc.php* (a monitoring script included in most APC packages that can be moved to your webroot, but should not be left there after use) in your browser to see the current statistics. What you want to see is little to no fragmentation of the cache, and there should be some amount (at least 16–32 MB) of free space available. At this point, you should also see hit rates at or close to 100%. If your cache is totally full or showing high fragmentation, or if the full count is more than 0, you should increase the amount of memory allocated to APC. Continue increasing the memory allocation until the cache is left with free space; once the site has run for a few days without filling up the cache, you're in good shape. It's important to check on this periodically to be sure that the cache isn't filling up or becoming fragmented.

Once your APC memory allocation has been set properly, there are many other configuration settings that allow some fine-tuning of how APC runs. As mentioned previously, these typically don't need to change for most sites (especially if you are only running one Drupal web root on a server). The full list of APC runtime settings is available at *http://www.php.net/manual/en/apc.configuration.php*. A few of the most commonly customized are:

apc._num_files_hint

> This setting tells APC how many files you expect to be cached. It uses this information when allocating cache storage space. The default is 1000, which is a pretty good rough estimate for a single Drupal site. However, if you are running multiple sites or a site with a lot of modules, increasing this could help reduce fragmentation.

apc.stat

> This setting controls whether or not APC will "stat" (check) a file to be sure it hasn't been updated since the cache entry was created. The default is 1, meaning that APC will perform this check. If set to 0, APC will not recheck files once they have been pulled into the cache. This means that if you change a file, you need to reload Apache in order for APC to read in that change. Obviously this is not ideal for development environments, but it can lead to performance improvements in infrastructures with

high I/O latency. This setting needs to be approached carefully, as there are quite a few other stats in the process of serving a request and they must all be disabled for you to see much improvement.

 So far, our description of APC has been entirely as an opcode cache. However, APC also supports "user" caches, meaning that you could use APC to store Drupal cache data. We discussed that possibility in Chapter 16.

Again, it's important to monitor APC status to ensure the cache does not fill or become too fragmented (usually fragmentation is caused by the cache being at or close to full). There are, for example, Munin scripts that scrape the APC stats from a local PHP script (a great candidate to live in an *adminscripts* directory!) and graph them over time. If you notice the usage approaching full on the APC cache, it's likely that you'll want to increase the cache size.

php.ini Settings

There are a few settings in *php.ini* that are important to consider when bringing up a site. The most important of these settings is memory_limit, which controls how much memory a single PHP process is allowed to consume. It is important to gauge this setting correctly because if a process consumes more than this amount of memory, it will error out at the point where it attempts to allocate more memory, and the entire page load will fail. For many Drupal sites, the maximum memory usage is somewhere around the 128 MB range. While it's not uncommon for this to be set at 512 MB or 768 MB on larger websites, if you are using that much RAM in PHP, you may have a problem in your code that needs attention. The downside to setting this to a very large value is that a memory leak or "runaway" process can end up consuming quite a bit of system memory, potentially causing the server to run out of memory.

Watch the memory use of your PHP processes (or httpd processes if you're running PHP as a module) to see how much they are using on average by running *top* and sorting by memory usage (type 0 to see sort options, then n to sort by resident memory). However, that just tells you what the current processes are doing and doesn't tell you what the maximum usage may be. For a more precise view of PHP memory usage, consider enabling XHProf, described in Chapter 6, and use it to profile the different page types on your site. With this setting, it's best to err on the large side because setting it too low will cause some user-visible errors with the site should you ever hit the limit.

The display_errors setting controls whether or not PHP errors will be shown on the output of the page where an error occurs. This is clearly something you want to disable on your production servers, but it can be very useful to enable on your development servers.

While you shouldn't display errors to users on a production site, you likely want to keep track of errors if they do happen. For this reason there is a log_errors setting that controls whether or not errors are logged. If you are running PHP as an Apache module, setting this to On will log PHP errors to Apache's error log.

Both display_errors and log_errors are selective about what types of errors they show. Both of them are affected by the error_reporting setting, which lets you define which types of errors to show/log and which to ignore. Settings here are applied *bit-wise*, meaning you can combine different message types with "and," "or," and "not" in order to achieve the type of error reporting you desire. Generally on production servers, you would only care about actual errors and not about warnings, notices, or language deprecation messages. On development servers, it's more useful to track everything so that you can see things like PHP notices when variables are used before being set, etc. *php.ini* files ship with a large section of comments explaining the various message types along with suggested settings for production versus development.

It's also important to set the time zone in *php.ini* (or in your *.htaccess* file). As of PHP 5.3, a warning message will be sent when the date.timezone setting is unset—and importantly, it defaults to unset. Valid time zone values are listed here (*http:// www.php.net/manual/en/timezones.php*).

PHP Apache Module Versus CGI

PHP is most commonly run as an Apache module called mod_php. This is the easiest way to run PHP, as it can be installed as a package that includes a very minimal Apache configuration to enable the module for PHP scripts. There are two main issues to understand when running mod_php:

1. The PHP module will be loaded into each httpd process, increasing resource usage and making the processes heavier. This means that every access to httpd, even for a static (non-PHP) file, will have the overhead of the PHP module residing in the httpd process.

2. PHP scripts will all be run as the same user, generally *apache* or *www-data*, that the httpd processes are run by. This is generally fine when you only host a single site on a server, but it's not secure for multisite environments, where it is best to keep the sites separated as much as possible. One way to work around this issue is to run multiple instances of Apache, each with a different user. This is easily accomplished with the default configuration in Debian-based distributions, though it is not as easy with Red Hat-based-distributions.

It is possible to run PHP as an "external CGI," which just boils down to having some way for httpd to call an external PHP process when it needs to execute PHP code. In order for this to work in production environments, you need to run a CGI manager such as mod_fastcgi to manage the PHP processes. This requires a bit of extra configuration over the built-in module, but you gain flexibility. For alternative web servers such as Nginx, you must run PHP as a CGI—more on this at the end of this chapter.

PHP now includes the FastCGI Process Manager, or *FPM*, also referred to as *PHP-FPM*. Prior to PHP-FPM, it was difficult to ensure PHP CGI processes shared an opcode cache, which was not great for performance. The addition of PHP-FPM allows its PHP processes to share a central APC cache, making it a stronger option for those who are looking for an alternative to running mod_php.

Many sites choose to skip the extra configuration needed to run PHP as a CGI binary, and instead stick with the default mod_php. mod_php can scale well and has the performance advantage of being in the same process space as Apache. However, it does add additional memory overhead in the httpd processes, and it's not quite as tune-able as having PHP completely separated as a CGI. For example, in a PHP-FPM setup, you can limit the amount of memory and/or threads each FPM pool has available to it. If you need this extra configurability, are hosting multiple sites that need to run as different users, or cannot offload static file serving (such as by using Varnish or a CDN), FastCGI and PHP-FPM are options worth considering. For our purposes, we will continue to assume the use of mod_php since it is the most popular method to run PHP.

Apache MPM Settings

Apache is one of the most configurable and flexible HTTP servers in existence. It is in fact so configurable that you can even change its process model via your choice of multiprocessing module (MPM). The two major core MPMs are Prefork and Worker:

- Apache Prefork can be considered the "classic" multiprocessing module. It works by having a single parent httpd process managing a pool of child processes. Each request that comes into the server is "assigned" to a child process, which then takes over communication with the client and fulfillment of the request. If more processes are needed, the parent process will create them and will clean up old processes.

- Apache Worker is a newer multiprocessing module that relies on threads instead of processes. It works in much the same way as the Prefork module, except that instead of maintaining processes, it maintains threads. The advantage to this is that its lighter weight. The disadvantage is that you must ensure your code is entirely thread-safe.

In most cases, the choice between these two modules is made for you. If you are using mod_php, you should use the Prefork module. There are many non-thread-safe PHP modules, and some are required by many Drupal installations. On the other hand, if you are running PHP as a CGI, you have the option of using Apache Worker and making Apache a bit more lightweight. The remainder of this chapter will assume the use of the Apache Prefork module using mod_php.

Prefork Thread Settings

The Prefork module has a number of settings that control its behavior. Generally, the defaults for the settings controlling the number of spare servers to start and leave idle work fine for most sites. However, it's important to focus on the settings that control the number of processes and how often they are cycled, as these are the settings that have the potential to bring your server crashing down if not configured correctly. They are:

StartServers

This setting defines how many processes will be started when the httpd service starts. For Prefork, this defaults to 5. For most sites this is fine, since httpd will spawn new processes as needed. In cases where you know your server will always be serving more than five clients at once, you might want to increase this so that there isn't a wait involved when spinning up additional processes.

MinSpareServers and MaxSpareServers

These settings control how many idle (not actively serving requests) httpd processes will be kept around. They default to 5 and 10, respectively, meaning that if there are less than five idle httpd processes, new processes will be spawned (at a maximum rate of one per second) until there are five idle. Contrarily, if there are more than 10 idle httpd processes, the additional processes will get killed off by the parent httpd process. Again, for most sites these defaults work fine, although on some sites it may be worthwhile to increase these settings somewhat so that you can better deal with traffic spikes. Setting these values very high means that you will have a lot of processes on the system using up RAM even when traffic is rather low.

MaxClients

Defines the maximum number of httpd processes that can be running. It can "make or break" your site, in that if it is set too low, the server will queue incoming HTTP connections (eventually dropping them once a threshold is hit), and if it's set too high, the server may swap itself to death during periods of high traffic. The default value for *MaxClients* for Prefork is 256. For static websites or very minimal PHP scripts, 256 processes may be fine, but for most Drupal sites, this is way too high. The reason that this value is too high is because when using mod_php memory is allocated inside of each httpd process, and for larger Drupal sites, it's not unusual to see httpd processes using somewhere from 64–150 MB (or more!) each. If your httpd processes are each averaging 150 MB of RAM, then at 256 processes, that's nearly 38 GB of RAM. Some of us are lucky to have servers that large, but it's not common, or inexpensive. Also, that doesn't take into account memory usage by other processes on the system. The trick to setting MaxClients appropriately is to first figure out how large your httpd processes are. You can get a general number for this by running *top* and looking at the RES (resident memory) column. Once you know how large your httpd processes are, you can use the following formula to see how many httpd processes you can support:

```
((System RAM) - (RAM used by other processes)) /
    (httpd process size) = MaxClients
```

"RAM used by other processes" would take into account any other major services running on the web server, plus some amount for basic OS-level processes. Generally we use 512 MB as a rough estimate for OS resource needs, and then add any additional service requirements to that. This 512 MB estimate is intended to cover resources used by the kernel as well as periodic processes that may be run on the server. Long-running services should be analyzed separately.

As an example, suppose your web server is running Varnish, httpd, and no other major services. The server has 8 GB of RAM. Varnish is allocated 2 GB of memory. Your average httpd process is around 85 MB. To provide some safety in our estimate, we'll round that up to 100 MB. In this case, we would calculate MaxClients as follows:

```
((8 GB System RAM) - (512 MB OS resources + 2 GB Varnish)) /
    (100 MB httpd process)
= 5632 MB / 100 MB
= 56.32
```

You should always round down at the end for safety, so you would end up with 56 as your MaxClients setting.

ServerLimit

This setting defines the maximum value that you can set MaxClients to during the life of the parent httpd process. In most cases, if you have calculated MaxClients as shown above, you can set this to the same number. If you want to give yourself some wiggle room in order to potentially increase MaxClients without having to fully restart Apache, you could set this to be the maximum that you would increase MaxClients to. In either case, MaxClients must be less than or equal to ServerLimit.

MaxRequestsPerChild

This setting controls how many requests a child httpd process will serve before it is killed. The Apache default is 10000, although many distributions ship with other values in *httpd.conf*. Both 4000 and 0 (disabled) are used by common distributions. When this is set to 0, httpd child processes are never killed (except as part of MaxSpareServers, as described above). As with most Apache settings, there is a trade-off involved when setting this. Setting this value on the high side can cause your httpd processes to consume more RAM over time due to memory leaks in PHP or other scripts, or due to a process that loads different code bases over its lifetime. On the other hand, setting this value too low will lead to a lot of overhead on the server caused by killing and respawning httpd processes. Generally, we would consider somewhere in the 1000–4000 range to be a safe value for this setting, based on the traffic your site experiences. 2000 is a good middle-of-the-road value that is high enough that you won't see process thrashing in most cases, but low enough that httpd processes won't stick around forever eating up a lot of memory.

KeepAlive

KeepAlive allows a client to reuse the same connection with the server multiple times instead of having to open up a new connection for each request. For example, if you had a web page with a number of images and CSS files all served locally, the client would download the web page and then reuse the same connection to download the images and CSS. This saves time and resources on both ends of the connection. However, there is a downside to using KeepAlive, which is that the server needs to keep connections open for a certain amount of time (defined by KeepAliveTimeout). This can lead to a lot of open connections sitting around waiting and not actually serving any content. For this same reason, KeepAlive can make it easier for someone to launch a denial of service (DoS) attack against your site—once there are enough connections open waiting for clients, no other requests to the site can be served.

To be clear, KeepAlive is very beneficial for client-side performance. However, it can bring down sites if misconfigured, or if enabled at all during large traffic spikes. This is one of the benefits of having a caching reverse proxy, such as Varnish, as it is far more capable of handling KeepAlive connections to clients without adversely impacting Apache stability.

If you choose to use KeepAlive, be sure to also look at the KeepAliveTimeout setting, which defines how long a process will wait for an idle client to send another request. The default KeepAliveTimeout is five seconds, which in most cases is rather high. Ideally, set this as low as possible without having it force new connections on existing clients. One or two seconds can work generally, but it's worth a bit of trial and error to figure out the correct setting for your site and the majority of your visitors. Also, we highly recommend providing KeepAlive to clients through a proxy and not directly with Apache.

Cache Headers

There are a number of headers that are used to inform client browsers and intermediate caches whether or not to cache content, and if so, for how long. Configuring these headers properly can make a difference in user-visible performance on your site. The headers you will want to keep an eye on when setting up a production site are ETags, Expires, Cache-Control, Last-Modified, and Vary. These headers work together to determine just how aggressively a client can cache a page or static file. We will discuss each of these headers individually:

Last-Modified
> This header is used exactly as you might expect, to check whether a page has been modified since it was last fetched. By default, Drupal adds this header to pages with a timestamp generated during the Drupal bootstrap process when serving a page.

ETag
> The ETag, or entity tag, is meant to uniquely identify a single version of a page. When the ETag matches on two versions of a document, they are assumed to be the same. This tag can be as simple as an MD5 hash of the document or as complicated as hashes of various aspects of the request. What it should not be is the default Apache ETag, which includes server-specific information. If you use Apache's default ETag, if you have four web nodes the ETags generated on each node will be different, and reverse proxy caching will be significantly worse.

Expires
> This header indicates when the page will expire from any cache it is in. In Pressflow and Drupal 7 or later, you can set this date by configuring the page cache maximum age. This is a legacy header, and if Cache-Control (which we will discuss next) exists, this header is ignored by newer browsers and proxies.

Cache-Control
> This header controls caching options and is set by Pressflow and Drupal 7 later when they are configured to use an external page cache. The name is not as creative as one might have hoped. The header contains keywords and settings that impact caching, for example:

max-age=N
> This informs downstream proxies of the maximum number of seconds this page can stay in its cache.

no-cache
> This completely disables caching.

private
> This allows for browser caching, but not intermediate proxy caching.

Logging

Apache allows you to set multiple log outputs for different types of information, though the majority of sites are configured only with a general access log and an error log. Most often, in the case of multiple sites on a single server, logs are defined per-virtual host so that it's easy to track information for each individual site.

The format of the log files can be defined using the `ErrorLogFormat` and `LogFormat` directives. Generally, the default `ErrorLogFormat` is fine for most sites, and for the access log, most sites use one of the log formats that comes predefined in default Apache configuration files—either "common" or "combined." The combined log format adds header information for `Referer` and `User-Agent`. If you decide to use your own custom log format, you can define the format and give it a name using the `LogFormat` directive, and then refer to that name in a `CustomLog` directive:

```
LogFormat "%h \"%r\"" hostandrequest
CustomLog logs/request.log hostandrequest
```

This example defines a *hostandrequest* log format that includes only the remote host and the requested URL, and then uses that format to log to the file *logs/request.log*.

 Log destinations are defined relative to the *ServerRoot* unless the path begins with a slash. *ServerRoot* defaults to */etc/httpd* on Red Hat-based distributions or */etc/apache2* on Debian-based distributions. Red Hat includes a symlink from */etc/httpd/logs* to */var/log/httpd* in order to ensure logs end up in the standard location on the system.

While the built-in Apache logging works great for many sites, it's not quite as flexible as some sites require. For these situations, Apache supports using external logging tools. Cronolog (*http://cronolog.org/*) is one example of an external logging application used in conjunction with Apache. It has some nice features, such as dynamic log file naming using date fields, making it possible to output to a log file with the current date in its filename. When the date changes, Cronolog will automatically start writing to a new file, meaning you get "built-in" log rotation as well as having log files nicely organized by date. Because new log files are written to every day, there's no need to reload httpd to perform log rotation. You most likely will want to add your own scripts to compress these log files, and eventually to remove/archive them. The following is an example Apache configuration to use Cronolog:

```
ErrorLog "|/usr/sbin/cronolog /var/log/httpd/error/%Y%m%d-error.log"
CustomLog "|/usr/sbin/cronolog /var/log/httpd/access/%Y%m%d-access.log" common
```

You can add the following script to cron.daily on the server to compress old log files:

```
#!/bin/bash
export PATH="/usr/bin:/bin"

if [ -d /var/log/httpd ]; then
  find /var/log/httpd -name "*.log" -mtime +1 -exec gzip -9 "{}" ";"
fi
```

and this one to eventually remove them:

```
#!/bin/bash
export PATH="/usr/bin:/bin"

if [ -d /var/log/httpd ]; then
  find /var/log/httpd -name "*.log.gz" -mtime +60 -exec rm "{}" ";"
fi
```

Server Signature

There are a couple of places where Apache may output information about its version, and potentially version information for modules such as PHP. One of these is the "server signature" line that optionally shows up at the bottom of Apache-generated pages (e.g., 503 errors or directory listing pages); the other is the Server HTTP response header that gets sent by the server. Some people may consider this a security risk in that it makes it easy for potential attackers to know what software versions you are running and target you with specific attacks. Others would say that security through obscurity is not security at all, and if someone is dedicated enough, hiding information like this is only going to make it take a few minutes longer for them to figure out an attack. Whatever your view is, you may want to hide this information either for security reasons or just because you don't like the way it looks to potential visitors.

The Server header and server signature lines are controlled by two different settings:

ServerSignature
> This is an on/off setting that controls whether or not to show the server signature line on Apache-generated pages. Setting this to Off means that the server signature will not be shown on those pages.

ServerTokens
> This is the setting that controls what information is shown in the server signature line and placed in the Server HTTP response header. The default setting for ServerTokens is Full, which will show Apache version information as well as module and version information for running modules (e.g., PHP). While you can't set this to be empty without modifying the source code, you can limit the information sent to be only the "Product" string, "Apache," by setting ServerTokens to Prod. Remember that changing this not only changes the server signature on documents, but also controls the text used in the Server HTTP header.

Administrative Directory or VirtualHost

Often times, you'll need to store various web-accessible scripts on a server used for monitoring or management. For example, it can be useful to have access to *apc.php* to review APC settings and statistics, but you typically don't want to leave that in your publicly accessible web root. There are a couple of easy solutions for how to securely store those scripts: you can either use a locked-down directory or a separate virtualhost to store the scripts. In either case, securing the scripts directory using a list of authorized IPs and/or an htaccess username and password is critical.

 Some sites go so far as to only allow access from *localhost*, meaning you need to do something like proxy your traffic through SSH in order to load the administrative scripts. If you do lock down a directory to only *localhost*, ensure that you're factoring any reverse proxies you may be running into your thinking. These will make many connections appear to be coming from *localhost*.

Storing these types of scripts in their own separate directory has a couple of great benefits. First, you don't need to temporarily copy files into your production web root and remove them when you're done. (How many times have you copied a `phpinfo()` script or similar into the web root and then forgotten to remove it?) Secondly, keeping them in their own virtualhost or directory means they are easily accessible by authorized users (or monitoring scripts) at a permanent URL that you can use across all of your web servers.

An example administrative scripts directory configuration looks like this:

```
Alias /adminscripts /var/www/adminscripts
<Directory "/var/www/adminscripts">
    Options -Indexes
    AllowOverride None
    # Control who can get stuff from this directory.
    Order Allow,Deny
    Allow from 127.0.0.1
</Directory>
```

Nginx

Apache's web server, httpd, is the most popular web server in use today, and has been for many years. Recently, however, some other open source web servers have gained some traction. Nginx (*http://nginx.org/en/*) is one alternative to Apache's httpd that has become very popular.

There are a number of reasons why you might consider using Nginx for your site instead of Apache. Nginx is newer, and there is a lot of discussion around the Internet suggesting that Nginx is generally faster and lighter, especially for serving static files. While some tests may back this up, it's by no means conclusively faster for all requests. One thing that may make Nginx faster than Apache for serving static files in our default setup (using mod_php) is that with mod_php Apache would have a full PHP process in memory for each httpd process. Nginx doesn't have to worry about this, because it relies on an external PHP setup. This is one reason we recommend offloading static file serving if you are using Apache and mod_php.

One of the main differences in Nginx is its event-based model for dealing with new connections. Instead of dedicating a process or thread to each request, this process model only services a request when an event triggers (data read from disk, etc.), and then moves on to another request. This model has become very popular recently, due to how efficient it can be when executed well. Apache 2.4 now includes the *event* MPM, which works somewhat similarly to Nginx.

The most common Nginx setup for Drupal involves using PHP-FPM (see "PHP Apache Module Versus CGI" on page 174), which provides a pool of PHP processes that Nginx connects to over a Unix or TCP socket. This architecture provides a method to scale and tune Nginx separately from the PHP processes, keeping the Nginx processes very lightweight and able to quickly serve static requests.

 mod_php won't work with Nginx. You must use PHP as a CGI when running Nginx.

Why Not Use Nginx Everywhere?

Nginx and PHP-FPM can provide a performance enhancement and a reduction of resources as compared to the most common Apache configuration, so it may seem like there is no reason to ever use Apache. This may be true in certain cases, but there are indeed reasons why many people still prefer Apache. One major reason is that when you start caching static items in a reverse proxy and/or CDN—more on this in the next chapter—the web server is being hit much less often for those types of requests, and the performance difference for static files is only noticeable when first loading an item into the external cache. This leaves Apache and mod_php to be just an application server, which limits the advantages of Nginx as a static file server. Another major reason for people to use Apache is if they require htaccess files in their setup, as these are not supported by Nginx. At the end of the day, the question of which httpd server to use is usually decided by team familiarity and other requirements.

## CHAPTER 19

Reverse Proxies and Content Delivery Networks

We've discussed a number of ways to speed up Drupal sites by improving code, optimizing infrastructure, and speeding up database queries. These changes can make a huge difference in website performance, but they can only go so far. Site performance can be improved even further by caching content before requests even reach Apache (and Drupal, PHP, or MySQL). Reverse proxies provide a way to do just that—cache static items such as images, JavaScript, and CSS, and potentially even full pages—and serve those items in a fraction of the time it would take if the request had go into Apache, PHP, and MySQL. This chapter focuses on reverse proxies with built-in caches, also referred to as *web accelerators*.

Content delivery networks (CDNs) take the idea of a reverse proxy a step further by moving cached content physically closer to website visitors. In addition to offloading network traffic from your infrastructure, this also makes your site seem much faster to visitors by reducing their network latency.

Using a Reverse Proxy with Drupal

When implementing a reverse proxy cache in front of your web servers, there are many options to consider. First up is which reverse proxy to use. Varnish (*https://www.varnish-cache.org/*) has become very popular in recent years and its configuration language is extremely powerful, allowing for very specific caching configurations. Varnish has generally become accepted by the Drupal community as the reverse proxy of choice, so we'll concentrate solely on Varnish here. The overall ideas apply to any reverse proxy, but the specific configuration examples will apply to Varnish only.

Other Popular Reverse Proxy Caches

Of course, Varnish isn't the only option out there. Other popular reverse proxy caches include the following:

Nginx
> In addition to functioning as a web server in place of Apache, Nginx (*http://nginx.org/en/*) is also frequently used as a standalone reverse proxy.

Squid
> Squid (*http://www.squid-cache.org/*) is one of the oldest reverse proxies still available today, though its use has declined in favor of Varnish in recent years.

Apache Traffic Server
> Originally developed at Yahoo!, Traffic Server (*http://trafficserver.apache.org/*) was donated to the Apache Software Foundation and is now fully open source.

Secondly, you need to decide how much you want to cache and how integrated the proxy will be with your website. For example, caching static content items like images and JavaScript is relatively easy and can be done "out of the box" with minimal configuration, using pretty much any reverse proxy. If you want to take things a step further and start caching full pages served by Drupal, that requires a bit more configuration. Going even further, you can closely integrate Varnish and Drupal such that when an object is edited, Drupal can immediately purge pages containing that object out of Varnish's cache to prevent stale content from being served. While the more advanced actions may take a bit more configuration, it's not terribly difficult once you get comfortable with the configuration language—and there are a number of contributed Drupal modules that will help ease the process as well.

Let's look at an example of using Varnish to cache. Figure 19-1 shows Varnish handling incoming HTTP requests for the site. When Varnish has a valid item in its cache, it will serve that item from the cache immediately with no backend request to the web server. When Varnish does not have an item cached, or has an out-of-date item cached, it will make a request to the web server for the item, store it in the local Varnish cache if it's cacheable, and then return it to the client.

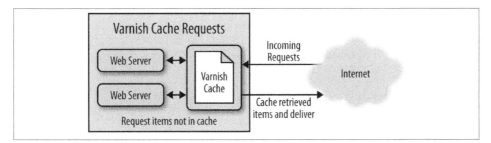

Figure 19-1. Varnish reverse proxy

Understanding Varnish Configuration Language

Varnish Configuration Language (VCL) is used to define how Varnish will handle requests, cache items, and connect to one or more backends (web servers). You don't need to be an expert in VCL in order to use Varnish, but understanding at least the default subroutines and their behavior will make it much easier to customize a VCL file for your specific needs. VCL was designed to be similar to C and Perl, and therefore is easy to pick up for most developers and system administrators.

 Changes to the VCL file used by Varnish do not take effect immediately; they must first be compiled and then loaded into Varnish. This can be done with commands through the Varnish admin interface, or happens automatically when the Varnish daemon is restarted.

Loading VCL Changes

In order to pull in changes to your VCL file, you will need to compile it in Varnish. Compiling the VCL in Varnish is preferred over fully restarting the Varnish daemon for a couple of reasons. First, you won't interrupt existing connections. Second, if you restart Varnish and the new VCL file has an error, Varnish will refuse to start; however, if you manually compile a new VCL file with an error, Varnish will report the error but continue to run with the old, working configuration.

To compile a VCL file, you need to connect to the Varnish administrative interface. This can be done either with *telnet* or with the *varnishadm* utility. Here's an example using *varnishadm* to connect to the Vanrish admin port to compile and then load the updated VCL file */etc/varnish/example.vcl. newconfig* is a name to reference the configuration and can be whatever name you want to use:

```
$ varnishadm
200
-----------------------------
Varnish Cache CLI 1.0
```

```
----------------------------
Linux,3.9.10-100.fc17.x86_64,x86_64,-sfile,-smalloc,-hcritbit

Type 'help' for command list.
Type 'quit' to close CLI session.

> vcl.load newconfig /etc/varnish/example.vcl
200 13
VCL compiled.
> vcl.use newconfig
200 0
```

Defining a Backend

The first step when setting up Varnish is to configure it with your backend information. The backend declaration supplies Varnish with information on how to connect to your backend web server(s). The declaration can be as simple as providing a hostname and port, but it also allows you to configure additional options such as connection timeouts, max connections, and probe checks, which are used to check whether the backend is healthy or not. An example backend server declaration looks like this:

```
backend default {
  .host = "10.0.1.15";
  .port = "80";
  .connect_timeout = 20s;
  .first_byte_timeout = 20s;
  .between_bytes_timeout = 10s;
  .max_connections = 120;
  .probe = {
    .request =
      "GET healthcheck.php HTTP/1.1"
      "Host: www.example.com"
      "Connection: close"
      "Accept-Encoding: gzip" ;
    .interval = 5s;
    .timeout = 3s;
    .window = 5;
    .threshold = 3;
  }
}
```

This example defines a backend named *default*, which will connect to port 80 on host 10.0.1.15. Varnish will throw an error if any of the timeouts are hit while making a request to the backend. The max_connections setting allows a way to limit the number of connections that Varnish will make to the backend—this should not be more than your Apache MaxClients setting on the web server, discussed in the previous chapter.

When running a single server with both Apache and Varnish, you will need to have Varnish listen on port 80 and move Apache to listen on an alternate port (via the Listen setting in *httpd.conf*). Also be sure to set the correct Apache port in your VCL backend settings.

The probe section is optional; it defines a periodic health check for the backend. Using a probe gives you a proactive way to check the status of a backend—otherwise, the status will only be updated if it hits a timeout when making a backend request for a client. Obviously, that particular client request will be served a Varnish error. It's best to define a probe, especially if you have multiple backends, so *sick* backends are automatically avoided with the use of a director. Once a probe detects that the backend has returned to a healthy state, the backend will be made active again in the director.

Inside of the probe definition, you are able to specify a URL to request, along with any other headers that should be used for the request. In addition, you define how often to run the check, what its timeout is, and window and threshold values. In order to declare a backend as *healthy*, Varnish will look the past *X* probe responses, where *X* is your window value: at least threshold of them must be successful. In our example, Varnish will look at the previous five probe requests, and if three or more of them were successful, the backend will be marked as healthy. If two or fewer probe requests were successful, the backend will be marked as *sick*.

Your probe should use a simple page as a check. You don't want to use a page that will put a large load on your web server or take a long time to respond, though it's best to choose a page that verifies the full stack is working. For example, use a simple Drupal page instead of using a static HTML page, which might succeed even if there were problems with Drupal, PHP, and/or the database.

Directors: Dealing with Multiple Backend Servers

If you have more than one web server, you can define each in its own backend declaration, but then you'll need a way to group them together and tell Varnish how to direct traffic between them; that's where *directors* come in. In Varnish, a director is a logical grouping of backend servers. There are a number of different director types that use different algorithms to decide which backend to use for a given request. To declare a director, you need to give it a name, tell it which director type to use, and then define which backend servers to include.

Varnish Director Types

The types of director available in Varnish include:

Random
Picks a backend at random, though weights can be used to adjust the chance of using a particular backend.

Client
Uses the client's identity to choose a backend.

Hash
Chooses a backend based on the request URL hash. This is useful if you have one Varnish instance load balancing in front of multiple Varnish servers and want to split the cache among them; it prevents cache duplication between the servers.

Round-robin
Cycles through a list of backends, directing one request to each, then moving on to the next.

DNS
Allows you to specify a list of IPs or a netblock to use for backend servers. This backend makes it easy to define a large number of backend servers with minimal configuration in the VCL.

Fallback
Provided with a list of backends, this director will start at the top of the list and use the first one that is considered healthy.

The following example shows how to define a round-robin director, which will simply loop over all the backends listed, directing a single request to one backend and then moving to the next backend for the next request. Assume we've already defined two backends, *web1* and *web2*:

```
director main round-robin {
    {
        .backend = web1;
    }
    {
        .backend = web2;
    }
}
```

This defines a director named *main*, which will direct traffic evenly between both of the backends. Another commonly used director is the *random* director, which will randomly select a backend from a list, though you can also weight the backend servers in order to send more or less traffic to them. This can be useful if your web servers are not uniform and one has more processing power than another. An example definition looks like this:

```
director loadbalance random {
  {
    .backend = web1;
    .weight  = 3;
  }
  {
    .backend = web2;
    .weight  = 1;
  }
  {
    .backend = web3;
    .weight  = 1;
  }
}
```

This example declares a director named *loadbalance* that randomly selects a backend server from those listed, but will give the *web1* backend a weight such that it will be selected roughly three times as often as either of the other two backend servers.

Once you define a director, Varnish needs to be told when to use that director. This is configured within the vcl_recv subroutine, described in more depth in the next section. At its simplest, all you need to do is set the req.backend variable to the backend or director you want to use. The setting used is the same whether you are setting it to a single backend or to a director:

```
sub vcl_recv {
  set req.backend = loadbalance;
}
```

This example sets the default backend to the *loadbalance* director we defined in the previous example.

Built-in VCL Subroutines

There are a number of subroutines used by Varnish to handle requests. You can override or "prepend" any of these subroutines with your own definitions. Most of the time, only one or two of these subroutines needs to be modified in order to work well with your site. However, some sites need a bit more customization and end up overriding most or all of the built-in subroutines. It's important to know that if you don't define one of the built-in subroutines in your VCL file, that subroutine will still exist in its default configuration. Here is a quick overview of some of the predefined subroutines used in the VCL file that are commonly modified with site-specific configurations:

`vcl_recv`

This subroutine is called to deal with an incoming request. It contains the logic to tell Varnish if and how to serve the request—for example, whether it should return a cached item or bypass the cache and fetch an object from a backend server in order to fulfill the request. `vcl_recv` is also where you declare which backend (or director) to use for a given request.

`vcl_fetch`

This subroutine is called after an item has been fetched from a backend. Generally, things to check for here include if a cookie is being set, or some other response that indicates the item should not be cached.

`vcl_error`

This subroutine is called when an error is hit either within Varnish or with the backend response. Here you have the option of calling a *restart* on the request to try again, in the hopes of not getting an error the second time. This subroutine is also used to customize the Varnish error output and to deal with custom error codes that may have been set elsewhere in the VCL.

`vcl_hash`

This subroutine creates a hash for the cached item. The cache is used internally by Varnish for future lookups and by default includes the URL and either the HTTP host or IP address. If you are doing some custom caching (e.g., splitting the cache) based on a cookie or a certain header in the request, then you would likely do so by including that item in your hash calculation. This is useful, for example, if you want to cache mobile requests separately from regular "desktop" requests based on a device type cookie or header.

 For Varnish 3.0, the VCL reference located here (*https://www.varnish-cache.org/docs/3.0/reference/vcl.html*) gives an overview of all VCL subroutines and shows the default configuration for each. The default VCL example here (*https://www.varnish-cache.org/trac/wiki/VCLExampleDefault*) provides a flowchart showing how a request flows through the various VCL subroutines.

Customizing Subroutines

When you add code for any of the built-in subroutines in your VCL configuration, by default you will only prepend the default for that subroutine. If your custom code terminates with an action (e.g., some sort of `return` statement), then the default won't be run for that subroutine. Sometimes there are reasons you want to bypass the default routines, though generally it is best to only prepend them by not including a `return` statement at the end of your code.

As an example, let's write a few custom vcl_recv subroutines with one difference: one will return at the end of the subroutine (bypassing the default vcl_recv stub), and one will not return by default, meaning the default stub will get executed. For starters, here is the default vcl_recv stub:

```
/*
 * Copyright (c) 2006 Verdens Gang AS
 * Copyright (c) 2006-2011 Varnish Software AS
 * All rights reserved.
 *
 * Author: Poul-Henning Kamp <phk@phk.freebsd.dk>
 *
 * Redistribution and use in source and binary forms, with or without
 * modification, are permitted provided that the following conditions
 * are met:
 * 1. Redistributions of source code must retain the above copyright
 *    notice, this list of conditions and the following disclaimer.
 * 2. Redistributions in binary form must reproduce the above copyright
 *    notice, this list of conditions and the following disclaimer in the
 *    documentation and/or other materials provided with the distribution.
 *
 * THIS SOFTWARE IS PROVIDED BY THE AUTHOR AND CONTRIBUTORS ``AS IS'' AND
 * ANY EXPRESS OR IMPLIED WARRANTIES, INCLUDING, BUT NOT LIMITED TO, THE
 * IMPLIED WARRANTIES OF MERCHANTABILITY AND FITNESS FOR A PARTICULAR
 * PURPOSE ARE DISCLAIMED.  IN NO EVENT SHALL AUTHOR OR CONTRIBUTORS BE
 * LIABLE FOR ANY DIRECT, INDIRECT, INCIDENTAL, SPECIAL, EXEMPLARY, OR
 * CONSEQUENTIAL DAMAGES (INCLUDING, BUT NOT LIMITED TO, PROCUREMENT OF
 * SUBSTITUTE GOODS OR SERVICES; LOSS OF USE, DATA, OR PROFITS; OR
 * BUSINESS INTERRUPTION) HOWEVER CAUSED AND ON ANY THEORY OF LIABILITY,
 * WHETHER IN CONTRACT, STRICT LIABILITY, OR TORT (INCLUDING NEGLIGENCE
 * OR OTHERWISE) ARISING IN ANY WAY OUT OF THE USE OF THIS SOFTWARE,
 * EVEN IF ADVISED OF THE POSSIBILITY OF SUCH DAMAGE.
 */

sub vcl_recv {
  if (req.restarts == 0) {
    if (req.http.x-forwarded-for) {
      set req.http.X-Forwarded-For =
        req.http.X-Forwarded-For + ", " + client.ip;
    } else {
      set req.http.X-Forwarded-For = client.ip;
    }
  }
  if (req.request != "GET" &&
      req.request != "HEAD" &&
      req.request != "PUT" &&
      req.request != "POST" &&
      req.request != "TRACE" &&
      req.request != "OPTIONS" &&
      req.request != "DELETE") {
        /* Non-RFC2616 or CONNECT which is weird. */
        return (pipe);
```

```
    }
    if (req.request != "GET" && req.request != "HEAD") {
      /* We only deal with GET and HEAD by default */
      return (pass);
    }
    if (req.http.Authorization || req.http.Cookie) {
      /* Not cacheable by default */
      return (pass);
    }
    return (lookup);
  }
```

Let's walk through what the default code does. First, it appends to the X-Forwarded-For header if that is set. Next, it checks for nonstandard request types; if it encounters something unexpected, it will return pipe, meaning that the request will be piped directly to the backend instead of going through the normal request flow in Varnish. After that, if the request type is anything except GET or HEAD, Varnish will pass it through without caching (you wouldn't want to cache a POST request, for example). In the final check, Varnish checks if there is an Authorization header or if a cookie is set. If either of those are in place, the request is returned with pass, meaning it won't be cached. Finally, after going through all that, the subroutine returns lookup, meaning it will forward the request to the backend and attempt to cache the result.

For the sake of this example, let's assume that you want to add one additional check to vcl_recv. Specifically, there is a URL, */update.php*, which you want to tell Varnish never to cache. Seems reasonable enough. Let's see how that would be handled in vcl_recv:

```
  sub vcl_recv {
    if (req.url ~ "^/update.php$") {
      return(pass);
    }
  }
```

Once you've loaded that code into Varnish, your custom vcl_recv will be run for incoming requests. In this case, if a request comes in for */update.php* Varnish will return pass, meaning that it will bypass its cache for the request. Requests for any other URL on the site will fall through your subroutine and, because you did not include a return at the end of the subroutine, the default stub shown earlier will be executed as well. Compare that to the following:

```
  sub vcl_recv {
    if (req.url ~ "^/update.php$") {
      return(pass);
    }
    return(lookup);
  }
```

The code in this version includes return(lookup) in the subroutine. In this case, requests for URLs other than */update.php* will be cached in Varnish and delivered to clients. The problem is that because the default stub is not run, it's possible that you are caching an item even in cases where you probably shouldn't (for example, if the request contains a session cookie).

The difference may seem minimal, but it can have quite an impact. It's not "wrong" to override/bypass the default subroutines, but you should be aware when doing so, and be sure you understand the consequences. Some sites copy and paste the defaults below their custom code as a way to better visualize the code path (and not forget what the default stub is doing, even though it may be hidden behind the scenes).

Cookies and Varnish

In its default configuration, Varnish will not cache any request that has a cookie set. This means any logged-in user traffic will not be cached in Varnish, but it also means that any custom or contrib modules that set any type of cookie (session or otherwise) may cause Varnish cache misses. One common example of this is Google Analytics, which sets a tracking cookie for every visitor. With a default Varnish configuration, enabling Google Analytics would cause all page visits to miss the Varnish cache because of the cookie. That's obviously not ideal behavior, so let's take a look at how to modify the Varnish configuration to ignore certain cookies when deciding whether or not to serve a cached item.

The way to do this is to do a regular expression replacement (this is one of the few built-in functions available in Varnish) on the request cookie in order to strip out cookies that we know should be ignored as far as caching is concerned. Stripping out certain cookies should be dealt with in the vcl_recv subroutine, as that is where Varnish makes the request cookie object available. Consider this example:

```
sub vcl_recv {
  # Remove Google Analytics cookie.
  # These are all of the form "__utm[a-z]=<value>".
  set req.http.cookie = regsuball(req.http.cookie,
                        "(^|;\s*)__utm[a-z]=[^;]*", "");
  # Remove a ";" prefix, if present.
  set req.http.cookie = regsub(req.http.cookie, "^;\s*", "");
  # Remove the cookie if it is now empty or contains only spaces.
  if (req.http.cookie ~ "^\s*$") {
    unset req.http.cookie;
  }
}
```

The preceding code will allow Varnish to cache pages even if a Google Analytics cookie is present. If you have multiple cookies you want to remove, simply add additional calls to regsuball to strip out known cookies that don't affect caching.

Caching for Authenticated Users

We mentioned in the previous section that by default, requests from logged-in users will not be cached by Varnish. For many cases, that's actually the preferred behavior. For example, you wouldn't want to cache per-user or per-role page customizations and then serve those cached items to an anonymous user. However, there are some files that remain static for all requests, such as image, JavaScript, and CSS files. There is no reason not to cache those in Varnish and serve them for any request, regardless of whether or not the user is logged in.

There are a couple of different approaches to solve this particular issue. One option is to create a list of file extensions that should always be cached. The second option makes the assumption that any files served out of the *sites/* subdirectory can be cached regardless of whether the user is logged in. Either way, the implementation is very similar: add a check in `vcl_recv`, and if the check is met, unset any cookies that might be present and return a `lookup`. `return(lookup)` will return an item from the cache or, if it's not present, fetch it from the backend and store it in the cache for future requets. Here's a VCL example for serving cached items for common "static" file extensions:

```
sub vcl_recv {
  if (req.url ~ "\.(js|css|jpg|jpeg|png|gif|gz|tgz|bz2|tbz|mp3|ogg|swf)$") {
    unset req.http.Cookie;
    return (lookup);
  }
}
```

Edge-Side Includes

There are many cases where it would be possible (and ideal!) to cache a page in Varnish for authenticated users, but where there is some small amount of personalized content in that page that can't be shared between users. Edge-side includes (ESI) provides a way to work around this problem by referencing the personalized data in a separate ESI tag. The full page without the personalized content can then be cached in Varnish, and that content can be pulled in separately and integrated with the cached content.

Imagine the simple case of a logged-in user block that displays the user's name. This is something you wouldn't want to cache and serve to other users, for obvious reasons. However, if the rest of the page contents are not user-specific, then Varnish could cache the entire page and dynamically pull in an ESI block containing the user-specific block content.

ESI is a very powerful tool that can greatly increase your cache hit rate by allowing much more of the site to be cached for authenticated users. However, misused or misconfigured, ESI could have the opposite effect and greatly reduce your site's client-side performance, so be sure to thoroughly test any deployment. We could easily span an entire

---

chapter (or book!) discussing ESI, but because of space constraints, we won't go into it in more depth here.

 The Drupal ESI (*http://drupal.org/project/esi*) module provides example documentation for how to integrate Drupal ESI into Varnish.

Serving Expired Content

Sometimes it makes sense to serve cache content that has already expired. This isn't quite as bad as it sounds; cached content is not like expired milk, and certainly smells better. Actually, there are a couple of good reasons that you might want to serve expired content:

- The backend server is down or unreachable.
- Varnish has sent a request to the backend for an object, but that request is slow to process on the backend. Meanwhile, Varnish could serve an old version of that same object to any incoming requests for the same object.

Both of these situations are handled by setting a *grace* period for requests to live in Varnish after they have expired. This can be set using the `req.grace` variable in `vcl_recv`. You'll also need to set `beresp.grace` in `vcl_fetch`. `req.grace` controls the grace period for an object. `beresp.grace` affects the maximum grace time allowed for an object, controlling when the object will be purged from the cache. Consider the following VCL snippet:

```
sub vcl_recv {
  if (req.backend.healthy) {
    set req.grace = 20s;
  } else {
    set req.grace = 30m;
  }
}

sub vcl_fetch {
  set beresp.grace = 30m;
}
```

In `vcl_recv`, we check if the backend is healthy (health is based on backend probes or recent failed backend requests). If the backend is healthy, a grace period of 20 seconds is used for requests — this applies to cases where a cache item has expired and a new request has been sent to the backend for the updated object. In this case, any subsequent requests for the item will be served the expired content while the backend request is waiting to complete. On the other hand, if the backend is considered sick, the grace time is increased to 30 minutes. This allows Varnish to serve content up to 30 minutes past its expiration time, allowing time for the backend server to recover without taking the website entirely offline. After the grace period has run out, Varnish will return to the default behavior of fetching from the backend—in the case of a backend server downtime, this likely means Varnish will start returning errors after the grace period has expired.

The beresp.grace setting in vcl_fetch should simply reflect the maximum time that you use for req.grace, which is 30 minutes in this case.

Error Pages

More likely than not, you've seen a default Varnish error page. It probably was pretty ugly and would seem quite confusing to regular users of your website. Thankfully, the default error pages are quite easy to customize within the vcl_error function. All you need to do is use the synthetic keyword to define an HTML document to output for errors, and then have Varnish deliver that document. Here's how this is achieved in the default VCL:

```
sub vcl_error {
  set obj.http.Content-Type = "text/html; charset=utf-8";
  set obj.http.Retry-After = "5";
  synthetic {"
<?xml version="1.0" encoding="utf-8"?>
<!DOCTYPE html PUBLIC "-//W3C//DTD XHTML 1.0 Strict//EN"
 "http://www.w3.org/TR/xhtml1/DTD/xhtml1-strict.dtd">
<html>
  <head>
    <title>"} + obj.status + " " + obj.response + {"</title>
  </head>
  <body>
    <h1>Error "} + obj.status + " " + obj.response + {"</h1>
    <p>"} + obj.response + {"</p>
    <h3>Guru Meditation:</h3>
    <p>XID: "} + req.xid + {"</p>
    <hr>
    <p>Varnish cache server</p>
  </body>
</html>
"};
  return (deliver);
}
```

Notice how the synthetic keyword is simply passed a long string containing HTML output. This can be easily overridden with your own HTML, but ideally this would not include external CSS or images since your backend may be down when this error page is served. Be sure to add the return (deliver) at the end of your custom vcl_error so that the default vcl_error isn't used.

Memory Allocation

Varnish provides two stable methods for memory allocation: file-backed, or completely in-memory. With file-backed memory allocation, Varnish depends on the OS memory caching/paging system to keep recently used items in RAM; with in-memory allocation ("malloc"), Varnish claims a dedicated chunk of RAM and stores all cache items there. There are trade-offs to either option. Using a file-based backend means you can generally have a much larger cache, but certain cache items may be slower than others if they end up getting paged out to disk by the operating system. In the case of malloc, cached items are guaranteed to be in RAM, but if you are caching a lot of items, you may need more space than you have available RAM.

You will nearly always get better performance when using malloc. For that reason, we recommend using malloc except in the cases where you need to cache more than you have space for in RAM (and are unable to add more RAM). That said, Varnish is actually very smart about how it caches to disk: it relies on the operating system's file cache, and frequently used cache items end up in the FS cache under optimal circumstances.

In order to figure out how much RAM is required for your website, it's easiest to simply allocate something like 512 MB or 1 GB, and then let Varnish run for a while. Monitor the memory usage using *top* and *varnishstat*, specifically looking at the `SMA bytes al located` output of *varnishstat*. If you see that the cache has filled up or are seeing many nuked objects, then you should increase the memory allocation.

 Varnish will use a bit more memory (or file system space) than allocated, due to internal overhead. When setting the amount of memory to use, you are only limiting the size of the cache; the overhead size is not configurable.

Logging and Monitoring Varnish

Once you have Varnish in place, there are a number of tools you can use to log requests and monitor hit rates, usage, and other information:

varnishncsa

Many administrators like to have a simple request log (much like Apache's access log) for tracking all requests handled by Varnish. Varnish ships with the *varnishncsa* daemon, which provides just that. Simply start the *varnishncsa* service (command-line options include a file to output to), and it will start logging.

varnishstat

Run without any options, *varnishstat* will provide a continuously updated snapshot of statistics. This will give you an idea of your current cache hit rate, cache usage, and other request and backend statistics. If you run *varnishstat* with the -1 flag, it will output all statistics once and exit; this is useful for capturing the output to a file.

varnishhist

This will provide you with a visual representation of how long requests take to be served. Items graphed toward the left side are served faster than those on the right side. This can help give you an idea of your cache hit rate and help you spot any outliers that take an unusual amount of time.

varnishlog

varnishlog reads out of Varnish's shared memory and outputs information about each request handled. You have the option of filtering out certain requests based on things like the request URL, which is almost always how this utility is used because otherwise it just gives way too much information.

All of these tools are very useful for tracking how well Varnish is working to cache your site's content, and especially useful when you are making changes to your VCL file and want to see the effects. Using *varnishstat* to watch cache hits and misses and then tracking down misses using *varnishlog* or watching the request/response headers in your browser can be very useful when troubleshooting VCL issues.

Sample VCL for Drupal

To wrap up our discussion of Varnish, let's take a look at a sample VCL file that can be used on a Drupal site with just a few configuration changes—you will need to adjust the backend declaration to point to your web server, and add additional backend definitions and a director if you have more than one backend server.

There are a few things included in this VCL file that weren't covered in this chapter:

1. In vcl_deliver, we add response headers to track whether or not the item returned was cached. In the case of a cache hit, we also add a header with the number of cache hits for that particular item. This is very useful for tracking your hits and misses, especially when first setting up Varnish in a new environment.

2. There is a list of file extensions in vcl_recv that we always want to cache, so we unset any cookies for these requests. This same list is duplicated in vcl_fetch so that if the backend attempts to set a new cookie with the response, that Set-Cookie will be caught and dropped by Varnish ensuring that the item will be cached. The important thing to note here is that if you edit the list in vcl_recv, you should update the list in vcl_fetch to match.

3. vcl_fetch includes a check for a few different error codes (404, 301, 500), which correspond to *page not found*, *moved permanently*, and *internal server error*. By

default, the backend will return these with a TTL of 0 so they won't be cached by Varnish. But because these requests can actually cause a full Drupal bootstrap and database queries, it's actually beneficial to cache the responses for some amount of time. In this example, we set the TTL to 10 minutes so that Varnish will maintain the responses in the cache.

Our sample Drupal VCL file looks like this:

```
# Sample VCL based on VCL created by Four Kitchens, available at
# https://fourkitchens.atlassian.net/wiki/display
#      /TECH/Configure+Varnish+3+for+Drupal+7
/*
 * Copyright (c) 2013 Four Kitchens
 * All rights reserved.
 *
 * Redistribution and use in source and binary forms, with or without
 * modification, are permitted provided that the following conditions
 * are met:
 * 1. Redistributions of source code must retain the above copyright
 *    notice, this list of conditions and the following disclaimer.
 * 2. Redistributions in binary form must reproduce the above copyright
 *    notice, this list of conditions and the following disclaimer in the
 *    documentation and/or other materials provided with the distribution.
 *
 * THIS SOFTWARE IS PROVIDED BY THE AUTHOR AND CONTRIBUTORS ``AS IS'' AND
 * ANY EXPRESS OR IMPLIED WARRANTIES, INCLUDING, BUT NOT LIMITED TO, THE
 * IMPLIED WARRANTIES OF MERCHANTABILITY AND FITNESS FOR A PARTICULAR
 * PURPOSE ARE DISCLAIMED.  IN NO EVENT SHALL AUTHOR OR CONTRIBUTORS BE
 * LIABLE FOR ANY DIRECT, INDIRECT, INCIDENTAL, SPECIAL, EXEMPLARY, OR
 * CONSEQUENTIAL DAMAGES (INCLUDING, BUT NOT LIMITED TO, PROCUREMENT OF
 * SUBSTITUTE GOODS OR SERVICES; LOSS OF USE, DATA, OR PROFITS; OR
 * BUSINESS INTERRUPTION) HOWEVER CAUSED AND ON ANY THEORY OF LIABILITY,
 * WHETHER IN CONTRACT, STRICT LIABILITY, OR TORT (INCLUDING NEGLIGENCE
 * OR OTHERWISE) ARISING IN ANY WAY OUT OF THE USE OF THIS SOFTWARE,
 * EVEN IF ADVISED OF THE POSSIBILITY OF SUCH DAMAGE.
 */

# Default backend definition.  Set this to point to your content server.
backend default {
  .host = "127.0.0.1";
  .port = "81";
}

sub vcl_recv {
  # Use anonymous, cached pages if all backends are down.
  if (!req.backend.healthy) {
    unset req.http.Cookie;
  }

  # Allow the backend to serve up stale content if it is responding slowly.
  set req.grace = 6h;
```

```
# Do not cache these paths.
if (req.url ~ "^/status\.php$" ||
    req.url ~ "^/update\.php$" ||
    req.url ~ "^/admin$" ||
    req.url ~ "^/admin/.*$" ||
    req.url ~ "^/flag/.*$" ||
    req.url ~ "^.*/ajax/.*$" ||
    req.url ~ "^.*/ahah/.*$") {
    return (pass);
}

# Always cache the following file types for all users. This list of extensions
# appears twice, once here and again in vcl_fetch, so make sure you edit both
# and keep them equal.
if (req.url ~
    "(?i)\.(pdf|txt|doc|xls|ppt|csv|png|gif|jpeg|jpg|ico|swf|css|js)(\?.*)?$") {
    unset req.http.Cookie;
}

# Remove all cookies that Drupal doesn't need to know about. We explicitly
# list the ones that Drupal does need, the SESS and NO_CACHE cookies. If after
# running this code we find that either of these two cookies remains, we
# will pass as the page shouldn't be cached.
if (req.http.Cookie) {
    # Append a semicolon to the front of the cookie string.
    set req.http.Cookie = ";" + req.http.Cookie;

    # Remove all spaces that appear after semicolons.
    set req.http.Cookie = regsuball(req.http.Cookie, "; +", ";");

    # Match the cookies we want to keep, adding back the space we removed
    # previously. "\1" is first matching group in the regular expression match.
    set req.http.Cookie = regsuball(req.http.Cookie,
                       ";(SESS[a-z0-9]+|SSESS[a-z0-9]+|NO_CACHE)=", "; \1=");

    # Remove all other cookies, identifying them by the fact that they have
    # no space after the preceding semicolon.
    set req.http.Cookie = regsuball(req.http.Cookie, ";[^ ][^;]*", "");

    # Remove all spaces and semicolons from the beginning and end of the
    # cookie string.
    set req.http.Cookie = regsuball(req.http.Cookie, "^[; ]+|[; ]+$", "");

    if (req.http.Cookie == "") {
        # If there are no remaining cookies, remove the cookie header
        # so that Varnish will cache the request.
        unset req.http.Cookie;
    }
    else {
        # If there are any cookies left (a session or NO_CACHE cookie), do not
        # cache the page. Pass it on to the backend directly.
```

```
      return (pass);
    }
  }
}

sub vcl_deliver {
  # Set a header to track if this was a cache hit or miss.
  # Include hit count for cache hits.
  if (obj.hits > 0) {
    set resp.http.X-Varnish-Cache = "HIT";
    set resp.http.X-Varnish-Hits = obj.hits;
  }
  else {
    set resp.http.X-Varnish-Cache = "MISS";
  }
}

sub vcl_fetch {
  # Items returned with these status values wouldn't be cached by default,
  # but by doing so we can save some Drupal overhead.
  if (beresp.status == 404 || beresp.status == 301 || beresp.status == 500) {
    set beresp.ttl = 10m;
  }

  # Don't allow static files to set cookies.
  # This list of extensions appears twice, once here and again in vcl_recv, so
  # make sure you edit both and keep them equal.
  if (req.url ~
    "(?i)\.(pdf|txt|doc|xls|ppt|csv|png|gif|jpeg|jpg|ico|swf|css|js)(\?.*)?$") {
    unset beresp.http.set-cookie;
  }

  # Allow items to be stale if needed, in case of problems with the backend.
  set beresp.grace = 6h;
}

sub vcl_error {
  # In the event of an error, show friendlier messages.
  set obj.http.Content-Type = "text/html; charset=utf-8";
  synthetic {"
<html>
<head>
  <title>Page Unavailable</title>
  <style>
    body { background: #303030; text-align: center; color: white; }
    .error { color: #222; }
  </style>
</head>
<body>
  <div id="page">
    <h1 class="title">Page Unavailable</h1>
    <p>The page you requested is temporarily unavailable.</p>
```

```
    <p>Please try again later.</p>
    <div class="error">(Error "} + obj.status + " " + obj.response + {")</div>
  </div>
</body>
</html>
"};
  return (deliver);
}
```

Content Delivery Networks

CDNs can be used either in place of or in addition to a reverse proxy. As we mentioned in the introduction to this chapter, a CDN can dramatically increase the speed of your website, not only by caching your content, but also by dispersing that content geographically and making it available on a fast network link in order to optimize performance for visitors from all over the world.

In the most simple configuration, a CDN can be set up to serve all static content from your site. However, CDNs are capable of doing much more: for example, they can handle all traffic to your website (imagine pointing your website's domain to a CDN server instead of it pointing to your web server) and even potentially handle SSL requests, which is something that Varnish can't do.

Serving Static Content Through a CDN

The easiest (and cheapest!) way to integrate a CDN with your site is to use the CDN as a static cache store. Generally this means storing images, JavaScript, and CSS on the CDN, but serving all page requests from your own servers. When a request comes in for a page on your site, the request is handled by your web server, but all static content is referenced with a URL that points to the CDN server so clients will fetch all of that content from the CDN server(s) directly. When missing or expired content is requested on the CDN, it makes requests directly to the backend server(s) to update its cache. The CDN (*https://drupal.org/project/CDN*) Drupal module makes this configuration very easy by automatically rewriting URLs for you.

In the case of a CDN set up to *pull* content, rewriting the URLs is all that is needed because the CDN will automatically request items from your web server if it doesn't have them in its cache. Another type of CDN is a *push* CDN, where you must manually upload content to the CDN servers before it will be served. The Drupal CDN module also handles such CDNs (with additional configuration), though pull-based CDNs are much more common.

When to Use a CDN

CDNs can provide an amazing performance boost to your site with very little configuration overhead. Cached items are served faster to visitors, and load is reduced on your
servers as more requests are dealt with by the CDN. In general, if you can afford the
cost of a CDN, then there is no reason not to use one. While the cost for larger sites and
those needing special features can grow quite large, there are many affordable CDN
providers for small- to medium-sized sites.

Choosing Between a CDN and a Reverse Proxy

There is actually no reason that this needs to be an either/or decision. If you have a
reverse proxy in place, you will still see benefits from adding a CDN. The caches can
layer well, and any special request handling that needs to happen can easily be configured
with some custom headers passed on by the CDN and handled in the reverse proxy (or
vice versa).

## CHAPTER 20

Load Testing

We mentioned in Chapter 1 that performance improvements are not a one-time task, but are something that should be revisited in iterations throughout the lifetime of a website. Load testing is an important aspect of any project: it provides insight into how your site and infrastructure will react under load. While critical to the launch process of any project, load testing is also useful to integrate into your standard testing procedure. It can help you locate bottlenecks and generic performance regressions introduced in the evolution of a site after launch (due to code and infrastructure changes).

There are many different methodologies and applications for performing load tests, but generally this testing involves accessing various pages on the site with enough traffic to start causing degradation. From there, work can be done to isolate bottlenecks in order to improve performance. If you perform periodic load tests, you are much more likely to catch something while it's still a minor performance issue, not after it becomes a major problem.

Different Types of Load Tests

There are a number of different load testing configurations (sometimes referred to as *test plans*) that can be used individually or in conjunction to provide insight into site performance. Generally, we end up running three different types of tests:

Baseline tests
> These tests are run with a relatively low amount of traffic in order to obtain some baseline information about site performance. These are useful for tracking general user-facing performance (time to first byte, time for a full page load) and for comparing against a higher-traffic load test result, as well as for tracking regressions in the standard case.

High traffic tests

Tests with relatively higher traffic are run in order to see when site performance begins to degrade as traffic increases. These tests can give you an idea of how many requests a site can handle before performance deteriorates to an unacceptable degree. At the same time, these types of tests are very good for uncovering bottlenecks in a site; many times issues with underlying services or service integration require a higher load in order to trigger. Generally speaking, this type of load test is the one that is run most frequently.

Targeted tests

Most tests are designed to cover all different request types and page types for a site. Targeted tests take a different approach; they are designed to test one or several specific features or user paths. For example, if you are working to improve the performance of a certain page type on your site, you could run a load test that only focuses on that particular area.

Depending on the load testing tool in use, these tests could all be based on the same test plan by tweaking the amount of traffic generated and/or by enabling or disabling certain parts of the test plan in order to focus testing on only a subset of the site.

Creating a Valid Test

One of the most difficult aspects of load testing is creating a test that represents real site traffic. If the test diverges greatly from real traffic patterns, the performance results and bottlenecks found during the test may not help you improve real-world performance in a meaningful way. By starting with a test that as closely as possible matches real-world traffic (or expected traffic, if you are looking at a new/growing site), you'll more reliably uncover performance issues on your site. Fine-tuning a load test can happen over time in order to keep it in line with shifting traffic patterns and new features added to a site. Things to take into consideration when creating and reviewing a load test plan include:

User browsing patterns

What pages are visited most often? How long do users spend on different page types? What are the most common entry points into the site?

Logged-in traffic

What percentage of traffic is logged in versus anonymous users? Do logged-in users visit different pages than anonymous users?

Amount of content

When creating a new site, do you have enough content on the site to perform a valid test? If not, then consider creating content programmatically before running a test. The Devel (*https://drupal.org/project/devel*) module is great for this purpose (among other things).

When to Test

There are many ways to approach load testing for a given website and infrastructure. How frequently tests are run is entirely up to you. Some sites may run a load test manually once per month, while others may run tests multiple times per day. Whatever you decide, it's important to run a baseline test occasionally to understand what "normal" performance looks like. Only once you have baseline numbers for user-facing and server-side performance during a load test can you define what is "good" or "bad" in a particular test result.

Continuous Integration (CI)

Testing can be tied into your development process using a tool such as Jenkins (described in more depth in Chapter 9). Tests could be set up to run each time a new release is pushed to the staging environment, or if you have sufficient resources, tests could even be run each time new code is pushed to the site's code repository.

Periodic Testing

For those who don't want to deal with the overhead of testing for each new code push, an alternative approach is to test on some predetermined schedule. This could be daily, weekly, or even monthly. The more frequently tests are run, the easier it will be to directly link a change in performance to a specific change on the site. If you go too long between tests, it can become much harder to pinpoint the cause of a performance problem.

Manual Targeted Testing

In addition to the previously described approaches, it can be useful to run manual tests occasionally, especially if you are trying to test a specific aspect of the site with a targeted test plan. For example, if you are planning a media event that will drive a lot of new users to your site, it might be beneficial to run targeted tests against the main site entry points and features that may receive higher than normal traffic, such as user registration.

Interpreting Test Results

One problem that many people encounter with load testing is that they are bombarded with too much data in the results, and it's not always clear what information is important. In most situations, you will at least want to examine:

Time to first byte
> Also referred to as *latency* in some load testing applications. This is quite important as it usually represents the actual Drupal execution time (or caching time), whereas other data points are less focused.

Full page load time
> Also referred to as *response time* in some applications. The difference between time to first byte and this is mainly due to the size of the page, the network path, and other issues.

Requests per second
> The number of page requests per second is an important statistic to look at when planning for traffic loads and infrastructure scaling.

Error responses
> These are another very important data point, and also the most likely to be ignored. A failing site will often load test very well; however, those results are obviously not providing very useful information and misrepresent the actual site performance. Paying attention to the error responses can give you an idea of where problems may be occurring. For example, Apache may have timeouts waiting on backend requests such as connecting to MySQL when the DB server is overloaded, and in those cases may return a 503 error.

Depending on what the goals are for your load test, you may also be looking at additional information such as bytes transferred or throughput for a particular page.

No matter what data you choose to track, it becomes even more valuable if you are able to track it over time. By comparing multiple test results, you'll get a much better idea of your site's performance as well as gaining the ability to see trends in the performance data. It can be very useful to observe things like page load time to see how it varies over time, or how it might increase or decrease in response to a specific code or infrastructure change.

Another important consideration is to understand how requests from load testing software differ from requests made by a user using a standard web browser. For example, JMeter, which we cover later in this chapter, does not execute JavaScript, and by default it will not download linked assets on a page (more on this in "Example Load Test Using JMeter" on page 212). In general, those differences are acceptable as long as they are understood. However, it can be worthwhile to perform some sort of additional testing with a tool that more accurately represents a browser. These tools are not always capable of high-traffic load tests, but they can at least be used to establish a baseline.

Server Monitoring During Load Tests

When you run a load test, you'll be presented with a list of results that focus entirely on client-side performance, since that is all that the load testing application can see. It's important to monitor servers and services during load test runs in order to get the most from your tests and to be able to track down infrastructure bottlenecks. Of course, this sort of monitoring could be left to the automated systems you set up while reading Chapter 8, but it can also be useful to manually watch the servers during test runs to see how things are affected and adjust what you are monitoring. Different sites will suffer from completely different infrastructure bottlenecks, so it's best to keep an eye on as much data as possible, but for starters we recommend:

Web servers
> Watch overall system load, memory usage, swap usage, network traffic, and disk I/ O. Also keep track of things like the Apache process count to see if you are approaching (or hitting!) the MaxClients setting. As always, don't forget to watch logs for Apache to see if any errors are being reported.

Reverse proxies and other caches, such as memcached
> Watch load, network traffic, and caching statistics. Is your cache hit rate higher or lower than normal? Try to understand why that might be (e.g., a test plan that only hits a very small subset of the site's pages would likely cause higher cache hit rates). Watch memory usage and evictions to be sure that the cache isn't becoming overly full and forced to delete items before they've expired.

Database servers
> Watch the server load and connection count, and watch the MySQL error log for any unusual errors. Ensure that the MySQL slow query log is enabled, and watch it for potential query improvements that can be made (see e.g. *pt-query-digest* in the Percona Toolkit). You can also watch MySQL statistics directly or with tools such as *mysqlreport* to monitor things like InnoDB buffer usage, lock wait times, and query cache usage. Watch the MySQL process list to see if there are certain queries running frequently or causing waits for other queries.

Where to Test

There are a number of options to determine which environment to run load tests against: development, staging, production, or potentially some environment dedicated to load testing. In an ideal world, tests should always be run against the production environment to obtain the most valid data possible. However, site users (not to mention investors) tend to dislike the website becoming unusably slow due to a load test. While some people may be able to run tests against production, even if it means scheduling the test for 3 a.m. or some other low-traffic time, others won't have that option. Our advice is to take into account what the goals and requirements are for your load testing and, based on that, run the tests against an appropriate environment.

> One other consideration when planning which environment to run a load test against is whether or not the test will be creating and/or deleting data on the site. In general, testing things like user comments against a production site can be very difficult to do in a way that doesn't interfere with your users.

As we mentioned in Chapter 7, the more closely your staging environment mimics production, the more useful it will be. In the case of load testing, staging can be a very fitting place to run load tests. While your staging servers may not be as numerous and high-powered as those in the production environment, you can still easily track down many performance issues and infrastructure bottlenecks by running tests against the staging environment if it is similar to your production environment.

Another option is to run tests against a development environment. This is especially valid for tests integrated with CI. While the performance numbers here will, expectedly, differ from in production, it's still a great way to test for performance changes when code changes occur.

 When running tests against an environment that is not your production environment, be aware that any user-facing performance numbers should be taken with a grain of salt. That is, performance will likely be slower than in your production environment, but the numbers can still be useful when comparing test results over time.

In cases where test or staging environments are under heavy use, it may not be possible to run load tests against those environments. For those situations, usually the only alternative is to have a dedicated "load testing" environment used specifically for load tests—or potentially also for other automated tests, such as acceptance testing). As always, the more closely this environment can mimic production, the more valid your test results will be. For those infrastructures that run mostly in the cloud, this environment might be spun up on demand when tests need to be run, but otherwise left offline.

Some sites might insist on running load tests against production in order to have "real" numbers. While this can make sense in certain situations, it's rare that a dedicated staging environment won't be sufficient to get the data required. Generally, our recommendation would be to only run low-traffic tests against production in order to obtain user-facing performance information. If you are trying to put the site under a heavy load in order to catch performance bottlenecks, then doing so in a staging environment should yield useful results.

Example Load Test Using JMeter

While there are many load testing applications and services available, JMeter (*http://jmeter.apache.org*) is one open source option that we have used extensively. JMeter tests are fairly flexible, and the ability to run tests either from a GUI or directly from command line makes it convenient for running tests remotely. As an example, we'll configure a simple load test plan with JMeter that logs into a Drupal site, visits a few pages, and then logs out. Once this is complete, you can configure how many concurrent threads you would like to run and for what duration, and you should have a good understanding of how it might be adapted to run against your own site.

 JMeter has some downsides: it doesn't execute JavaScript, nor does it render the HTML for pages it retrieves. You can still get useful performance information from JMeter tests, but be aware of those limitations and plan for another way to test JavaScript and rendering times if needed. There are multiple options for this type of testing, including Selenium and PhantomJS.

First, we need to understand the structure of the site we'll be testing. Our example is a standard Drupal 7 site with some "static" node pages, a forum section, and a front page that dynamically displays custom content to logged-in users, or a list of featured articles for anonymous users. For our load test, we'll want to test each of these different page types—plus, it's always important to focus attention on the front page, both for anonymous and logged-in users. You don't want people leaving your site because the front page took too long to load!

Global Test Settings

When you first launch JMeter, you will be presented with an empty test plan. We'll start by naming the test plan something original, like *Drupal*, by editing the Name field. Next, we'll start adding some global settings that we'll refer to in other parts of our test. Settings are stored in objects that JMeter refers to as *Config Elements*, and in this case, we're going to add one of the type *User Defined Variables*. To add this to the test, right-click on the test plan icon in the left toolbar and select Add→Config Element→User Defined Variables. The new element should appear as a child under the test plan.

Select the new object, and change the name to something useful like *Global Settings*. Next, we're going to add the variables listed in Table 20-1.

Table 20-1. JMeter global settings

Name	Value
site.hostname	d7.example.com
site.port	80
testlength	300
drupal.user	testuser
drupal.pass	verysecurepassword

Of course, you'll want to set the hostname to your site's real hostname, and set the user account and password to some existing (nonadmin) account. We will use that account for the test threads to log into the site. The `testlength` variable will be used to control how long the test runs (in seconds). Once complete, the settings should look something like Figure 20-1.

 We are using only a single account in this test in order to keep the example as simple as possible. You should consider using many (dozens, or hundreds, depending on your site's user base) user accounts to more accurately reflect real-world traffic.

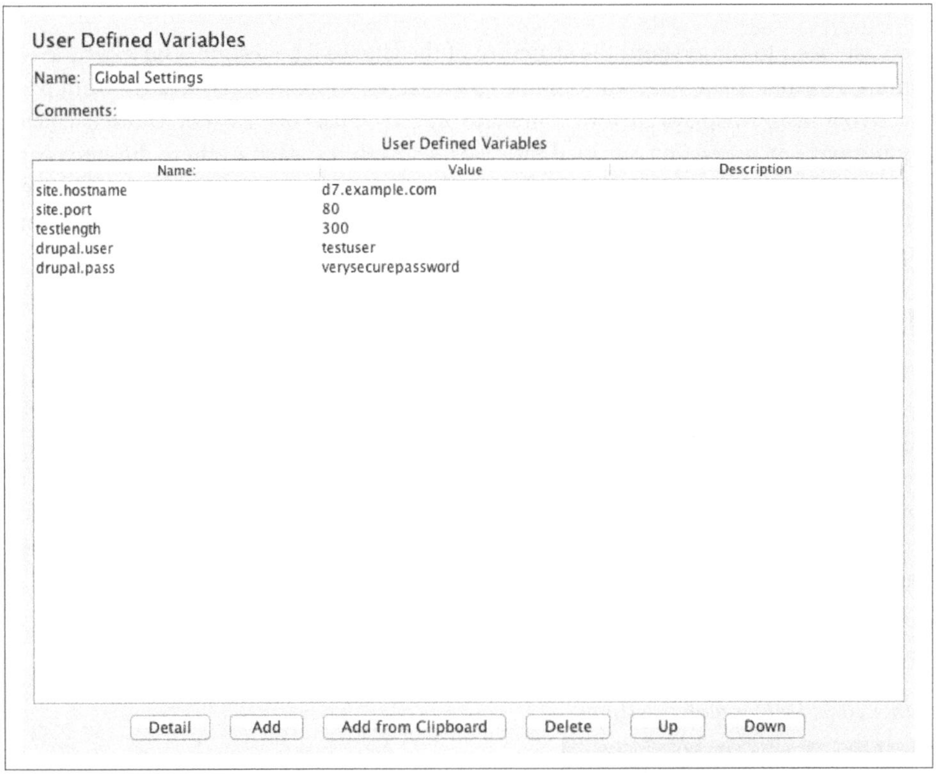

User Defined Variables

Name: Global Settings

Comments:

User Defined Variables

Name:	Value	Description
site.hostname	d7.example.com	
site.port	80	
testlength	300	
drupal.user	testuser	
drupal.pass	verysecurepassword	

Detail | Add | Add from Clipboard | Delete | Up | Down

Figure 20-1. JMeter global settings

Next, we'll create an *HTTP Request Defaults* Config Element in order to store default values for all of the HTTP requests we'll make later in the test. This saves us having to enter things like the server hostname in every single request, since if it's not specified, it will fall back to these default values. Right-click on the test plan and go to Add→Config Element→HTTP Request Defaults. In the HTTP Request Defaults configuration, set *Server Name or IP* to our global variable, *${site.hostname}*, set *Port Number* to the variable *${site.port}*, and then set *Implementation* to *HttpClient4*, *Protocol* to *http*, and

Content encoding to *utf-8*. Once complete, your settings should look like those in Figure 20-2.

HTTP Request Defaults

Name: HTTP Request Defaults

Comments:

Web Server
Server Name or IP: ${site.hostname}   Port Number: 80

Timeouts (milliseconds)
Connect: Response:

HTTP Request
Implementation: HttpClient4   Protocol [http]: http   Content encoding: utf-8

Path:

Parameters

Send Parameters With the Request:

Name:	Value	Encode?	Include Equals?

Detail   Add   Add from Clipboard   Delete   Up   Down

Proxy Server
Server Name or IP: Port Number: Username   Password

Optional Tasks
☐ Retrieve All Embedded Resources from HTML Files   ☐ Use concurrent pool. Size: 4

Embedded URLs must match:

Figure 20-2. HTTP Request Defaults

As mentioned previously, JMeter will not download linked assets by default. This includes CSS, images, applets, and iframes. This differs greatly from what happens when an actual user accesses your site, since the user's browser will download all of those assets. The setting for controlling this behavior in JMeter is *Retrieve All Embedded Resources from HTML Files*, located in the *Optional Tasks* section of HTTP Request Defaults or any individual HTTP Request. Many sites leave this setting disabled since most slowdowns and infrastructure bottlenecks are caused by serving the page itself, not the linked assets. This is especially true when you have incorporated a reverse proxy or a CDN to cache static assets. That said, if you choose to leave this option disabled for standard test runs, we advise running periodic tests with it enabled to ensure that asset delivery is happening as fast as expected.

Thread Groups

JMeter has the concept of *thread groups*, which is a way to group together a set of threads that will perform certain requests (anything defined as a child of the thread group) against the site. This can be useful for splitting up the test into different sections—e.g., tests for things like authenticated users versus anonymous users. Because thread groups each have configurable settings for timing and number of threads, it's also possible to use them to put different traffic loads on different parts of the site. In our case, we're going to define a single thread group for authenticated traffic, though it will also include an anonymous visit to the site's front page. For a more complete test plan, it would be useful to also add at least one more thread group to handle anonymous traffic, but we leave that as an exercise for the reader.

 JMeter threads are *not* the same as real users on your site. While a single thread may seem like it closely represents a user, remember that JMeter is not rendering pages or reading content once it's displayed — it's just loading pages as fast as possible and then going on to load the next page in the test plan. This can give you an idea of how many requests per second your site can handle, but it does not directly translate into the number of users your site can handle.

To add a thread group, right-click on the test plan icon in the lefthand toolbar and go to Add→Threads (Users)→Thread Group. The new thread group should appear below your global settings in the left toolbar, as shown in Figure 20-3. Name it *Authenticated Users* so that you know what type of testing it will be handling. Now we'll want to configure the number of threads—let's go with 10 for now, as that's a relatively small amount of traffic but should still give us a good baseline on performance. The *Ramp-Up Period* is how long JMeter takes to create all of the threads. Let's set that to 20 seconds, meaning JMeter will create a new thread every two seconds until it hits the 10 total threads we've configured.

There are a couple of options for how to control the test duration. First, you could set a loop count on the thread group. This controls how many times each thread loops over the test plan within the thread group. In our case, we'll set this to 'Forever', and instead we'll set a limit on the time duration of the test. To do this, click the 'Forever' checkbox next to 'Loop Count', and then click the 'Scheduler' checkbox to enable the scheduler. It will fill in 'Start Time' and 'End Time' with the current date and time; that can be ignored. In the 'Duration' setting, add the value *${testlength}* which will use the testlength variable that we defined in our global settings. Once complete, the test plan order and thread group settings should look like Figure 20-3.

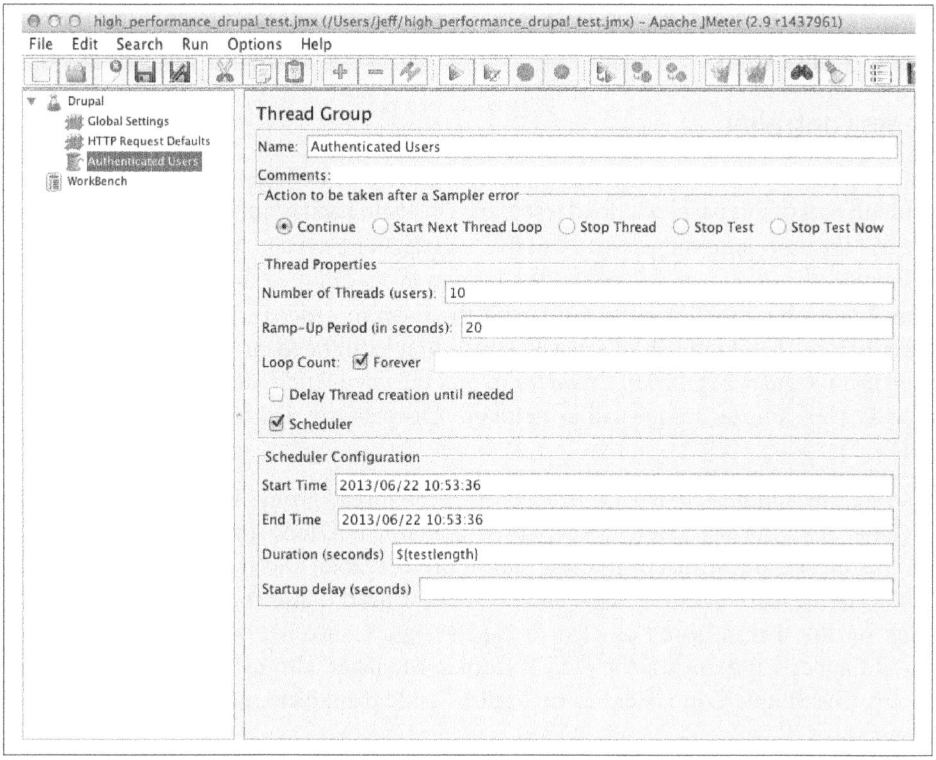

Figure 20-3. JMeter thread group[]

Handling Cookies

This thread group is intended to simulate authenticated traffic, which means that we'll need to handle the session cookies used by Drupal. In JMeter, this can easily be accomplished by using an *HTTP Cookie Manager*. This is a configuration element similar to the User Defined Variables element we are using to store global variables. In this case, however, we'll keep the HTTP Cookie Manager as a child of the Authenticated Users Thread Group instead of using it globally, since it is private to this thread group.

In order to add an HTTP Cookie Manager, right-click on the thread group and go to Add→Config Element→HTTP Cookie Manager. It should show up indented to represent that it is a child of the Thread Group element—if it doesn't show up in the correct location, you can drag and drop it within the left toolbar to add it as a child of the thread group.

Configuration of the HTTP Cookie Manager is very simple. The only setting that we need to change from the defaults is to select *Clear cookies each iteration*. That will remove any cookies from a thread after it's gone through one loop of the thread group tests, meaning that each thread starts fresh (similar to a new user) each time it loops through the thread group.

Login Controller

Although it's not too complicated, performing the Drupal login is probably the most difficult part of this particular load test plan. The login itself is quite simple: we just need to POST the username and password to the */user/login* form page. What makes this more difficult is that the form also contains a hidden *form_build_id* input containing a random hash, which we'll need to POST with the form in order for Drupal to accept the submission. To accomplish this, we'll need to first load the form (located at */user*), and then use a *Regular Expression Extractor* to pull the *form_build_id* string out of the page source. This same technique will work for any Drupal form. Do you feel like a spammer yet?

Let's start by adding a *Simple Controller* under the thread group. We'll use this to group together all of the login logic to keep it self-contained. It doesn't matter to JMeter if we do this or not, but it makes the test plan more readable, and it also makes it easy to duplicate the form handling logic should we ever need it elsewhere on the site. Right-click on the thread group and go to Add→Logic Controller→Simple Controller; it should appear underneath the HTTP Cookie Manager, also as a child of the thread group. The Simple Controller has no options aside from its name; we'll name this one *Login*.

Now we can add the request elements needed in order to fetch and submit the login form. The process consists of requesting the */user* page, pulling out the *form_build_id* string from the response data, and then submitting the form with a POST request to */user/login*. We'll start by creating an *HTTP Request* element to request the */user* page. Right-click on the new Login controller we just created and go to Add→Sampler→HTTP Request. Change the name to *User Form*. Since we have a global HTTP Request Defaults object set up, there's no need to fill in most of the request fields. The only thing we need to set is the Path, which needs to be set to */user*.

In order to get the *form_build_id*, we'll need to create a *Regular Expression Extractor* as a child of the User Form request. Right-click on the User Form request and go to Add→Post Processors→Regular Expression Extractor. It should show up as a child of the User Form request, but drag it there if not. Name the extractor *Drupal form build id*. We'll keep the defaults for the other settings, and then we just need to create a regular expression to extract the *form_build_id* string. The string appears in the page source like this:

```
<input type="hidden" name="form_build_id"
    value="form-P6bhzmdBofDC_AZ-yjHn6ZB-R35b5ljF1hmTEwXbDF0" />
```

Everything after `form-` in the value string is a random hash specific to that particular form, but we'll want to grab the whole string including the "form-" at the beginning. To do this, we can use the following regular expression:

```
name="form_build_id" value="(.*?)"
```

For the *Reference Name*, enter *form_build_id* — this is the variable name we'll be able to use later to refer to this value. Next, for Regular Expression, enter the regular expression just shown. For Template, enter *1* — this tells JMeter to assign whatever is in the first reference (in between the parentheses in the regular expression) to the variable we're creating. Finally, for Match Number, enter *1* — this tells JMeter to apply this regular expression to the first match it comes across. Note that if you have multiple forms showing up on the login form (such as a search box in the header), you may need to adjust this.

Now we'll create a second request for submitting the form. Right-click on the Login Controller and go to Add→Sampler→HTTP Request. If needed, drag it so that it appears underneath the User Form request, but still as a child to the Login Controller. Name this request *Submit User Form*, change the *Method* setting to *POST* since we're submitting a form, and then set the *Path* to */user/login*. Next, we'll need to add a list of parameters to send with the request. These can be added by clicking the Add button below the parameters list. Add the parameters shown in Table 20-2.

Table 20-2. User login parameters

Name	Value	Encode	Include Equals
name	${drupal.user}	No	Yes
pass	${drupal.pass}	No	Yes
form_build_id	${form_build_id}	No	Yes
form_id	user_login	No	Yes
op	Log in	Yes	Yes

For `name` and `pass`, we are referring to the variables we set in the global settings earlier. `form_build_id` uses the results from our regular expression extractor to submit the appropriate *form_build_id*. `form_id` is another hidden field that we need to submit, and `op` is the name of the submit button for the form. The top portion of the Submit User Form request should look like Figure 20-4—nothing needs to be changed below the parameters list.

HTTP Request

Name:	Submit User Form
Comments:	

Web Server

		Timeouts (milliseconds)	
Server Name or IP:	Port Number:	Connect:	Response:

HTTP Request

Implementation: [   ] Protocol [http]: [   ] Method: [POST] Content encoding: [   ]

Path: /user/login

☐ Redirect Automatically ☑ Follow Redirects ☑ Use KeepAlive ☐ Use multipart/form-data for POST ☐ Browser-compatible headers

[Parameters] [Post Body]

Send Parameters With the Request:

Name:	Value	Encode?	Include Equa...
name	${drupal.user}	☐	☑
pass	${drupal.pass}	☐	☑
form_build_id	${form_build_id}	☐	☑
form_id	user_login	☐	☑
op	Log in	☑	☑

[Detail] [Add] [Add from Clipboard] [Delete] [Up] [Down]

Figure 20-4. Submit user form

Browse Controller

Now that we have the ability to log into the site, we'll create a list of a few pages that we want to test. Start by creating another Simple Controller as a child of the Authenticated Users thread group, and name it *Browse* — this will be used as a container for our authenticated user page browsing requests. Be sure that this controller is below the Login Controller, but as a direct child of Authenticated Users, not as a child of the Login Controller. Next, we'll create individual HTTP Request elements for each page that we want to test.

> Another approach to this is to create a CSV file listing URLs to visit. This can be easier to maintain for a large number of paths. We won't describe this approach in detail, but it can be done by using a *CSV Data Set Config* element to read the CSV file into a list of variables.

For each page we're going to test, we'll create an *HTTP Sampler* by right-clicking on the Browse controller and going to Add→Sampler→HTTP Request. Since we're using the HTTP request defaults, the only settings that need to be changed for each request are the name and path. In the case of our example site, we'll want to test the front page, the forum index, a forum post, and a couple of article pages. We'll do this by adding request elements for the name/path combinations listed in Table 20-3.

Table 20-3. Page requests

Name	Path
Front Page	/
Article 1	/somearticle
Article 2	/anotherarticle
Forum Index	/forum-index
Forum Post 1	/forum/post-1

These are actual paths on our test site, but you'll obviously want to adjust these to fit your site, being sure to cover all the various page types you have in place.

We're now testing a full set of pages as an authenticated user. However, it would also be useful to test at least the front page as a nonauthenticated (anonymous) user, since many people will visit the front page directly before logging in. To simulate this, create a duplicate of the Front Page request element, rename it *Front Page (Anon)*, and drag it just above the Login Controller. This way, each thread will request the front page before logging in and proceeding to visit the other pages. Once we've done this, our test plan looks like Figure 20-5.

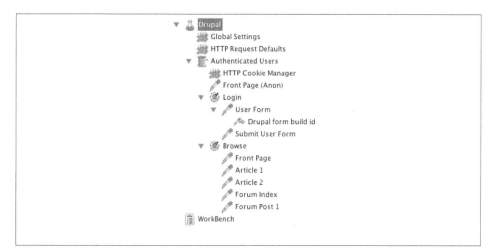

Figure 20-5. Test plan

Output Configuration

Now that our test plan is complete with a set of page requests, the only piece missing is to save the request results. This is done by creating a *Simple Data Writer* element within the test plan. The data writer could be created at the global level in order to save all requests from a test, or it could be placed within a thread group in order to save results only from that set of requests. This is useful if you have multiple thread groups (e.g.,

Authenticated Users and Anonymous Users) and want to write out to different data files for each of them. You can have data writers at as many levels of the test as you like. In our case, we'll add one global data writer to catch all requests. To do this, right-click on the test plan and go to Add→Listener→Simple Data Writer. Name it *Full Test Output*, and enter a filename for it to save to, such as */path/to/jmeter-test/full-output.jtl*.

Data writers have many options regarding which data to save in the file. Note that if you are saving the full responses, the file can get large rather quickly if you're doing a large number of requests. In general, settings such as those shown in Figure 20-6 will be sufficient; however, if you are debugging issues with requests or responses, it can be useful to save the request and/or response headers and the full response data. We'll describe how to view the output data momentarily, in the section "Reading Test Results."

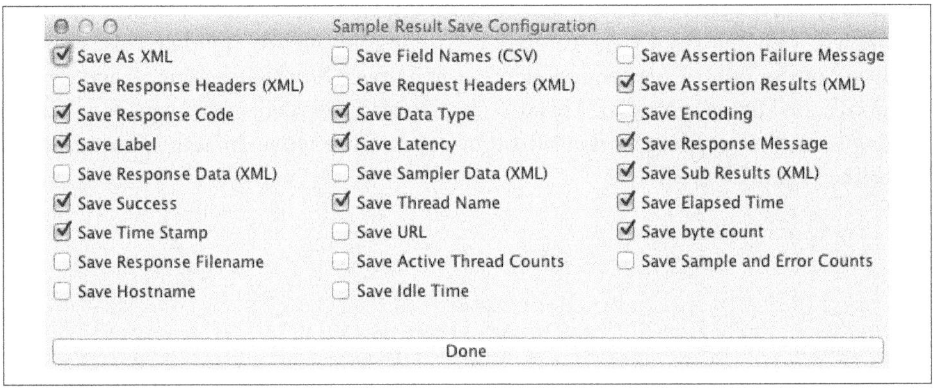

Figure 20-6. Data writer configuration

Running a Test

Tests can be run either by opening the test in the JMeter GUI and clicking on the Play button in the toolbar, or from the command line. If you're running the test from a remote server, simply run the following:

```
$ /path/to/jmeter/bin/jmeter -n -t /path/to/test/loadtest.jmx
```

In this command, -n tells JMeter to run in non-GUI mode, and -t tells it the path to the test plan file you want to execute.

Reading Test Results

Now for the fun part, reading the test results to see how our site performed! There are a number of reports available for reading results, though for an overall picture, the best choice is to use the *Summary Report*. Add one of these to JMeter by right-clicking on *Workbench* and then going to Add→Listener→Summary Report. Once that is created, click on the Browse button next to the Filename input, and select the output from your test run. JMeter will load that data and display a summary report, as seen in Figure 20-7.

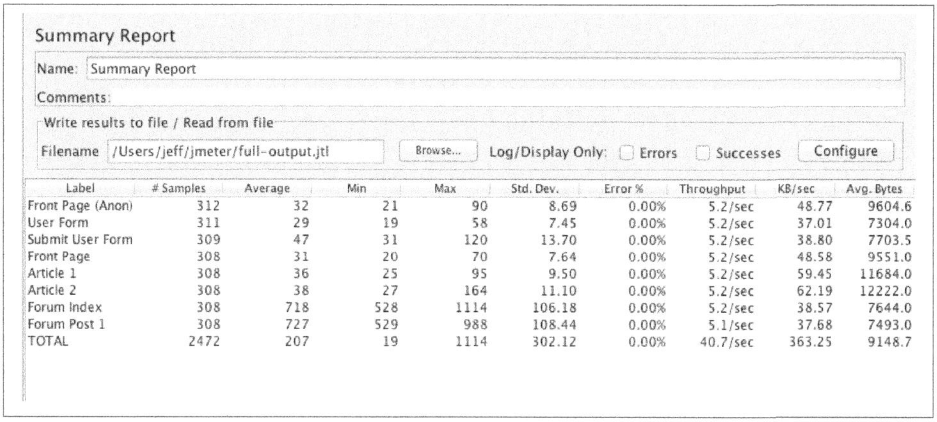

Label	# Samples	Average	Min	Max	Std. Dev.	Error %	Throughput	KB/sec	Avg. Bytes
Front Page (Anon)	312	32	21	90	8.69	0.00%	5.2/sec	48.77	9604.6
User Form	311	29	19	58	7.45	0.00%	5.2/sec	37.01	7304.0
Submit User Form	309	47	31	120	13.70	0.00%	5.2/sec	38.80	7703.5
Front Page	308	31	20	70	7.64	0.00%	5.2/sec	48.58	9551.0
Article 1	308	36	25	95	9.50	0.00%	5.2/sec	59.45	11684.0
Article 2	308	38	27	164	11.10	0.00%	5.2/sec	62.19	12222.0
Forum Index	308	718	528	1114	106.18	0.00%	5.2/sec	38.57	7644.0
Forum Post 1	308	727	529	988	108.44	0.00%	5.1/sec	37.68	7493.0
TOTAL	2472	207	19	1114	302.12	0.00%	40.7/sec	363.25	9148.7

Figure 20-7. JMeter summary report

In our case (this was run over a LAN), we can see very fast page load times for all pages on the site. The forum index and forum post are by far the slowest pages, so if we were looking to make improvements, that would be the place to start; however, they are by no means slow at an average load time of around 700 ms.

If you want to dig down into individual requests, you can use the listeners *View Results in Tree* or *View Results in Table*, which allow you to click on each individual request to see the details. As we mentioned earlier, this can be a good way to troubleshoot errors with the test—for example, if your login isn't working properly, you could use these listeners to track the headers sent and received in order to debug what might be going wrong.

In addition to the built-in listeners, there are some great third-party plug-ins that provide a nice set of graphs for viewing things such as latency (time to first byte) and full page load time within your results. We highly recommend using *jmeter-plugins* (*http://jmeter-plugins.org/wiki/Start/*)—specifically, the graphs for *Response Latencies over Time* and *Response Times over Time* are very useful for visualizing how the page load times vary for different pages throughout the test. Figure 20-8 shows an example of the response times graph for our test—here, it's easy to see the performance difference between the forum pages and the rest of the site.

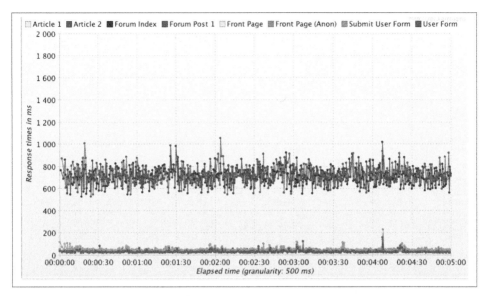

Figure 20-8. Response times graph

## CHAPTER 21

Where to Next?

We hope that this book has given you an actionable approach to improving the performance of your Drupal website. Website performance is a very broad topic, and while we hope we have given enough information about common performance issues, it's just not possible to cover everything in detail. Here, we present a number of resources for additional reading on many of the topics we've covered in the book, as well as general resources for Drupal performance and scalability.

Official Book Website

This book has an official website (*http://shop.oreilly.com/product/0636920012269.do*) that links to code snippets and configuration files discussed in the book.

High Performance Drupal Group

There is a Drupal Group focused on high-performance Drupal issues (*https://groups.drupal.org/high-performance*). This is a good place to see what other people are doing and to ask performance- and scalability-related questions.

Drupal Watchdog

Drupal Watchdog (*http://drupalwatchdog.com*) is the only print magazine specific to Drupal. The magazine includes articles from many well-known Drupal contributors focusing on many different topics, including Drupal performance. Articles are made freely available online sometime after each issue is released in print.

Revision Control with Git

The *Pro Git* book is available here (*http://git-scm.com/book*). The Git Flow extensions that are built around the branching model mentioned in Chapter 9 are available at here (*https://github.com/nvie/gitflow*). A general comparison of Git and Subversion can be found here (*https://git.wiki.kernel.org/index.php/GitSvnComparison*).

Varnish

The Varnish Reference Manual (*https://www.varnish-cache.org/docs/3.0/reference/index.html*) is the authoritative source for configuring Varnish and writing VCL. There are a number of Varnish Modules and Extensions (VMODs) located at *https://www.varnish-cache.org/vmods* that can help you easily extend the functionality of your VCL files.

Configuration Management

One advantage of using modularized configuration management systems is that it is easy to share and reuse code. The Chef community (*http://community.opscode.com/cookbooks*) is perhaps one of the best at this, with its vast collection of cookbooks. Puppet (*http://forge.puppetlabs.com*) also has a growing list of community modules.

Vagrant

There are a number of prebuilt Vagrant virtual machine "boxes" available online. Vagrantbox.es (*http://www.vagrantbox.es*) provides links to many of them, including "official" boxes provided by PuppetLabs, Opscode (Chef), and Ubuntu.

Jenkins

Jenkins (*http://jenkins-ci.org/*) has a number of plug-ins that make it even more useful. Some of the ones we use most frequently include:

- The GitHub plug-in (*https://wiki.jenkins-ci.org/display/JENKINS/GitHub+Plugin*), which lets you tie into GitHub repos and kick off jobs based on activity there
- The Build Keeper plug-in (*https://wiki.jenkins-ci.org/display/JENKINS/Build+Keeper+Plugin*), which allows you to configure rules to keep or discard builds
- The Performance plug-in (*https://wiki.jenkins-ci.org/display/JENKINS/Performance+Plugin*), which ties into JMeter or JUnit test runs in order to display test data and can trigger a build error condition based on errors during the test run

MySQL Performance

The MySQL Performance Blog (*http://www.mysqlperformanceblog.com*) is an excellent source for tips, tools, and some very interesting benchmarks and test cases.

InnoDB Index Structures

To extend on the index structure overview that was given in Chapter 15, check out Jeremy Cole's blog post "B+Tree index structures in InnoDB" (*http://blog.jcole.us/2013/01/10/btree-index-structures-in-innodb/*).

Index

We'd like to hear your suggestions for improving our indexes. Send email to index@oreilly.com.

EntityQuery, 162
EntityQuery() API, 32
error responses, tracking, 210
ETag cache header, 179
event handling, 10
evictions, 160
    least recently used (LRU), 154
Expire, 25
Expires cache header, 179
external requests, 5, 49
external scripts, 17

F

Facebook, 5, 49, 66
failover configuration, 125–130
    for cloud deployments, 124
    Heartbeat, 127
    IP vs. DNS, 126
    service-level issues and, 126
failover infrastructure, 91
failover, as hosting consideration, 92
false optimizations, 30
FastCGI Process Manager (FPM), 175
field API, 161
field storage
    CRUD, 162
    EntityFieldQuery, 162
    EntityQuery, 162
    MongoDB, 162
field_sql_storage module, 161
File Systems in User Space (FUSE), 114
file-backed memory allocation, 199
files, adding to pages, 11
Firebug, 10, 13, 58
Firefox, 58
first-time visitors, 5
frontend performance, 5, 9–19, 25
    audits of, 10–12
    cacheable headers, 15
    CDNs and, 16
    compression, 15
    display times, 3
    external scripts and, 17
    HTTP requests, limiting, 9–12
    image requests and, 12
    jQuery and, 16
    minification, 13
    PageSpeed (Google), 55
    real user monitoring, 58

SPOFs and, 17–19
third party libraries and, 16
verifying changes in, 55–59
waterfall charts, 56
YSlow, 55
frontend proxies, 82
full page loads, 3
function calls, 69

G

geographic distribution, as hosting consideration, 92
getMultiple() API, 38
Git, 104–106
    repository, setting up, 104
    Subversion vs., 226
    workflow with, example, 108
Git Flow extensions, 226
Git Hub plug-in (Jenkins), 226
GitHub, 102
GlusterFS, 114
    configuring, 115
goals, 2
    realistic, 4
    setting, 4
Google, 9
    CDN, 16
Google Analytics, 59, 195
grace period for expired content, 197
gzip compression, 15

H

HA NFS clusters, 116–120
    configuration for, 117
    DRBD, setting up, 117–118
    Heartbeat, 119
    NFS, setting up, 119
    testing, 119
ha.cf configuration file (Heartbeat), 128
HAProxy, 82
haresources configuration file (Heartbeat), 128
hb_standby tool (Heartbeat), 129
hb_takeover tool (Heartbeat), 129
Heartbeat, 119
    configuration, 127–129
    failover configuration with, 127
    installation, 127
    tools/options for, 129

About the Authors

Jeff Sheltren has been involved with open source since 2001. He started using Linux professionally at the University of California at Santa Barbara, where he was a senior systems administrator and programmer for the computer science department. His previous position at the Oregon State University Open Source Lab (OSU OSL) was as the operations manager, providing technical and organizational leadership to the OSU OSL while working closely with the many open source projects hosted there, including Drupal.org, the Linux Foundation, and the Apache Software Foundation. Currently, Jeff works as a performance engineer at Tag1 Consulting.

Jeff has extensive infrastructure experience, gained over the years. As the operations manager at OSU OSL—the largest open source hosting infrastructure of its kind—he led the infrastructure and development teams; he is deeply involved in the CentOS Linux build and release process as a member of the QA team, and he works as a volunteer for the Drupal.org Infrastructure Team. Jeff currently maintains a number of packages for the Fedora Project and Fedora's Extra Packages for Enterprise Linux (EPEL), and he serves as the lead systems engineer for multiple Tag1 clients. He lives in Vancouver, Washington.

Narayan Newton is a co-owner of Tag1 Consulting who joined the team in 2008. He was introduced to Drupal during his tenure at the Oregon State University Open Source Lab, where he was the co-lead system administrator—and served as the database administrator of over 180 MySQL databases; he has also held the positions of freenode server administrator and Drupal.org server administrator. Narayan is a permanent member of the Drupal Association as their systems coordinator, and is the lead systems administrator for the Drupal.org Infrastructure Team. He is also a co-maintainer of the Pressflow high-performance Drupal distribution.

Outside of Drupal, Narayan has been deeply involved in the FreeBSD, Gentoo, and Slackware communities. More recently, he acted as infrastructure lead for the Examiner.com 2.0 relaunch, infrastructure lead for the Drupal.org redesign launch, and infrastructure lead/performance lead for Drupal.org Git migration. Narayan is currently chief technology officer at Tag1 Consulting and resides in Portland, Oregon.

Nathaniel Catchpole has been using Drupal since version 4.5 and has been a regular contributor to Drupal core since 2006; along with extensive code profiling, he has contributed over 400 patches to the Drupal 7 release. Nathaniel also maintains the core entity, cache, and taxonomy subsystems, as well as the Memcache and Entity Cache contributed projects. In September 2011, Nathaniel became branch baintainer and release manager for the Drupal 8 release cycle.

Nathaniel has been with Tag1 Consulting since September 2010. Prior to that, he worked on the Examiner.com Drupal migration and launch and as a consultant for CivicActions, with clients such as Sony BMG and Amnesty International.

Colophon

The animal on the cover of *High Performance Drupal* is the Red-shouldered Hawk (*Buteo lineatus*). The Red-shouldered Hawk can be found in North America, specifically in eastern North America, the coast of California, and northern Mexico. They live in wooded areas and stay within a confined range within those areas.

Adult male Red-shouldered Hawks are 15 to 23 inches in length and tend to weigh 550 grams. Females, on the other hand, are a bit longer than males by just a few inches, and weigh 700 grams. The wingspan of the adult Red-shouldered Hawk ranges from 35 to 50 inches. They have brown heads, red chests, red bars along their bellies, and white bars along their tails. Like many hawks, they have great vision and will swoop down on their prey. They eat rodents, squirrels, rabbits, amphibians, small birds, and large insects.

The Red-shouldered Hawk is a monogamous bird. A breeding pair will typically build a stick nest and will use the same nest every year. The female Red-shouldered Hawk typically gives birth to three to four eggs and after being born the young are dependent on their parents for up to 19 weeks.

The cover image is from Johnson's *Natural History*. The cover fonts are URW Typewriter and Guardian Sans. The text font is Adobe Minion Pro; the heading font is Adobe Myriad Condensed; and the code font is Dalton Maag's Ubuntu Mono.

Get even more for your money.

Join the O'Reilly Community, and register the O'Reilly books you own. It's free, and you'll get:

- $4.99 ebook upgrade offer
- 40% upgrade offer on O'Reilly print books
- Membership discounts on books and events
- Free lifetime updates to ebooks and videos
- Multiple ebook formats, DRM FREE
- Participation in the O'Reilly community
- Newsletters
- Account management
- 100% Satisfaction Guarantee

Signing up is easy:

1. Go to: oreilly.com/go/register
2. Create an O'Reilly login.
3. Provide your address.
4. Register your books.

Note: English-language books only

To order books online:
oreilly.com/store

For questions about products or an order:
orders@oreilly.com

To sign up to get topic-specific email announcements and/or news about upcoming books, conferences, special offers, and new technologies:
elists@oreilly.com

For technical questions about book content:
booktech@oreilly.com

To submit new book proposals to our editors:
proposals@oreilly.com

O'Reilly books are available in multiple DRM-free ebook formats. For more information:
oreilly.com/ebooks

Spreading the knowledge of innovators   oreilly.com

Have it your way.

CPSIA information can be obtained at www.ICGtesting.com
Printed in the USA
LVOW02s1430311013

359479LV00046B/384/P